AF560120

Forest Project Analysis and Management

Forest Project Analysis and Management

Pawan Pattanaik

RANDOM PUBLICATIONS
NEW DELHI (INDIA)

Forest Project Analysis and Management

ISBN 978-93-5111-831-2

Published in 2016 in India by

RANDOM PUBLICATIONS

4376-A/4B, Gali Murari Lal, Ansari Road
New Delhi-110 002
Phone : +9111-43580356, 011-23289044, 011-43142548
e-mail: sales@randompublications.com,
info@randompublications.com, randomexports@gmail.com

Reprinted 2024

Type Setting by : Friends Media, Delhi-110089
Digitally Printed at : Replika Press Pvt. Ltd.

Preface

The Forest Project, or "Programme for the Management of Natural Forests and the Establishment of Communal Plantations" aims to satisfy requirements in the new decentralization context by enhancing forest resources of the decentralized communities and through the development of communal plantations.

Similar to agriculture, forests also reveal the wealth of a nation. Investment in forestry and realisation of returns is taken care of by the state, due to the long gestation period and several laws governing the exploitation of forest resources. However, efforts are taken by the government to widen the forest cover through several afforestation programmes and agroforestry projects.

Monitoring and evaluation are particularly important in forestry projects for local community development because of the diversity and innovative nature of these projects. These projects, taking place on lands that have not conventionally been used for forestry, require new skills of foresters and involve different participants. Monitoring focuses on a project's inputs, activities, management and outputs to improve the operation of the project as designed. Evaluations re-examine the design of the project and assess its impacts. Ongoing evaluations support mid-course corrections while ex post evaluations address mitigation and follow-up activities in the project area and offer lessons for the design of other projects.

A comprehensive inventory of forest resources is essential for land management planning, but by itself is not sufficient. An inventory provides a detailed picture of the resource at one point in time. The forest is not a static entity, but a dynamic biophysical system. A full description of such a system must contain not only an estimate of its present state, but also a description of its potential future change.

This book is prepared with the undergraduate students of forestry in mind and hence the sophisticated mathematical applications are limited. It is believed that this book will be useful to them.

– Author

Contents

Preface .... *v-vi*

1. Forest Policy and Project **1**

Policy Objectives 1
Country Assistance Programs 1
Bank Financing 2
Plantations 2
Commercial Harvesting 2
Adapting Forest Policy and Legislation 4
Adapting Forestry Institutions 6
Designing Projects to Meet Local Needs 8
Project Design 9
Policy and Legislation Issues 10

2. Participatory Approaches to Planning for Community Forestry Project **14**

The Focus of the Proejct 14
Participatory Planning 15
Community Forestry Projects 20
The Malakand Social Forestry Project 23
The Two Dimensions of Participatory Planning: Local And Institutional 40
The Begnas Tal Rupa Tal Watershed Management Project in Nepal 54
The Previnoba project in Senegal 61

3. Interregional Project for Participatory Upland Conservation and Development **85**

The PUCD Project in Forest 86
Approach, Methods and Tools 87
Results and Lessons Learned 89
The PUCD project in Rwanda 101

4. The Evolution to Participatory

Assessment, Monitoring and Evaluation in Community Forestry 115
Particpatory Assessment, Monitoring and Evaluation and Commmity Forestry ... 116

The Benefits of Participatory Assessment, Monitoring and Evaluation 116
The Focus of Participatory Assessment, Monitoring and Evaluation 117
Field Workers as Facilitators of Participatory Assessment, Monitoring and Participatory Assessment, Monitoring and Evaluation 118
Description and Purpose of Community Selection by Outsiders 119
Methods for Comity Selection 119
Community Problem Analysis 121
Communities Setting Project Objectives. 125

5. Valuing The Forest and its Uses: The Available Techniques and their Usefulness in Practice 126

The Techniques for Estimating Measures of Economic Value 126
Valuing Forest Goods and Services in Practice 130
Identifying Interested Groups their Value Perspectives 137
Economic Values: Usefulness and Limitations 143
Financial Values and Economic Values 147
Valuing Forest Properties 148

6. Forest Project Management Planning 150

Forest Management Planning 150
Examples of Yield Prediction Modelling Technology 156
Forest Management Planning 164
Implementation of Forest Management Operations 170
Implementation of Post Harvest Operations 187

7. Indian Forest Law and Policy 193

Forest Policy 194
Policies in India on Production Forestry 195
National Forest Policy of Joint Forest Management 205
Rights Over Forest Resources 208
The National Forest Policy 211

8. Forestry Conservation Management Practices 216

Forest Conservation and the Rural Poor 219
Environmental Change and Biodiversity Conservation 227
Conservation and Management of Biomass Resources Management 236
Adaptation and Mitigation Practices in Forest Management 239

9. Global Discourse on Forestry 245

Distribution of the World's Main Vegetation Types or Biomes 253
Recent Estimates of Global Forest Area 256
Forest Conditions and Area 259
Forest Ecosystem Services and Underlying Processes 261
World Energy Resources and Consumption 264

***Bibliography* 270**

***Index* 272**

1

Forest Policy and Project

POLICY OBJECTIVES

The management, conservation, and sustainable development of forest ecosystems and their associated resources are essential for lasting poverty reduction and sustainable development, whether located in countries with abundant forests or in those with depleted or naturally limited forest resources. The objective of this policy is to assist borrowers to harness the potential of forests to reduce poverty in a sustainable manner, integrate forests effectively into sustainable economic development, and protect the vital local and global environmental services and values of forests.

Where forest restoration and plantation development are necessary to meet these objectives, the Bank assists borrowers with forest restoration activities that maintain or enhance biodiversity and ecosystem functionality. The Bank also assists borrowers with the establishment and sustainable management of environmentally appropriate, socially beneficial, and economically viable forest plantations to help meet growing demands for forest goods and services.

SCOPE OF POLICY

This policy applies to the following types of Bank-financed investment projects:

(a) Projects that have or may have impacts on the health and quality of forests;

(b) Projects that affect the rights and welfare of people and their level of dependence upon or interaction with forests; and

(c) Projects that aim to bring about changes in the management, protection, or utilization of natural forests or plantations, whether they are publicly, privately, or communally owned.

COUNTRY ASSISTANCE PROGRAMS

The Bank uses environmental assessments, poverty assessments, social analyses, Public Expenditure Reviews, and other economic and sector work to identify the economic, environmental, and social significance of forests in its borrowing countries. When the Bank identifies the potential for its Country Assistance Strategy (CAS) to have a significant impact on forests, it integrates strategies for addressing that impact into the CAS.

BANK FINANCING

The Bank does not finance projects that, in its opinion, would involve significant conversion or degradation of critical forest areas or related critical natural habitats. If a project involves the significant conversion or degradation of natural forests or related natural habitats that the Bank determines are not critical, and the Bank determines that there are no feasible alternatives to the project and its siting, and comprehensive analysis demonstrates that overall benefits from the project substantially outweigh the environmental costs, the Bank may finance the project provided that it incorporates appropriate mitigation measures.

The Bank does not finance projects that contravene applicable international environmental agreements.

PLANTATIONS

The Bank does not finance plantations that involve any conversion or degradation of critical natural habitats, including adjacent or downstream critical natural habitats. When the Bank finances plantations, it gives preference to siting such projects on unforested sites or lands already converted (excluding any lands that have been converted in anticipation of the project). In view of the potential for plantation projects to introduce invasive species and threaten biodiversity, such projects must be designed to prevent and mitigate these potential threats to natural habitats.

COMMERCIAL HARVESTING

The Bank may finance commercial harvesting operations only when the Bank has determined, on the basis of the applicable environmental assessment or other relevant information, that the areas affected by the harvesting are not critical forests or related critical natural habitats.

To be eligible for Bank financing, industrial-scale commercial harvesting operations must also

(a) Be certified under an independent forest certification system acceptable to the Bank as meeting standards of responsible forest management and use; or
(b) Where a pre-assessment under such an independent forest certification system determines that the operation does not yet meet the requirements, adhere to a time-bound phased action plan acceptable to the Bank for achieving certification to such standards.

To be acceptable to the Bank, a forest certification system must require:

(a) Compliance with relevant laws;
(b) Recognition of and respect for any legally documented or customary land tenure and use rights as well as the rights of indigenous peoples and workers;
(c) Measures to maintain or enhance sound and effective community relations;
(d) Conservation of biological diversity and ecological functions;
(e) Measures to maintain or enhance environmentally sound multiple benefits accruing from the forest;
(f) Prevention or minimization of the adverse environmental impacts from forest use;
(g) Effective forest management planning;
(h) Active monitoring and assessment of relevant forest management areas; and
(i) The maintenance of critical forest areas and other critical natural habitats affected by the operation.

In addition to the requirements, a forest certification system must be independent, cost-effective, and based on objective and measurable performance standards that are defined at the national level and are compatible with internationally accepted principles and criteria of sustainable forest management.

The system must require independent, third-party assessment of forest management performance. In addition, the system's standards must be developed with the meaningful participation of local people and communities; indigenous peoples; non-governmental organizations representing consumer, producer, and conservation interests; and other members of civil society, including the private sector. The decision-making procedures of the certification system must be fair, transparent, independent, and designed to avoid conflicts of interest.

The Bank may finance harvesting operations conducted by small-scale landholders, by local communities under community forest management, or by such entities under joint forest management arrangements, if these operations:

(a) Have achieved a standard of forest management developed with the meaningful participation of locally affected communities, consistent with the principles and criteria of responsible forest management; or
(b) Adhere to a time-bound phased action plan to achieve such a standard. The action plan must be developed with the meaningful participation of locally-affected communities and be acceptable to the Bank.

The borrower monitors all such operations with the meaningful participation of locally-affected communities.

ADAPTING FOREST POLICY AND LEGISLATION

To achieve these new aims, governments will have to adapt existing forest policies and legislation. National forest policies-a general overview of a government's approach to forest management-cover production objectives and environmental and developmental goals. The aim of these policies is often to maximize revenues and foreign exchange from wood and timber, and ensure supplies of raw materials to large forest-based industries. To achieve these aims, legislation has been passed in many countries giving governments and private companies exclusive use of forest land and timber reserves.

If the food security of people living in or near forest areas is to be increased, forestry management policies must be redesigned to accommodate national, industrial and local forest resource needs.

This requires that:

- Traditional forestry management goals of production and protection be expanded to encompass the needs of local people;
- Governments be prepared to give up exclusive management of forest lands and transfer certain areas to local control;
- Existing legislation restricting forest access to local people and discriminating against small forest enterprises be modified to allow local people to use the forest for gathering forest products, and for growing food and cash crops; and
- Forestry departments work in collaboration with other government departments, NGOs and local people to develop agroforestry projects that meet local food needs.

Five particularly important changes in forest policy and legislation will help increase food security.

FOREST POLICY SHOULD INCLUDE THE PRODUCTION OF NON-TIMBER FOREST PRODUCTS

In many countries forest policy prevents or discourages people from using forest lands to produce non-timber products. The people affected are typically local inhabitants operating small-scale enterprises to produce food and locally-valued items that can be sold for cash. The priority development of such products through national forest policies would he of great benefit to local people.

Local agroforestry schemes could be developed within national forests to allow for the production of bushmeat, rattan, bamboo, fuelwood, traditional medicines, fruits, honey and other forest foods. This would be achieved by setting aside areas in the forest for wildlife habitats or for growing locally-valued crops, or by growing such crops between rows of trees in government plantations.

RESTRICTIONS ON FOREST ACCESS FOR LOCAL PEOPLE SHOULD BE LIFTED

Better access to forests is essential if local people are to be able to participate in and benefit from the cultivation of food crops and locally-valued products on forest lands.

In any project to develop non-timber products, the expertise of local people and their experience of growing and harvesting these products is vital to the forest authorities and can be used to pave the way for local participation in forest management, or cooperative management by local people and forest authorities.

RIGHTS OF OWNERSHIP OR STEWARDSHIP OF FOREST LAND SHOULD BE TRANSFERRED TO LOCAL INDIVIDUALS OR COMMUNITIES

Food security needs are often best met if forest land for agriculture or the cultivation of locally-valued products is transferred from the forest authority to local individual or collective control. Local management can respond more quickly to changing needs and circumstances, and local people are more likely to invest their time and resources on land if they have secure tenure.

LEGISLATION SHOULD BE MODIFIED TO SUPPORT SMALL-SCALE INCOME-GENERATING ACTIVITIES B ASED ON THE FOREST

Many people depend on gathering and processing tree and forest products for income. Forest policies and government legislation in support of these activities could make them more profitable and sustainable, thus improving the livelihood and food security of the people concerned. The people who would benefit most would be those who depend most on these activities-typically the landless and other disadvantaged groups.

In the short term, government subsidies on raw materials and other forms of financial support to forest-based industries are an option, though longer-term solutions should be promoted simultaneously to ensure economic stability for such enterprises.

Suitable government action to support small-scale forest industries would include:

- Guaranteeing supplies of raw materials from government forests at fixed or reduced prices;
- Protecting small enterprises from competition from larger industries;
- supporting local processing activities that add to the value of the forest products;
- Encouraging producer cooperatives;
- Developing and promoting new technologies to improve production;

- Providing financial incentives to establish and run small businesses; and
- Providing market support in the form of transportation, market information and access to market dealers and outlets that guarantee fair returns on sales.

FOREST POLICIES THAT ENCOURAGE THE NON-SUSTAINABLE USE OF FOREST LANDS SHOULD BE ELIMINATED AND SUSTAINABLE LAND-USE PRACTICES ENCOURAGED

Practices such as non-sustainable timber harvesting and inappropriate forms of agriculture have led to serious degradation of forest lands and have had disastrous effects on local food security. Long-term, sustainable land use and forestry practices need to replace those that bring only short-term results. This requires that governments:

- Remove incentives for non-sustainable projects-such as clearance of fragile tropical rainforest for cattle ranching-that cause long-term environmental damage;
- Adopt a more careful and creative approach when selecting forest land for conversion to agriculture;
- Regulate land use in areas of forest opened up for agriculture, commercial enterprise or settlement;
- Investigate and promote sustainable land uses combining the cultivation of trees and crops; and
- Encourage alternatives to land clearance, such as retaining forests and increasing opportunities for local people to use forest lands.

Forestry policies based on these principles should be integrated with government policies on agriculture, livestock, industry, development and the environment so that all sectors complement rather than compete with one another for resources.

ADAPTING FORESTRY INSTITUTIONS

Forestry institutions will also have to change if they are to put the new forestry policies into effect. They will have to take a wider view of the role of forest management, become more aware of the effects of forestry policies on the food security of local people, and cooperate with non-forestry sectors such as education, health and nutrition in the research and implementation of food security projects.

Forestry staff will need to take on a new role as intermediary between the government and local people, to educate and inform forest users of the most appropriate use of forest lands, and to work with local people to devise and implement agroforestry projects.

- Forestry institutions will have to be prepared, where appropriate, to transfer management of forest lands to local communities.

- New types of training will be needed for forestry professionals and extension workers to help them to ascertain and represent local food security needs to forestry institutions, and to help local people organize and participate in forest management.
- Forestry professionals will need to be trained to cooperate with and use the expertise of Egos already operating within rural communities.
- A change in the aspirations of forestry personnel will be needed if they are to become advocates for the poor and disadvantaged. A separation of the 'police' and extension functions within forestry departments could help bring about such a change, and the development of policing involving local people could aid mutual cooperation.
- More women need to be involved in research, planning and extension agencies to reflect the central role women play in forestry and agricultural activities in many societies. Possibilities for integrating local women into projects to enhance food security would be increased if institutions employed more women staff and extensionagents; projects would have a greater chance of success if they took into consideration the concerns of local women and were designed to fit into women's working routines.
- Adequate institutional support for new programmes and for staff working at the community level will also be essential.

RESEARCH

All aspects of the links between forestry and food security require research. Of primary importance is research on how foresters can integrate food security objectives into their activities by developing forest products for food and income, improving existing agricultural techniques for growing non-timber products, examining Marketing options for non-timber forest products and minimizing any negative impacts of national forestry policy on small-scale forest enterprises.

All research should be firmly grounded in local circumstances and needs. A better understanding of how local people use and manage forests is the basis of present and future research. Local knowledge of forest ecology is invaluable to researchers, but investigation into this is urgent because local knowledge is disappearing as forest resources diminish and traditional practices die out.

Researchers need to broaden their methods, and undertake interdisciplinary studies covering biological and socio-economic aspects of forest management and food production. Research into the following subjects is being given priority:

- Ways in which rural people currently use forest and farm trees, and to what extent they are dependent on them for their food security;
- Methods by which existing patterns of cultivation could be improved to produce higher quality timber and non-timber products;

- Techniques for arresting land degradation and preventing soil damage using trees or agroforestry methods;
- Methods of sustainable agricultural production that maximize the use of natural nutrients and reduce the need for fertilizers and pesticides;
- The ecology of different plant and animalspecies, and techniques for their sustainable production;
- The identification, conservation and management of under-exploited species;
- The effect of forest and trees on groundwater and rainfall availability for agriculture; and
- The sustainable management of forests for multi purpose uses.

DESIGNING PROJECTS TO MEET LOCAL NEEDS

The challenge for forestry project workers is to devise programmes that are relevant to each individual community, and provide local people with an opportunity to increase their incomes and improve their food security. Programmes based on traditional and new forms of agroforestry on farm and forest land are some of the most promising. Trees can provide food, animal fodder and income, improve conditions for growing food and cash crops, and enhance livestock productivity.

Projects need to be developed and tested under the local conditions on which their success depends. This means identifying, at the planning stage: the nature of existing land ownership arrangements; customs relating to the growth and use of trees; the nature of the community's food shortage problem; and the people the project is intended to benefit.

The complexities of ownership and tenure of land and trees determine who can reap the benefits of tree cultivation. They are therefore of vital importance at the project planning stage. Common property systems under which families or communities own areas of land, including substantial forest areas, are found in many parts of the world, particularly Africa. Many of the poorest members of society may, in fact, own no land themselves and therefore be totally reliant on communal lands for food and income. In the past, this has been an effective way of managing land, but population growth is now putting a strain on communal lands. Agroforestry programmes which improve such traditional arrangements have been far more effective in increasing food security than programmes which are based on externally-imposed property systems.

Land ownership arrangements are less oriented towards the community and the poor in Latin America and Asia, for instance, where land ownership tends to be concentrated amongst a small percentage of the population. Most small farmers rent their lands or practice shifting cultivation within the forests. Population pressure has led both to much wider dependency on forest lands and products, and to the clearance of forest lands for agriculture. Possible solutions include increasing security of tenure for people farming forest lands and helping them to use their land more intensively. Some Asian governments have begun to issue long-term leases of forest lands to local people and to cooperate with them in developing agroforestry schemes to increase food security.

Successful schemes of this type have been carried out in the Philippines and Java, and Thailand. In Thailand, people traditionally reliant on shifting cultivation systems are employed by the forest department to establish plantations, and may plant and harvest crops between the trees. Each family is also given several hectares of land to farm for themselves. No land title is issued, but permits that entitle the holder to use the land can be inherited, though not sold.

Land ownership is not the only issue affecting food security, however. In many countries, land ownership rights do not necessarily also confer ownership of the trees that grow on the land. Large trees in Kenya, for example, are often regarded as the property of extended kinship groups, even though they may be situated on what is essentially privatelyheld land. Planting or owning trees in other areas, such as West Africa, however, does confer ownership of the land and, for that reason, farmers are often prohibited from planting trees on the rented lands they farm.

In some societies, the right to exploit tree products, whether on farm or forest lands, is not associated with ownership of trees. In the Dominican Republic and Honduras, the ownership of all trees, including those planted on farm land, is vested in the State. Farmers may be prevented from cutting trees on their land and thus discouraged from planting them.

Even in areas where local people have rights of tenure or of access to forest lands, they may have the right to gather only certain products. Traditionally, medicines and foods can often be gathered, while cutting trees may be prohibited.

If food security programmes are to be successful, an understanding of nutrition is also essential so that local deficiencies in diet can be identified. Each community needs to be studied individually because dietary problems can range from specific vitamin deficiencies to general undernourishment due to seasonal shortfalls in any or all types of food.

PROJECT DESIGN

In accordance with OP/BP 4.01, *Environmental Assessment*, the environmental assessment (EA) for an investment project addresses the potential impact of the project on forests and/or the rights and welfare of local communities.

For projects involving the management of forests proposed for Bank financing, the borrower furnishes the Bank with relevant information on the forest sector concerning the borrower's overall policy framework, national legislation, institutional capabilities, and the poverty, social, economic, or environmental issues related to forests. This information should include information on the country's national forest programs or other relevant country-driven processes. On the basis of this information and the project's EA, the borrower, as appropriate, incorporates measures in the project to strengthen the fiscal, legal, and institutional framework to meet the project's economic, environmental, and social objectives. These measures address, among other issues, the respective roles and legal rights of the government, the private sector, and local people. Preference is given to small-scale, community-level management approaches where they best harness the potential of forests to reduce poverty in a sustainable manner.

As appropriate, the design of projects that use forest resources or provide environmental services includes an evaluation of the prospects for the development of new markets and marketing arrangements for non-timber forest products and related forest goods and services, taking into account the full range of goods and environmental services from well-managed forests.

POLICY AND LEGISLATION ISSUES

The aim of this analysis of collective FMP and plan is to promote appropriate changes in forest policies and legislation which will support the effective scaling up of local forest governance.

USE OF BY-LAWS

Many decentralized local forest governance systems are based on use of local by-laws. Whilst by-laws may appear to offer legal backing to these arrangements, there are some risks involved as exemplified by the case study from Zanzibar by Lindsay, (1998). Collective forest managers do not necessarily have long-term legal security under by-laws because the legal authority of the local institution granting self-governance authority may itself be uncertain. This may cause problems relating to power relationships with other stakeholders outside the community (e.g. with timber concessionaires, neighbouring villages, nomads, local government) because by-laws cannot formally define the rules by which CFMs can interact with outsiders nor can locally derived rules define the limits of state power. The rights of CFMs to manage and utilize forests need to be exclusive to prevent access by outsiders. Clarity is needed as to what these rights actually are and that they cannot be taken away or changed unilaterally. The example from Zanzibar illustrates the fragile legal security of many CFMs.

Many community forestry initiatives have used the local by-law option as a means of operating within the local political context. This is often a positive choice to work with imperfect legal instruments and concentrate on persuasion and building alliances rather than pushing immediately for major legal changes that may upset delicate coalitions

In India, the JFM programme continues to be mostly a creation of state notifications and administrative orders . The national Forest Act of 1927 has not been revised, and there are almost no examples of revised State Forest Acts to provide a firmer legal basis for JFM. This has provided some initial flexibility in responding to experiences and problems encountered in implementation but it also fosters a sense that the rights of participants are malleable and temporary, and can be changed unilaterally government decides that conditions warrant it.

FOREST DEVOLUTION IN THE WIDER POLITICAL ENVIRONMENT

The use of simpler FMPs for more effective local forest management implies more devolved decision making since it is the local CFMs who will be ultimately responsible for preparing and implementing such plans. However, devolved forest management is not a politically neutral strategy. In most places it requires an agenda of political reforms to support it.

Devolved natural resource management has been particularly problematic where the sector is a net contributor to the state budget . This true for the forestry sector in many countries where forest revenues fund other sectors of government. Therefore, scaling up of small-scale initiatives in participatory forest management and their legitimization by the state does not normally take place without political backing.

There is now a general trend for top-down governance and resource management to be consciously replaced by more participatory and devolved approaches across all sectors – usually because the state is convinced of the economic, social and environmental benefits of these approaches. However, as Lindayati (2000) points out, policy formulation is not necessarily about a rational decision-making process and selecting the best (economically, socially and ecologically) policy options. For example, policy decisions are often determined by the interests and ideals of those who have power to make them. Some are a direct response to natural calamities or disasters whilst some are strongly influenced by the political mood in a society . Often a "sense of crisis" is needed to "unfreeze" policy makers and introduce changes.

As shown by this study, there are many examples of simpler forest management planning from many countries. The extent to which successful initiatives can provide a stimulus for effective policy change leading to a greater spread of benefits depends on a number of factors identified by Mayers and Bass (1999):

- Extent of 'gap' left by government;
- Viability of local forestry options;
- Viability of local institutions;

- Strength and equity of incentives, leaders and organization at local level;
- Degree and equity of devolution of power; and
- Degree of support from enlightened national/state elite.

Collective forest managers therefore need the opportunity, within policy frameworks, to experiment with such new ideas. Foresters can assist in the facilitation process by linking successful field-based initiatives with supportive policy changes.

OVERLOADED GOVERNMENT INSTITUTIONS

The supportive role of forest administrations is important for initiatives such as learning–oriented FMP preparation processes. It is common for frontline staff of such institutions to be overloaded with ever expanding service delivery for collective forest management approaches in addition to their other duties and their own subsistence needs.

Under conventional extension approaches, frontline staff are usually expected to be carriers of predetermined technical information and normally do not need to be highly qualified professionals with a range of skills. However, as has been described here, participatory planning processes require support and facilitation – invariably is the frontline staff who are expected to provide this despite the fact that they are frequently underpaid, de-skilled, poorly motivated and provided with little or no infrastructural support.

Shepherd (1998) argues that such frontline staff, standing at the extension-client interface, have to act as liaison persons, spokespersons, disseminators, resource handlers and negotiators between the forestry administration and collective forest managers. This is a complex job requiring ability, commitment and confidence.

Policy and legislative change in support of collective forest management (with all the implications of simpler FMPs), therefore needs to be backed up by organizational changes within forestry administrations which recognize the critical role being performed by frontline staff. Often this means rebuilding the organizational structure itself based on the new task requirements and, perhaps not surprisingly, decentralizing and devolving powers and responsibility within such government institutions.

DEALING WITH POWER DIFFERENCES

Local elites including large landholders, traders, traditional leaders, and other individuals who have had power to influence many of their neighbours in matters of forest management are often in the position of informal policy makers shaping the outcome of devolution policies – usually against the interests of the poor,. Frontline forest administration staff are expected to facilitate the sensitive process of realigning these local power arrangements as part of the decentralized forest management planning process – clearly not an easy job.

Local bureaucrats may be reluctant to challenge the position and interests of local elites because of historical "patron-client" relations between these groups. In this situation, the local representation process can be easily manipulated with participation of the forest-dependent poor in planning and decision-making being especially difficult and often an ideal rather than a prevailing practice. Ironically, the organization (forest administration) which has been given the responsibility for devolving control of forests to local communities has traditionally represented the interests of those same elites. One solution would be to improve the levels of skills and professionalism amongst frontline staff although some would argue that as this is never likely to be really effective a better model would be for other organizations (NGOs) or other service providers to become more involved – particularly with negotiation between local elites and other local people.

2

Participatory Approaches to Planning for Community Forestry Project

THE FOCUS OF THE PROEJCT

PEOPLE'S PARTICIPATION

Development projects are by definition external interventions. Why, when and how they are identified, formulated and approved depends on the policies and negotiation skills of the different parties involved, usually governments, non-governmental organizations (NGOs) or international institutions. Direct involvement of the intended target groups or their representatives in this process of project preparation and negotiation is not a common practice. At most, with the help of some local people, a general assessment of constraints and opportunities to be addressed through project interventions is made during project identification and formulation. As a consequence, when development projects become operational, their appearance is generally a surprise for the intended target groups. An *effort is* under way to change this state of affairs, however, using methods that come under the name of "participatory development" or "people's participation".

People's participation is now thought by many to be a prerequisite for sustainable development.

There are, however, a variety of different interpretations of what "people's participation" and "participatory development" should and do mean in practice, ranging from *"we want them to participate in what we do"* to *"we want to support them in the achievement of their goals"*.

Broadly speaking, depending on project objectives and strategies, two approaches can be distinguished. The first type is the "blueprint" or "target-oriented" approach, in which projects are defined in terms of mechanisms for the delivery of pre-defined packages of goods and services to specific target groups. Participation in this context is understood in terms of the willingness of people to undertake the required activities.

The second type can be called the "process-oriented" approach. In this approach, specific categories of activities are defined by the people themselves. This definition is made on the basis of local resources and needs, with support ("facilitation") from the project. The technical message is not a uniform, pre-defined recipe but a "menu" with various options. Participation in this context is understood to mean that the people themselves assume ownership and accountability for activities, which they have identified and developed with the support of the project.

According to the typology of participation developed by Pretty , two forms of participation derive from these two approaches. The first, found in blueprint approaches, can be called "passive participation", whereby people participate by being told what is going to happen. The second, found in process-oriented approaches, can be called "interactive participation" whereby people participate in joint analysis, which leads to locally formulated action plans. Other types of participation exist in between and outside these two.

Under various forms of passive participation, people can participate by providing information to outsiders, by providing resources (usually labour) in return for incentives and by forming groups to undertake planned activities. A common characteristic of these types of participation is that planning and decision-making are in the hands of outsiders and relate to externally predetermined objectives.

In the case of interactive participation, on the other hand, local groups or communities take control. Interactive participation is meant to lead to action plans at local level, as well as creating (or enhancing) an organizational setting for their sustained implementation. Local people and project staff jointly undertake the different steps in the planning process.

PARTICIPATORY PLANNING

In the context of community forestry projects, participatory planning can be defined as joint actions of local people and project staff with the objective of formulating development plans and selecting the best available alternatives for their implementation. It should be a two-way learning process of dialogue, negotiation and decision-making between insiders and outsiders, concerning activities to be undertaken by the insiders and supported by the outsiders. It is thus conceptualized in terms of what can be called a "negotiating dialogue" between local people and project staff, aimed at conforming project support to local needs, constraints and opportunities. Simply stated, participatory planning is an effort of the parties involved to elaborate a common agenda for future development actions. This agenda is not completely open: both parties already have their own agendas, mandates and responsibilities. The challenge is to identify and agree upon those actions that fit in with both. Special methods and tools have been developed that facilitate the identification and elaboration of common agendas.

CRITICAL ASSUMPTIONS UNDERLYING THE PARTICIPATORY APPROACH

A comparative analysis of case studies on participatory planning in community forestry may seem a difficult undertaking at first, in view of the diversity of situations and the variety of factors involved. However, several common parameters can be distinguished.

In all these projects, the rural poor are considered the key actors in improving their own living conditions, as well as in managing their natural resources sustainably. Thus, their participation is essential to the success of the project activities. Four basic assumptions regarding the outcome of this participation underlie the analysis.

Decisions affecting the management of natural resources are continuously being made at many different levels, from the local farm household to the national government and even to international regulating agencies or multinational corporations. Because of the particular and often conflicting interests of the parties involved, conflict management is frequently an important dimension of natural resource management.

In this context, local empowerment (in particular of disadvantaged groups) constitutes a basic condition for achieving sustainability. The first assumption, therefore, is that participatory approaches facilitate this process of local empowerment by creating opportunities for specific disadvantaged groups, such as women or the landless, to have access to external resources (training, credits) or to mobilize their own resources (organization, knowledge, skills). This enhances their capacity to take action to defend their own interests.

Participatory planning approaches aim at strengthening the local capacity for sustainable development in terms of knowledge, skills and organization. One of the important ways to ensure that local capacity is improved is through the recognition of the appropriateness of local knowledge in designing project actions. The second assumption is that the use of participatory approaches will allow the integration of local knowledge systems into local project planning and implementation. The project then complements these knowledge systems with technical support for the development of appropriate technical menus. Therefore, in particular during the planning process, emphasis should put on the mutual assessment and mobilization of local knowledge and management systems.

Participation does not just mean getting the basic information out of the community in order to "target" the project interventions effectively. This approach is oriented towards establishing horizontal relationships between external agents (the project) and the local community, as equal partners who are willing to learn from each other. The third assumption is that participatory planning facilitates a two-way learning process between the local community and the project. This two-way learning process should facilitate the timely adjustment of project support services to changing local realities. Similarly, it should strengthen local capacity to identify and mobilize local as well as external resources needed to undertake sustained actions.

Development projects operate within an existing institutional framework, and participatory approaches should provide planners and decision-makers with the necessary information for providing more adequate enabling environments and institutional support. The extent to which local communities are given the conditions for, are capable of and are interested in developing more sustainable resource management systems will determine the level of local capacity for claiming higher quality external services. The institutional environment should respond to these bottom-up claims for more decentralized planning. The final assumption is that participatory planning will enhance political commitment and institutional support for local planning by building a common understanding between institutions and local groups.

THE CONCEPTUAL FRAMEWORK

Participatory planning is defined above using the concept of a "negotiating dialogue" between the parties involved, which are the local community, groups or households (the insiders) and the project or institutions (the outsiders). This planning process should produce two sets of results.

- In the short term, the tools of. participatory of planning should generate a two-way learning process, wich will shape project interventions to local needs, oppurtunities and constraints.
- In the long term, this learning process should lead to a) local empowerment and. b) effective support at the institutional level.

These are considered preconditions for strengthening both institutional capacity for decentralized planning and local planning capacity. In the case of natural resource management, the strengthening of these two capacity levels should lead to more sustainable use and management of resources.

Lessons from community forestry indicate that local-level decision-making and planning are fundamental for sustainable development. It has become clear after decades of experience that environmental problems such as deforestation and ecological degradation cannot be solved simply by planting trees. Sustainable management of natural resources requires a more comprehensive approach, which includes strengthening the organizational and technical capacities of rural communities, as well as engendering at least passive support for sustainable resource use from the larger community group. Four critical and interrelated conditions in this context are: (1) the presence of strong local organizations and community support for sustainable management; (2) the ability to ensure access to and control over natural resources (appropriate tenure systems); (3) the conditions for undertaking participatory technology development (integration of local knowledge and management systems); and (4) the existence of local systems for distributing benefits equitably. This can be visualized as follows:

In designing a participatory project, particular attention needs to be paid during the planning process to local knowledge, skills, decision-making procedures and communication systems, as well as to existing organizational structures. It is important to understand the profiles and perceptions of the different power groups involved in local decision-making or excluded from it. Accurate knowledge of the critical factors of organizational development, technical capacity, rights to land, trees and water, and benefit distribution systems should guide the design process. This knowledge should form the basis for selecting the tools and incentives that will be used to respond to the specific needs of the local community and, in particular, to the needs of the most disadvantaged groups.

From the project point of view, two questions must be addressed at the time of project planning:

- To what extent are the project objectives and strategies explicitly oriented towards participatory planning (are they process-oriented or target-oriented)?
- Is the technical dimension of the project defined in terms of predetermined technical messages, or in the form of a range of possible technical menus, to be developed and verified during project imple mentation?

Project institutional capacity is also critical. It depends not only on the methodological and conceptual orientation of project personnel, but also on project procedures for planning, implementation, internal communication and feedback, and on linkages between these procedures and the local planning process. Thus, special attention needs to be paid to (1) project objectives and strategies, (2) project technical approach, methods and tools, (3) project organization and management and (4) the development of institutional linkages (networking). These aspects are interrelated and can be visualized as follows:

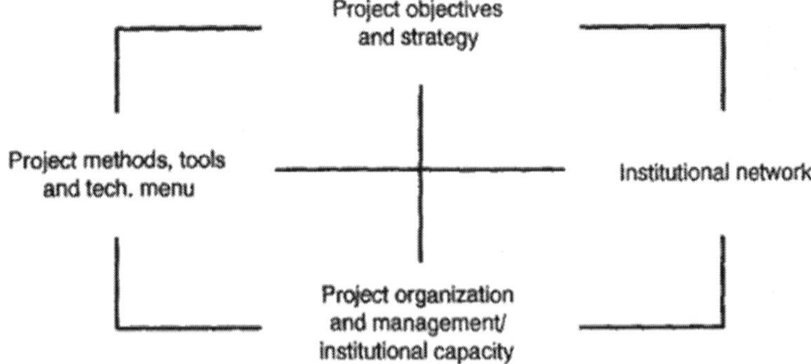

Fig. Critical Institutional Aspects for Participatory Approaches

The overall project design needs to be clearly oriented towards participatory strategies in the field. In order to promote interactive participation at the local level, project objectives and strategies need to be process-oriented. These strategies must be reinforced and further developed through the verification of methods, tools and technical menus in the field, as well as through the mobilization of institutional networks. This reinforcement depends on an appropriate project management structure and style, as well as on the adequacy of institutional capacity in terms of human: resources, funding and infrastructure.

The local community and the project, with their respective critical issues or conditions for participatory planning, can be thought of as "local enabling institutions" and "external enabling institutions". The critical areas will be interlinked when the local and the external systems interact. For example, integration of local knowledge systems depends on the nature of the project technical proposals. Likewise, institutional linkages and networking can generate the political commitment needed to overcome local land tenure constraints.

METHODS AND TOOLS

The methods and tools most frequently used in process-oriented development projects are those taken from rapid rural appraisal techniques. Ideally, these methods and tools strengthen the capacity of local people to identify and analyse priority needs, opportunities and constraints, and consequently to plan activities, implement them and evaluate the results. At the same time, they permit project staff to get a better understanding of the local realities and to learn from the local people's experience.

Rapid rural appraisal (RRA) and participatory rural appraisal (PRA), which make use of these instruments, have become fashionable in projects that are process-oriented. While it is beyond the scope of this study to elaborate on the differences between PRA and RRA, according to Chambers they can be placed on a continuum with at one end RRA, which is an instrument for data collection and learning by outsiders, and at the other end PRA, which is meant to enable local people to conduct their own analysis. In principle, the same appraisal methods and tools can be used in both RRA and PRA exercises. The main differences relate to the behavioural roles played in each by outsiders and insiders; in other words, to how and by whom these methods are used in the field.

A number of manuals or "toolboxes" have been published recently , and training courses or workshops on PRA and RRA methods and tools are multiplying rapidly in most parts of the world. There is, however, the risk that when manuals or toolboxes begin being used as recipes, they lose their ability to adjust to local situations. One of the most important qualities of these instruments is their flexibility and adaptability. Not all methods and tools can be used under all circumstances. Selective and creative use is more appropriate than mechanical application of the contents of a manual.

Therefore, in this study, no comparative analysis is made of the effectiveness of the different methods and tools. It is more important to consider how they are used, at both the local and institutional level. Important questions in this context are:

- To what extent has the use of these methods and tools contributed to a process of self-analysis, at both local and institutional levels?
- Does the use of these methods and tools indeed facilitate local planning and adequate design of project interventions?

INSTITUTIONALIZATION AND SUSTAINABILITY

Participatory planning is the initial step in the definition of a common agenda for development by a local community and an external entity or entities. Over a period of years, this initial step is expected to evolve for the parties concerned towards (1) a self-sustaining development planning process at the local level, and (2) the decentralization of national institutional planning. Through this process, these two planning levels should grow to be closely interrelated. The result will ideally be the continuing formulation of comprehensive and integrated plans for sustainable development of natural resources. As consolidated procedures and mechanisms for consultation and negotiation gradually evolve, the original participatory project approaches and methods will become institutionalized. This will lead to a sustained process of planning based on negotiation, in which all groups with a stake in the use and the conservation of natural resources will be involved on an equitable basis.

COMMUNITY FORESTRY PROJECTS

The community forestry projects include one from Africa, two from Latin America and two from Asia:

- The PREVINOBA project in Tivaouane, Senegal
- The Potosi Community Forestry Project in Bolivia
- The Los Maribios project in Nicaragua
- The Malakand/Dir Social Forestry Project in Pakistan
- The Begnas Tal Rupa Tal Project in Nepal

THE PREVINOBA PROJECT

The overall objective of the Village Reforestation Project in the Northwest of the Groundnut Belt in Senegal is to contribute to the battle against desertification through the improvement of the natural environment and the living conditions of the rural population. Specific objectives are to consolidate local capacity for integrated village land use and natural resource management, comprising the integration of forestry activities within agriculture and livestock systems, and to support the institutional strengthening of the forestry service. These activities should lead to the restoration of forest cover and enrichment of the soils to achieve sustainable self-sufficiency in forestry products for the local population, as well as raising incomes of farmers through silvicultural activities.

The approach of the project is to create the conditions for a permanent dialogue between the "primary actors" (local community members) and the "support actors" (external development workers), in order to enable and encourage local communities to take their development into their own hands (self-help). Based on an annual planning process, villagers progressively take charge of development activities through a re-examination of their own knowledge and skills and the application of new technologies. The approach aims to strengthen their capacity for appraisal, problem identification and analysis, organization, training, implementation and monitoring and evaluation. The steps followed are:

- Sensitization of different institutional authority levels about the project and its methodology;
- Selection of target villages and organization of awareness workshops in these villages;
- Prioritization and selection by the villagers of forestry activities to undertake;
- Farmers' training through exchange of experiences between the farmers and the project;
- Systematic monitoring by village forestry committees; and
- Evaluation: technical (by the forestry committee), qualitative (by the whole village) and global (by all the actors involved).

The results of the evaluation exercises are fed back into the planning process for the following year, returning to step 3 in an iterative process of plan improvement.

The experience of the Previnoba project shows that the participatory approach produces a progressive accountability of the villages, leading to an active participation of the villagers in forestry activities. Investments are made by the villages with their own resources, for example to finance the fencing of village woodlots and to purchase new materials. Village organizations have adopted measures such as sanction systems for the protection of the environment. New working and exchange relations are developed within the community and between it and the outside world.

THE POTOSI COMMUNITY FORESTRY PROJECT

The objective of the Potosi project in the Andean highlands of southwest Bolivia is the improvement of living standards of the peasants through the integration of sustainable forestry activities within existing production systems.

In order to achieve this objective, the project endeavours to (1) integrate tree planting and management into agricultural and livestock land use systems in order to improve productive outputs and to protect soils and water; (2) improve and adapt extension and training methodologies, verifying results in the field in order to develop an appropriate methodology for the Bolivian highlands; and (3) develop institutional capacity of governmental and non-governmental organizations for the promotion of community forestry.

The method used by the project is to promote a technical menu at the village level, which consists of agroforestry systems integrating tree production, planting and management and the commercialization of forestry products into existing production systems. Extension activities are oriented towards establishing a dialogue with the local communities on the basis of this technical menu. As soon as the communities have decided to start forestry activities, the extension worker starts supporting them in the preparation of their Community Forestry Plans. A clear distinction is made between the technical menu as an institutional proposal and the Community Forestry Plan as an elaboration by the community itself of the institutional proposal on the basis of local needs and priorities. In this approach, best described as participatory extension for community forestry, the extension worker assumes the role of promoter, facilitator and trainer, supporting and orienting the local communities in the planning, implementation and evaluation of their forestry development.

As a result of the project, local forestry planning capacity has been strengthened significantly: through practical experience the local communities are now in a better position to formulate their plans on the basis of local constraints and opportunities. Similarly, the project has strengthened its own capacity to respond more effectively to the community forestry plans: it has been able to adjust its own annual planning procedures based, within the framework of the project document, on the profiles of the community forestry plans. The project has also signed a number of agreements of collaboration with government agencies and NGOs that are promoting rural development programmes in the project area, with the aim of institutionalizing the methodological approach and technical menu of the project.

THE LOS MARIBIOS PROJECT

The full name of this project in northwest Nicaragua indicates its general objective: "Conservation and management of natural resources with community participation on the western slopes of the Maribios hill range". The specific objectives are: (1) to develop a replicable system of agroforestry extension based on farmers' participation and institutional participation; and (2) to promote the active participation of around 3 000 farmers (at least 25% women) who should develop an adequate capacity in planning, management and rational use of the natural resources in an area of 72 000 ha.

In the project approach, the extension worker uses RRA as a tool to make a first assessment of the "strong and weak" points of rural communities, leading to the selection of communities for project intervention. Next, more specific information is collected about the community to get to know the people and their problems. Information collected at individual level is clustered by group (landless, small, medium and big farmers, cooperatives) in order to identify both common and group-specific problem areas. This results in a selective list of the most important problems of the community, among which those that fall within the scope of the project are identified. On the basis of these group meetings, an initial appraisal is made of possible project support.

Before concrete plans are worked oat with individual peasants, a description and analysis is made of the opportunities ad constraints of their farms or off-farm activities, based on direct observation (transect walking) and interviews.

Then, for those with land, a farm management plan is worked out and put into an agreement between the farmer and the project. For the landless, groups are formed to manage the rational use of the resources (such as fuelwood) from which they earn their living. These steps constitute the process of participatory extension. As developed by the project, participatory extension is a continuous, progressive and iterative learning process for the extension worker and the peasant. The RRA is considered as a starting point of this process and is aimed at incorporating the farmers' perspective. The extension activities to orient and support this process are the execution of a participatory appraisal and the promotion of alternatives. The different phases of participatory extension are defined from both the institutional and the farmers' perspectives.

The response of farmers has been very positive and the project has contributed to the phenomenon of farmer group formation for improved land use management. Women, often on their own initiative, have started to prepare management plans for their vegetable gardens, introducing the production of fruit and forestry trees and applying soil protection measures. Landless peasants, such as the local fuelwood collectors, were very difficult to approach when the project started as they had always been involved in illegal tree cutting and fuelwood collection. Their positive response indicates that the project's technical menu responds to local opportunities and constraints. The project eases the basic problems of access to land, to appropriate technologies for land use management and to financial resources. The methodological approach helps the farmers to take control, the claiming and negotiating capacity of individual farmers or groups and provides them with the means to negotiate, and facilitates access to land, technology and credit.

THE MALAKAND SOCIAL FORESTRY PROJECT

The main objective of the Malakand Social Forestry Project in northwest Pakistan is to contribute to raising the standard of living in the region by improving the productivity and use of the hillsides and marginal farmlands. This is done through restoring suitable vegetation to the denuded hillsides, while developing a participatory extension system based on the "village land use planning" (VLUP) approach. The objective of VLUP is to assist the local population in the development of a management plan for privately and commonly owned hillsides and farmlands. The planning process is implemented by villagers and an interdisciplinary team of outsiders, and goes through the following phases:

(1) preparation; (2) analysis of village land use based on RRA techniques; (3) social organization; (4) development of management plans for specific land use units; and (5) implementation and monitoring of the plans. The outcome of this process is a village land use plan based on (1) the socio-economic and biophysical constraints and opportunities in the village, (2) the needs and wishes of land users, and (3) the services that the project can provide, summarized in what is called "the social forestry menu". This menu is developed for three types of land use: natural vegetation, vegetation established by the Forestry Department and agricultural lands. For each, potential technical project activities have been identified.

The next step is the formation of Village Development Committees (VDCs), comprising representatives from the different owner-lineages and, whenever village circumstances permit, involvement of representatives of non-owners as well.

Conflicts of interest and power at village level are one of the major constraints faced by the project, because the social structure of the villages is highly stratified, making it difficult to bypass the elite and reach other groups (other lineage groups, non-owners such as tenants and settled nomads, and women).

Explicit attention is being paid to gender issues, both by promoting women's activities and by trying to make the VLUP approach more gender specific. However, the traditional purdah system of gender segregation causes serious difficulties in this area.

Within the VDC, management committees are formed to develop the management plans. Once the plans have been approved, implementation starts and the parties involved assume their responsibilities. Once the plan is prepared, an agreement is signed between the VDC management committee and the project, in which the rights and obligations of each are specified. The plans are not considered a blueprint, but rather as indicative and flexible instruments to stimulate conscious decision-making about the management of an area. Over time, it has gradually become clear at the institutional level that the social forestry approach is a participatory planning process: the final outcome of the negotiations with the villagers can never be planned beforehand. In other words, the process can be planned but not the outcome.

THE BEGNAS TAL RUPA TAL WATERSHED MANAGEMENT PROJECT

In Nepal, in addition to the PUCD project in Ghorka, the Begnas Tal Rupa Tal Watershed Management project (BTRT) was selected for this report. The general objective of the BTRT is to stabilize the physical environment and increase the productivity of the project area through sustainable community management of its human and natural resources.

The specific objectives are: (1) adoption by farmers of soil conservation techniques and agroforestry practices; (2) rehabilitation of all identified critical soil erosion sites; (3) improvement of forest in the project area through protection, planting and management; (4) formation of user groups to identify, plan and manage their catchments; (5) involvement of women, occupational castes and minority groups of the community in the sustainable management of the human and natural resources, in order for all sections of the community to participate in and benefit from the project. Project strategy is aimed at training and assisting Community User Groups or Community Development Conservation Committees (CDCCs) to adopt sound land use management practices in order to address all the problems resulting in decreasing productivity and environmental decline.

Planning for the identification and implementation of development activities in the BTRT project area begins with the initiation of villagers themselves or the motivation of the villagers by BTRT project personnel. The final stage of this process of "programme development", as it is called in this project, is the implementation of local project activities and the sharing of the benefits among the participants. In between these two stages there are three other stages of programme development in which villagers and BTRT project personnel are involved: formation of the CDCC or user group; problem identification, needs assessment and prioritization; and programme formulation and negotiation.

BTRT staff members at the field stations have been successful in promoting a participatory approach and the formation of CDCCs in the communities. The CDCC has proved to be an adequate organizational structure for the elaboration of a global framework of watershed management planning in which a number of villages participate. At the same time, further detailed planning for implementation of specific activities is being delegated to the different committees. The CDCCs provide the opportunity to use local knowledge in the elaboration of the community forestry management plans. Villagers' knowledge of forestry resources and management skills in protecting and using the forest for the sustainable harvesting of forest products are demonstrated while preparing the plan for their village or ward.

The local socio-cultural context can limit the ability of participatory planning to contribute to the empowerment of disadvantaged groups. Although most of the CDCCs are made up of villagers belonging to different ethnic groups, socio-economic levels and educational levels, these committees tend to be dominated by the local elite. For example, literate villagers tend to take precedence over illiterate members and influence decision-making. It is not uncommon, therefore, that for disadvantaged groups, "participatory" planning is limited to participation in needs identification and assessment, and then to subsequent participation in implementation through labour contribution. On the other hand, the consolidation of different user groups into CDCCs for their better management has reduced overlapping of these groups in the community. Participatory planning of development activities is done through a series of general meetings of members of CDCCs or of the executive committee or of subcommittees for specific activities.

THE FOUR PARTICIPATORY UPLAND CONSERVATION AND DEVELOPMENT FIELD PROJECTS

The four case studies examined here are part of the Interregional Project for Participatory Upland Conservation and Development (PUCD). This project, started in 1991, has the aim of promoting the adaptation and application of participatory methods for the promotion of an integrated approach to watershed management. The PUCD has national field projects in Nepal, Pakistan, Rwanda, Burundi and Bolivia. Four out of five of these field projects were included in this study. They are located in Ghorka (Nepal), Quetta (Pakistan), Butare (Rwanda) and Makamba (Burundi).

The development objective of the PUCD interregional project is the transfer of responsibility for the management of upland catchments to local communities in accordance with the social, economic and production system requirements of these rural communities. The specific objectives are: to install five integrated upland conservation development projects in the selected countries incorporating the participatory approach; to coordinate the watershed management systems among these five countries, ensuring mutual strengthening of methodology and tool design, planning, implementation and evaluation; and to contribute to information dissemination on the subject of participatory watershed management.

The project approach is process-oriented and focused on local capacity building. Each project workplan is the outcome of a participatory planning process. Networking and interinstitutional linkages are used to broaden the scope of the technical support services that can be made available to local communities, including public works services from the government.

In each of the field projects, the first three to four months were reserved as a period for assessment, restitution and planning with the local population. To facilitate this participatory approach, tools of PRA and RRA were used by the local population and the project team together to prepare a workplan for immediate implementation. Implementation of activities started in most cases by the end of 1992. The projects had been designed with an initial pilot phase of two years in order to develop and verify the methodological approach. Therefore, during these first two years, special emphasis was given to the exchange between the field projects of experiences and lessons learned. At the end of the pilot phase, a technical review meeting of the project teams was convened.

THE PUCD PROJECT IN GHORKA

In Nepal the interregional project is working in the Bhusunde Khola Watershed (BKW), located in Ghorka District in the Western Development Region. So far, almost all planned activities have been implemented by 22 user groups. The project has provided the required material, financial and training inputs. The user groups assumed their responsibility for the organization and mobilization of the labour inputs. One of the major constraints faced by the project from the beginning has been the insufficient number of field staff and inadequate levels of training Although initial training for project staff took place, experience has shown that this was insufficient to promote the necessary conceptual orientation and participatory approach, or to impart adequate practical training in the use of PRA tools in the field.

The project also had to demonstrate its credibility as a serious partner, which meant that participants needed to see that activities took place and results were obtained. However, participatory planning needs careful assessment of proposed activities with the different interest groups before activities can be initiated, and this takes time. To avoid loss of interest, the process was speeded up. Activities were selected without a community environmental assessment and without a problem census. The opportunities for improved resource management in the area included a strong local awareness of problems of environmental degradation, the willingness and ability to organize into viable user groups, and a strong tradition of democratic discussion and group decision through consensus. In practice, the participation of the villagers (mostly the men) has been limited to the stages of appraisal and implementation, and to a lesser extent to the elaboration of the specific plans. The participatory approach should have encouraged local people to come together to determine development activities and their feasibility, and to define the responsibilities of the different individuals or groups. Broad-based village participation in the planning exercise is fundamental for the local people to get a clear understanding of what their "participation" in "planning" actually means in terms of their power to make decisions.

THE PUCD PROJECT IN QUETTA

In Pakistan the PUCD project, executed through the Balochistan Forest and Wildlife Department of the Ministry of Agriculture, is in the Kanak Valley southwest of Quetta. Water, because of its scarcity and the low rainfall levels, is the most important natural resource in the area. The most significant cash crop, fruits and vegetables, could not be produced without irrigation from tubewells, but these wells are lowering the water-table. After an analysis carried out by the villages, the project has been able to distinguish three areas for action: (1) increase the infiltration of rainwater by reducing runoff; (2) improve on-farm water harvesting techniques and water management; and (3) improve water-use regulations. A thorough cause-effect analysis was made of the issues mentioned by the villagers in order to arrive at a feasible plan of action for each of the villages.

It proved to be difficult to achieve an understanding of the participatory approach among the villagers. This region is near the Afghan border, where many projects are delivering relief to Afghan refugees. Villagers therefore tend to assume that outsiders are always the "givers", bringing "free" inputs to poor people. This is an attitude that needs constantly to be addressed by the project team. The villagers, and especially the women, generally consider themselves too poor to undertake action or not intelligent enough to assume responsibilities. When the appraisal exercises were conducted, the participants were usually in small groups, composed mainly of members of the local elite. In spite of the efforts of the project team to encourage the village heads to invite more people to attend the meetings, the results have not been satisfactory. An important factor in this context is the role and powerful position of the village chief. The language issue has been an important constraint, both within the project and between project and villages. At project level, in particular, it turned out to be difficult and sometimes impossible to translate some of the basic concepts into Urdu. All training sessions far the national field staff required translation into Urdu, weighing down the quality of these events.

The establishment of Village Associations constituted an important first step towards strengthening the local capacity to assume accountability for the planning, implementation and monitoring of specific activities. This institutional strengthening at local level is still in its initial stage and needs to be further supported by the project. The methods, techniques and tools used worked well in general. The PRA was meant to be an initial stage of the project, aimed at the preparation of the workplan. In practice it did much more than that. The PRA tools did generate relevant information for involving both sides in the planning process, but the intensive interaction between the villages and the project also stimulated a process of mutual confidence building.. Because of frustrating past experiences with the Forestry Department and projects, this confidence building is a fundamental step for participatory approaches to be effective. The interpersonal communication skills of the field staff and their ability to listen and to learn thus emerged as priority areas for training and support.

THE PUCD PROJECT IN BUTARE

In Rwanda, the PUCD interregional project is working in the municipality of Runyanya, Province of Butare, in the south of the country. From July 1992 onwards, the project together with the local population carried out an iterative process of participatory appraisal, planning and implementation of priority actions, and planning of more complex activities for the longer term. A detailed project workplan was elaborated and finalized on the basis of actions selected and planned by the population. During the appraisal phase, people were invited to express their needs and to propose actions. This resulted in a very long list of identified priorities related to agriculture, animal husbandry, water, infrastructure, crafts, extension and training, health and education. On the basis of this list three programmes were then formulated by the project: soil conservation and improvement, income generating activities and infrastructure improvement.

A total of about 150 groups, involving approximately 1 700 members, have initiated their respective projects in these three categories. The activities carried out so far have led to a number of results. Without any doubt, the capacity of the local population to direct its own development process has greatly increased. Although still incipient, there is an increased level of farmer organization. Production and conservation programmes have begun and physical works have been implemented. Also, methods and tools for planning and implementation have been tested and are being used locally.

One of the major constraints of this project has been the apparent lack of a long-term perspective within the local population: possibly because of the generalized poverty in the region, local people give priority to actions geared towards short-term results. The project has supported "spark actions" in order to respond to this short-term orientation, to strengthen its credibility as a serious partner and to create some space at the local level to develop a longer-term programme of activities for sustainable resource management.

Local communities appear to be gradually perceiving the project as their own. The most important instrument in this context has been the supportive role of the project in the area of training, and in the provision of equipment and materials for the implementation of mutually selected priority activities. Local communities are more and more capable of analysing their own problems and constraints, determining their priorities and mobilizing their own resources to implement their own projects. An open dialogue that manifests itself during appraisal, planning and evaluation meetings has been instituted between the local communities and the project staff. It has proven very useful for administrative authorities, farmer representatives and the project team to work together to review and analyse the participatory process and the results obtained.

THE PUCD PROJECT IN MAKAMBA

In Burundi, the interregional project is working in the Rwaba watershed, Makamba Province, in the south of the country. At the time of execution of the case study, approximately 130 families, organized in 21 groups, were involved in the preparation or implementation of their own project activities, covering a wide range of fields, from erosion control to social communication . These "microprojects" have been prepared and designed by the groups themselves with additional support from the project. This support has been provided with the objective of strengthening local capacity in the areas of analysis, planning, management of the resources in their environment, mobilization of their own financial, human and material resources, economic and financial management and self-evaluation.

The existing top-down attitude at the institutional level has been one of the principal initial constraints for the implementation of the participatory approach of the project. This legacy was perceived particularly in the attitudes and behaviour patterns of the field staff assigned to the project. In spite of careful training, progress in improving their interpersonal communication skills in the field has been very slow. Likewise, among the villagers. much time had to be invested in explaining how a participatory project would operate and building up its credibility as a serious partner as opposed to the usual top-down projects. For example, in spite of the bad experiences with the cooperative movement that was promoted in the past in the region, the traditional model of solidarity and collective action known as *"ikibiri"* is being taken up again by many groups, thanks to the PUCD project.

There is no doubt that local knowledge and skills have been mobilized and integrated within the identification, planning and organization of the microprojects, in particular during the appraisal phase of needs, constraints and opportunities. However, it is difficult to indicate exactly which elements have been integrated within which activities and how this was done. Apparently this process has followed a more or less "natural" course of sharing information, knowledge and skills between the local people and project staff.

THE APPROACHES

Although three of the projects started as blueprint or target-oriented interventions (Pakistan (Malakand), Nepal and Senegal), by the time these case studies were carried out all nine were process-oriented in approach, with emphasis on participation and sustainability. RRA and PRA tools as well as focused case studies were used effectively as instruments to obtain an understanding of local realities, to define project interventions and to enhance the empowerment of local people.

For project staff, the development, reorientation or verification of methods and tools functions as a permanent learning process. This process stimulates internal discussion, self-evaluation, feedback and analysis, contributing in turn to the further development of technical menus or "baskets of technical options. It leads to a more comprehensive understanding of community forestry and participatory resource management, generating an approach that integrates socio-economic, political, cultural, gender, technical and ecological aspects. Previous field experiences of local or international staff and the exchange of experiences among colleagues have been very useful in strengthening this process of reorientation, adjustment and verification. In all cases, conceptual and methodological issues have a high priority on the agenda of project staff.

The PUCD interregional project was designed on the basis of a process-oriented approach. Unlike some of the projects in this study, the PUCD projects started with a participatory assessment of needs, constraints and opportunities. They then promoted the formation of functional groups around the planning and implementation of specific activities. The explicit objective is to facilitate people's participation by promoting and facilitating local projects that can be identified, planned and implemented by the people themselves. The PUCD project provides technical and financial support to these local activities. One of the major challenges faced by these projects is to establish functional relationships between short-term activities for quick benefits and long-term sustainable management of natural resources. The PUCD case studies show that this long-term perspective cannot be developed properly with a project duration of only two years. The project experiences in Pakistan (Malakand), Senegal, Nicaragua, Bolivia and Nepal indicate that an initial period of at least five years is needed.

The viability of the process approach for community forestry projects depends on the existence of an institutional infrastructure in the project area. However, the cases of Bolivia, Nicaragua, Senegal, Burundi and Rwanda demonstrate that even in the absence of such infrastructure, innovative and creative mechanisms can be developed to mobilize complementary services from other institutions. These can satisfy the need for training, research and technical or financial support. In order to ensure that these mechanisms function effectively, financial and human resources must be put to work to develop active institutional networking. In addition, some of the studies indicate the usefulness of credit facilities (Nicaragua, Burundi, Rwanda, Pakistan). Access to credit can help establish the financial conditions to create local development initiatives, which lead to new income generating and employment opportunities.

METHODS AND TOOLS

In most of the projects, RRAs were conducted as a take-off activity by an interdisciplinary project team for the collection of basic information on the target villages and the region. These appraisals used various instruments, such as observation, interviews, meetings and secondary sources. The scope and length of the appraisal phase are the subject of differing opinions. The most common approach is to start with a concentrated effort of data collection over a few weeks, so that a first assessment can be made of the general opportunities and constraints. As soon as a working relationship has been established between the community and the project, complementary information is collected as part of the responsibilities of the field staff. Simultaneously, participatory assessments are conducted in specific problem areas, such as land use management, farming systems or forestry resources. In other words, the rapid appraisal in most projects collects general information using "traditional" research tools. The participatory assessment is problem-focused and action-oriented, conducted by the project and the concerned interest group and using more "didactic" tools of data collection in order to elaborate project plans.

There are, however, some important differences that can be illustrated when comparing the PUCD project (Quetta) and the community forestry project (Malakand) in Pakistan. In Quetta, map building, timeline and daily time exercises, semi-structured individual interviews and other RRA tools are used to collect general village data. This process takes several months. In the Malakand project, rapid appraisals are carried out in approximately eight days, with a clear focus on land use issues. On the basis of the results, general village management plans and specific land use unit management plans are developed by Management Committees with support from the project. During the elaboration of these plans, specific RRA tools are brought to bear on particular issues, such as map building (land use, land control, land management), timeline and daily time profile exercises for different interest groups, or the elaboration of agricultural or cultural/religious calendars.

The results of the rapid appraisal are often used for the selection of villages, as in Nicaragua, Bolivia and Pakistan. In the PUCD projects, the first three months were generally assumed to be sufficient for these exercises, after which implementation could start. Rapid appraisals were part of the project formulation exercise, which was to define the region of project interventions. This experience indicates that these exercises should not be seen as take-off activities, but as tools to be used throughout the life of the project. The period of three months may be sufficient for project take-off, but the use of RRA and PRA tools should continue, improving and adapting the project through experience to achieve specific objectives.

In general, all the projects follow a similar phasing of activities: (1) preparation, (2) data collection, (3) data processing, (4) analysis and restitution, (5) organization, (6) planning, (7) implementation and monitoring, and (8) evaluation. Some of the methods and tools are used for each of the phases, such as group meetings and working groups. Others, more specific to data collection, analysis and restitution, are used for the planning phase, such as the problem census, the transect walk, map building, timeline and daily time exercises, and so on. Similar methods and tools are often used for the PRA and the planning exercise. The experiences in Pakistan have shown that diagramming and visual sharing are effective tools to facilitate group discussion and analysis, and also that visual recording (video, slides and photos) can be an effective tool for restitution of appraisal results and further analysis and decision-making.

In all the projects examined, methods and tools for participatory assessment and planning are tried, verified and subjected to discussion and adaptation. In this way, existing toolboxes developed by others are used effectively as inputs. Manuals for PRA have been developed in most of the projects, often by modifying and adapting existing materials. They are used for the preparation of the field exercises and as training material for the field staff. It takes time to adapt these materials to the local setting and to verify their effectiveness in the field. The project experiences show that field staff should be involved in this process of adaptation, since this will help to develop their conceptual and methodological orientations.

Although there is not always evidence of systematic use of the different tools, the methodological orientation of the different projects is similar. The underlying intention is to create the conditions for an open dialogue between the local people and the project staff, in order to strengthen the people's capacity to orient their own development. Using the principles of self-help, the participants analyse the situation, identify priority needs, plan actions and mobilize local resources for implementation. This orientation is clearly focused on local-level planning within the context of village, group or private land use management systems.

Thus the case studies show that different RRA and PRA tools are frequently used in the field. It is also important to consider how they are being used, and in some cases, detailed records have been kept of the process. From the perspective of the outsiders (the RRA perspective), the use of these tools has been. effective in familiarizing project staff with the rural realities. From the PRA perspective, their use has also helped enable local people to play an active role in problem analysis, identification and planning of priority activities and implementation. Ideally, the use of these tools is gradually appropriated by the local people, as well as being institutionalized within existing government agencies, and the project staff assumes a facilitating role. In the case of the community forestry projects, two observations can be made in this respect. First, many of the tools have been incorporated into the community forestry extension methodology. Second, use of the tools has contributed to positive changes of behaviour and attitudes of field staff and technical support staff, facilitating listening, learning and sharing of information.

All the cases have shown that the use of RRA and PRA methods and tools have had a positive effect on developing participatory extension approaches in the field. Participatory and rapid rural appraisal tools have proven to be instrumental in extension approaches of both the established community forestry projects and the PUCD projects. In particular in the case of the established projects, these tools are important instruments for the extension staff. They constitute not only operational instruments (what to do), but also conceptual orientations (how to do it) regarding the role of the extension worker as facilitator. In this context, it is clear that both field staff and technical support staff should jointly participate in appraisal exercises, particularly at the initial stages.

For example, in the guidelines for participatory extension prepared by the project in Nicaragua, rural appraisal and participatory assessment are considered integral components of a system of participatory extension. In the Bolivian community forestry project, the focus of the extension approach is to support the villages in the formulation and implementation of their Community Forestry Plans, following the same steps as the appraisal exercises: needs assessment, organization, planning, implementation and evaluation.

In spite of universal previous experience with top-down approaches, the use of these tools has established relations based on mutual trust and respect between outsiders and local communities. However, the importance of explaining and evaluating the objectives of the "exercises" with the community emerged repeatedly. For example, conducting a transect walk with one or two farmers, without an adequate explanation at community level beforehand, can easily lead to misinterpretations by others. Initially, the women of the Quetta project were suspicious of the fact that individual interviews were proposed by the project team. The farmers of Pakistan (Malakand), on the other hand, complained about the general meetings conducted by the project because they saw nothing come out of these gatherings.

A lesson that can be learned is that the use of each of these tools has to be properly prepared, discussed, agreed upon and evaluated with the local people. One of challenges for further improvement is to develop adequate combinations and sequences of the different tools, such as linking mapping exercises with transect walks, or social mapping with identification of key informants and interest groups for group interviews. However, little has been done in this direction in the present case studies.

The case studies have shown that in the PRA process, particular attention must be paid to the issues of empowerment and equity. In all cases, but particularly in Pakistan and Nepal, it was difficult to involve equally the different interest groups; the disadvantaged groups tend to be excluded. Here, the challenge is to select those combinations and sequences of tools that facilitate the identification of these groups and permit them to express themselves freely. Although in some projects (e.g. Quetta), serious efforts have been made in this respect with promising results, there is still much to be done.

One of the major constraints to effective use of innovative tools is the training required to develop field staff capacity in the use of these tools. Much attention has been given to preparatory and in-service training of the field staff, though this is not always easy. A specific obstacle that emerged in some cases, for example, was the language problem, which prevents international (and sometimes even local) consultants from following group dynamics during the exercises in the field. As a consequence, field examples of tool use for feedback to field staff during training are only partially absorbed.

Interesting experiences have emerged from the innovative use and adaptation of the various tools, such as the case of the women's groups in Pakistan (Quetta). For the majority of these women, interacting with people from outside was an unfamiliar experience, as was getting together in groups to discover issues of common interest and discuss them. These were major changes in their lives, which needed to be processed and worked out. Project staff decided to use pictures taken by the women for the project album as a visual record of the new activities. However, some of the women were punished by their husbands because they had been photographed and their photos could be shown outside the village. In other cases photographs did not generate problems at all. Thus, an important result of the use of this tool with women was the emergence of significant differences between the villages in the area of gender relations. This led to identification of other intervillage differences, such as the daily time profiles of the women and their specific tasks.

PARTICIPATORY PLANNING AS A LEARNING PROCESS

Local-level participatory planning constitutes an iterative learning process (in which each step feeds into the next) for all parties involved. Appraisal and assessment, planning, implementation and evaluation are steps in a learning experience, and each is used as an input for the subsequent steps. This is true for both insiders and outsiders. In this context, project planning procedures and Project Management styles are important aspects of. participatory planning intervention strategies.

At the *project management level,* some of the study projects demonstrate variations in internal management styles regarding participation of the project staff in project planning. In the PUCD projects, for example, one of the obstacles to putting a participatory approach into practice is the fact that this methodological orientation has been insufficiently internalized by the project staff. The elaboration of annual workplans can be used as an important learning experience in this context, involving the participation of all levels of the project staff. Appropriate mechanisms have been established in some cases to make maximum use of field experiences and increased understanding of the different realities among the field staff. Three-monthly evaluation and planning workshops have proven to be exceptionally useful in developing a common understanding among the project team of the conceptual and methodological orientation of the project.

At the *local level,* participatory planning clearly has contributed to a strengthening of group self-confidence and capacity, particularly for disadvantaged groups such as the landless, women or the lowest castes. In many cases, training activities or study tours are organized by the project to support planning and decision-making. Study tours to other groups or villages where similar projects are being carried out can be a very effective training method. Aspects such as feasibility, pricing, Marketing and investment are part of this learning process of assessing the opportunities and constraints involved in achieving certain objectives.

At *government institution level,* field experiences contribute to a better understanding of the need to adjust internal organization and to develop planning procedures in line with the institutions' new roles as service agencies. Instead of "selling" development packages as development agents in order to achieve centrally established targets, the institutions are gradually redefining their role in terms of providing support services that respond to locally identified needs and opportunities, as in Burundi, Pakistan (Malakand), Nicaragua and Bolivia.

Ironically, it is more complicated to achieve decentralized, bottom-up planning in the institutions than to strengthen local planning capacities at village level. The case studies illustrate that institutional reorientation requires a lot of time, and that it is one of the most complex challenges. At the same time, a number of the studies demonstrate that progress is possible in this area. One efficient tool used by some case study projects was to establish from the beginning a permanent dialogue with the institutions. This requires efficient and timely feedback during project implementation, to ensure that the effectiveness of participatory approaches and local planning can be clearly demonstrated. Systematic monitoring of the process and evaluation of the results in the field is indispensable to support the learning process at institutional level.

LOCAL PLANNING AND EMPOWERMENT

The case studies show that the issue of local planning is closely related to organization. In all projects, questions have been raised regarding how to approach traditional power structures and, simultaneously, how to prevent monopolization of decision-making.

Community forestry and resource management projects are dealing with scarce natural resources such as land, water and trees. These resources are owned and/or exploited by the better off and are frequently the cause of disputes and conflicts. Organizational structures and decision-making mechanisms are generally dominated by the local elite.

In most of the case studies, this issue has been the subject of serious discussion and analysis. In Nepal it was decided to focus on "community development conservation committees" (relatively small functional groups) instead of the village development committees. In Nicaragua, the project menu has been developed in such a way as to respond to the specific needs and constraints of disadvantaged groups, such as landless fuelwood collectors. In Pakistan, the approval of the community development plan in a village-wide meeting represents a kind of political backing for the land use management plans of specific user groups. Separate women's activities are carried out in both the PUCD and the non-PUCD projects in Pakistan. In Bolivia, an anthropological study on the traditional organizational structures of local Indian communities (*Ayllus*) was carried out. The results of this study have been extremely important in relating local planning to the functioning of the *Ayllu* system, in such a way as to reach all community members. In Senegal, strong traditions of local organization have permitted the development of intervillage farmers' organizations.

In spite of the efforts to promote broad-based participation in local planning, the experiences discussed lead to the conclusion that there are some constraints that are difficult or impossible to overcome. Strong local organizations are not automatically an effective instrument far participation in planning. At times, on the contrary, they can be major obstacles. Therefore, in many cases the most active "counterparts" of project staff in the field are the members of relatively small groups with shared interests, such as management committees, working groups or women's groups. These functional groups can, if necessary, mobilize other villagers to attend meetings, give their opinions or Collaboratef with them in all kinds of activities.

The case studies demonstrate that these functional groups play an important role in local project planning and implementation. In the PUCD projects, these groups are established based on the results of the appraisal phase of data collection and analysis. The groups define their own rules and elaborate their plan of activities with support from the project. In the established projects, various mechanisms have been developed. In the Bolivian case, these groups, with support from the project, are responsible for the appraisal and assessment phase. In Nicaragua, the Fuelwood Collectors' Associations have developed their own mechanisms and calendar for their members to present their management plans. In Senegal, the project starts with awareness raising activities, followed by identification and selection of priority actions. Organization and programming of these priority actions is done by the villagers themselves through the Reforestation Committee, assigning specific tasks to different groups. In the Malakand project in Pakistan, general appraisal and assessment by the project is followed by specific data collection by each of the land use management units, comprising several families. Thus, a wide variety of organizational systems have been found in the field, corresponding to the opportunities and constraints of the specific situations.

By preferring to establish working relations with local functional groups, most of the projects have not worked much with the community as a whole. In Rwanda and Burundi this is because local communities do not exist as clear social or spatial organizations. In most of the other cases, local conflicting interests are so strong (class, ethnicity, gender, caste) that a community-wide participatory approach to planning is not feasible (Nepal, Pakistan, Nicaragua and to a certain extent Senegal). In spite of this situation, part of the planning process can be oriented towards the elaboration of a "community development plan" (Pakistan/Malakand). Although these community development plans do not have a direct operational significance, they do constitute an important political framework at local level for the implementation of the land use management plans of individual groups. This strategy has proven to be effective in creating opportunities for participation in the planning exercise by more disadvantaged groups, such as small farmers and the landless.

This example also demonstrates that a differentiated strategy and approach is needed to achieve empowerment of disadvantaged groups and equitable distribution of benefits.

One of the assumptions of the study is that participatory planning enhances the integration of indigenous knowledge and management systems in the local planning process. The most evident argument to support this assumption is the fact that local groups prepare plans themselves, making decisions based on their own collective reflection and analysis of their needs, opportunities and constraints. This process of collective reflection through exercises such as timelines, daily profiles and transects stimulates them to express their own perceptions and to share their knowledge and practical experiences.

In the case studies, however, it is difficult to assess the extent to which local knowledge systems are actually being integrated into the technical components of local plans. In general, no explicit attention seems to be given at project level to systematically explore and record specific local knowledge systems for natural resource management. It appears that the elaboration of local plans makes use of "common local knowledge" regarding such areas as tree species, soils, water sources, sites, seasons, or crop calendars. On the other hand, local organizational structures and decision-making systems do constitute the framework for approval and implementation of the local plans, integrating local management skills and organizational expertise.

INSTITUTIONAL SUPPORT AND DECENTRALIZED PLANNING

The issue of institutional support and decentralized planning must be examined at two levels: the project level and the institutional level. Participatory planning activities may refer to different moments in the project cycle and to different levels. The case studies show that local people usually have not been directly involved in the identification and formulation of the projects. This is common practice and does not necessarily have negative consequences for project implementation afterwards. During the identification phase, planning of project implementation is part of the project plan of operations and covers the expected lifetime of the project. The project Document and this global plan of operations constitute the framework for project implementation, and this framework needs to be highly flexible for participatory approaches in the field to be possible. This is clearly demonstrated in the PUCD cases, as well as in some of the other community forestry projects.

During project implementation, annual workplans are prepared, specifying which activities will be carried out and what kind of results can be expected. For these exercises "participatory planning" is central, since its outcome must be carried into the project plan. Most of the cases illustrate a growing capacity at project level to develop mechanisms for preparing annual workplans on the basis of the local plans. Three important points should be noted here. First, the preparation of "bottom-up" annual workplans should be seen as a participatory process at project level, facilitating inputs from both field staff and technical support staff during planning workshops. Second, a systematic analysis of the results obtained so far (monitoring and evaluation data) constitutes a fundamental tool for the further improvement (technical, methodological and operational) of project interventions. Finally, for participatory planning processes at project level to function effectively, Project Managementf must incorporate (1) the ability to delegate project management tasks, (2) smooth channels for internal communication and (3) the creation of opportunities for reflection, analysis and sharing of experiences.

At field level, operational project planning is carried out on a weekly or monthly basis in the form of individual workplans of the field staff. It is at this level that fine tuning should take place between the local (village) plan of activities and the individual workplans of the field staff. A "common agenda" between the two should appear and become operational. However, it is at this level that serious constraints with far-reaching consequences can occur. The identification of adequate opportunities in time and space to schedule work with the respective local groups requires careful listening, observation and planning, as well as a high level of flexibility and commitment on the part of field staff. Unfortunately, these conditions are not easy to satisfy, and the high turnover rate of field staff, which is typical in most of the projects, affects the achievement of progressive results.

In general, the case studies have shown that institutional development has been rather limited in terms of establishing mechanisms for decentralized planning. This will eventually jeopardize the institutional sustainability of the participatory approach. Apparently, it is much more difficult to establish and consolidate interinstitutional linkages for coordination, collaboration and support than to establish and consolidate working relationships with local communities. On the other hand, in most of the countries where the case studies were carried out, processes of decentralization and privatization are under way in the context of structural adjustment programmes, with far-reaching consequences for the institutional framework in terms of decision-making, policy formulation and planning. The case studies from Nicaragua, Bolivia, Senegal, Rwanda and Burundi contain examples of institutional networking between regional, provincial and municipal governmental and non-governmental organizations, clearly demonstrating that abundant new opportunities exist in this context.

THE TWO DIMENSIONS OF PARTICIPATORY PLANNING: LOCAL AND INSTITUTIONAL

Participatory planning, as mentioned earlier, should be viewed as a two-way learning process of dialogue, negotiation and decision-making between insiders and outsiders, concerning activities to be undertaken by the insiders and supported by the outsiders. Participatory development approaches aim at promoting sustainable development on the basis of local empowerment and the accountability of individuals, groups and communities. To achieve local empowerment and accountability, local capacities need to be strengthened (information, organization), access to and control over benefits from natural resources should be guaranteed (tenure systems and legislation), and claim-making power needs to be developed.

Participatory development approaches do not imply that projects should respond mechanically to whatever individuals or groups in the local community want them to do. Projects should have something to offer, not as pre-established packages but as proposals to be defined and negotiated on the basis of local priority needs, opportunities and constraints. This process of definition and negotiation of activities involves different interest groups and the definition of their respective responsibilities.

Participatory planning must be seen as an initial step in developing a negotiating dialogue between the local community and the project/institution in order to define a common agenda. After some years, this initial step should evolve towards self-directed local development planning and decentralized institutional planning. These two planning levels should be closely interrelated and work towards comprehensive and integrated plans for sustainable development of natural resources. This requires consolidated procedures for consultation and negotiation between the parties involved. When this stage has been reached, participatory approaches, methods and tools can be said to be in the process of being institutionalized. Current processes of decentralization and privatization of public services in many countries represent new challenges, which will need new strategies. More attention should be paid to institutional networking with both governmental and non-governmental organizations at different levels, such as municipalities, secondary-level farmer organizations and village associations.

On the basis of the case studies it can be concluded in general that more progress has been made in developing the local dimension of participatory planning than the institutional dimension. In the long run this situation will hamper comprehensive and integrated planning for natural resource management. Participatory planning needs effective institutional commitment and support, and a framework of conducive policies and legislation. These points should be worked out explicitly during the identification and formulation of participatory projects. They should be reflected in project design Documents, in the project objectives, strategies and expected impact.

APPROACHES, METHODS AND TOOLS

The case study projects all exhibit progressive capacity building in participatory appraisal and planning at both local and project level. They are working seriously with approaches, methods and tools in order to define project interventions that respond to local needs, opportunities and constraints. Although there are still many problems to be solved, there is no doubt that local groups are gradually assuming accountability for their own projects. The participatory methods and tools have proven to be effective in this area, particularly in those cases where a strong relationship has been developed between the local community and the project, based on mutual respect and confidence.

The ability of the project staff to internalize their role as facilitators and their corresponding behaviour patterns and attitudes in the field are of fundamental importance in achieving this confidence.

It was found that the direct involvement of the field staff in the development, testing and adaptation of the different methods and tools contributes to a better understanding of the participatory approach. The effectiveness of the methods and tools thus would appear to depend in particular on the internal dynamics of the project (feedback mechanisms, reflection, discussion and analysis). The way these tools are used in the field for data collection, sharing of information and facilitation of self-analysis, and restitution of the results of the exercises to the community members are also key elements in making them effective. In particular, this last point (restitution) seems to be extremely important. In many cases it was found that local people start wondering after a while why so much time should be "lost" in meetings, exercises or discussions. It is important for the project staff to return the results of this work to those directly concerned as early as possible. Visualization of the process and the results through video, pictures or printed materials was found to be an effective way to communicate the feeling that progress is being made.

Certain "unsolved" problems emerged at field level with regard to the four basic assumptions of the study regarding participatory processes. Although there have been individual examples of empowerment of disadvantaged groups (the first assumption), in general these groups have not been able to benefit equally from project activities. In order to facilitate more equal access to project facilities and services, the projects need to differentiate their approaches, strategies and technical menus to correspond to the specific characteristics of the different interest groups. For this to function, however, a political balance also must be found at the local level when moving between various groups. Institutional support is needed from local authorities and powerful groups in the community before elaborating development plans that respond to the more disadvantaged groups.

A related question that is often raised concerns the comparative advantages and disadvantages of working with small groups as opposed to working with the whole community. The case studies indicate that small groups with shared interests can serve as more effective vehicles for promoting participation, and produce better results. Community-wide approaches appear to suffer from weaknesses deriving from the hierarchical structure of most communities. However, the sustainable management of natural resources requires at least some degree of community-wide cooperation to achieve significant benefits. The question is, therefore, to what extent small functional groups can serve as vehicles for action at community level. Examples from Bolivia, Senegal and Pakistan seem to indicate that much depends on the internal organization of the local community. In particular in Bolivia, strong reciprocal relationships exist between the individual family and the community and, hence, Community Forestry Plans are implemented for the benefit of individual families, groups and the community as a whole.

Regarding the second assumption of this study, it can be observed in the study projects that while participatory approaches are implicitly enhancing local knowledge and skills, thus far little explicit attention has been given to the assessment of specific local knowledge systems related to natural resources. In the past few years, various international programmes and networks have been established in this field, and interesting results are becoming available. However, the case studies indicate that very little information has been collected in most of these projects. In depth studies may need to be undertaken in order to fill this gap.

Interactive participatory planning, by definition, enhances two-way learning processes (the third assumption). A necessary condition, however, is that the field staff should have internalized their role as facilitators, no longer acting as extension agents sending out "messages". In addition, participatory Project Management styles and annual project planning procedures should be developed in order to maximize the institutional capacity of the project at all levels.

Participatory planning in the field is not likely to take place if participatory principles are not applied at office level. The more important aspects of internal organization and functioning of the projects have not been sufficiently documented. For example, there would be the need for a report illustrating and analysing the different steps that have been followed for the elaboration of annual workplans.

Not enough attention is being paid by the projects to producing documents about the development and verification of their approaches, methods and tools. Most of the Documentation consists of drafts or preliminary working papers. Consolidated and systematized materials are lacking. Without minimizing the importance of recording the physical results in the field, projects should also attempt to properly document qualitative results. For example, the general impression is that logical sequencing in time and in space of the different methods and tools could be further improved. However, no "hard evidence" could be found to substantiate this observation and to use in making concrete suggestions. Similarly, participatory planning is meant to be an iterative and progressive process but in most cases it has yet to be demonstrated (documented) that this is indeed happening.

Initiatives to mobilize the institutional networks for analysis of approaches, methods and tools on the basis of results from the field should be further promoted. The objective should be to develop a minimum level of standardization, since the experience of a single project cannot be expected to achieve major breakthroughs at policy and planning levels. Although expectations of what can be achieved in this respect should not be overestimated, the case of Senegal has clearly illustrated that "pooling" of resources and experiences of different projects and programmes is a viable strategy.

PROJECT IDENTIFICATION AND FORMULATION

In almost all cases examined, methodological reorientations in project strategies have been introduced in the course of implementation, particularly in the "older" community forestry projects. In the process, important operational, technical, methodological lessons have been learned. First, it is now clear that these projects need to be implemented over a reasonable length of time if sustainable results are to be expected. The period of two years initially approved in the case of the PUCD projects, for example, constituted an important constraint to the identification and implementation of priority activities. Participatory resource management projects appear to need an initial period of at least five years in order to set up sustainable mechanisms of participatory planning and development. In some cases, depending on ecological and climate conditions, a second or even a third phase might also be needed.

Second, it is also clear that participatory projects need inputs from the social sciences. Although progress has been made in monitoring and evaluation of results at field level, little has been done to monitor environmental and socio-economic impact and sustainability. In the case of projects where approaches, methods and tools have been verified, high priority should be given to carrying out cost-benefit studies. Specialized expertise in this field is required, and existing studies carried out by various international agencies should be analysed carefully.

Third, it is interesting to note that none of the technical menus of the case study projects consider the production, planting or Marketing of trees as the single key issue. Rather, technical proposals are focused on developing sustainable land use management systems, where shrubs, grasses, crops, livestock, water and soils are considered on an equal footing with trees and forests. Therefore, a more interdisciplinary approach is required for these community forestry projects, which reinforces the need for institutional networking and for coordination among the different line agencies at field level. This should be considered carefully during project identification and formulation.

A drawback of this wide area of intervention has emerged from some of the PUCD projects, however. These projects have encountered difficulties in developing coherent technical proposals for either the short or the long term. An excessively wide variety of activities has been identified and initiated, ranging from income generating activities to soil conservation, water sources protection, gully control, tree production and livestock improvement. This has created a situation where the "profile" of these projects is not sufficiently clear at community level, leading to a feeling of confusion and distrust among intended participants.

The case studies have demonstrated the need to develop technical menus that respond to the specific needs, opportunities and constraints of the most disadvantaged groups. The available options should be carefully assessed during project identification and formulation, and the required inputs should be included in project design. In particular, specific groups such as tenants, the landless, women and nomads are easily excluded. If no viable technical options can be identified in the forestry sector from which these groups might benefit, then community forestry is not likely to provide an adequate alternative for improving their living conditions. In such cases, other proposals will need to be worked out.

In this connection, the importance of clearly defining the target group of project participants from the outset cannot be overemphasized. Success in reaching the most disadvantaged groups can be expected only when the target group is clearly defined and the project foresees the need for specific targeting mechanisms. This needs to be a part of project design.

SUGGESTIONS FOR FURTHER RESEARCH

Within the framework of this study, it has not been possible to elaborate on the important issues of impact and sustainability. During the past 15-20 years, a great many community forestry projects have been implemented. Community forestry is meant to be a feasible alternative for promoting sustainable development of forest and tree resources at the local level. It has yet to be demonstrated that this method fulfils these expectations from political, economic, technical and social points of view. Therefore, there is a great need to carry out ex-post studies on the impact and sustainability of past community forestry interventions. An interesting challenge would be to use RRA and PRA methods and tools for this purpose.

The present study focuses on a comparative analysis of approaches, methods and tools in different political, ecological and socio-cultural contexts. However, it has proven very difficult to reach detailed levels of analysis. For example, perceptions of the different groups of participants concerning the intervention process and results achieved have hardly been worked out (do they perceive themselves to be "empowered"?). Similarly, in most of the cases it was not possible to explore the extent to which the approaches, methods and tools were actually practised in the field. This would require more intensive and lengthy fieldwork than was possible for this study.

Therefore, it is suggested to select a limited number of projects (two or three) in which to carry out follow-up research that should generate a more detailed level of analysis of certain issues. Some issues that need further exploration are participatory technology development, the appraisal of local knowledge systems and benefit distribution mechanisms with reference to disadvantaged groups. At institutional/project level, further research is needed on internal management and organization, institutional networking and monitoring and evaluation.

THE LOS MARIBIOS PROJECT IN NICARAGUA

The official title of this project is *"Conservation and management of natural resources with community participation in the western slopes of the Maribios hill range."* The project is executed by the Ministry of Environment and Natural Resources (Marena; known as "Irena" before 1994) with technical assistance form FAO and financial assistance from the Dutch Government. The project started in March 1989, for a period of five years. A second phase of five years has been approved recently. The project is being executed in the northwestern part of Nicaragua.

THE PROJECT AREA

During the first phase, the project area was limited to the southern slopes of the Maribios hill range, with a territorial coverage of some 37 500 ha. From the second phase onwards, activities have been extended to the eastern slopes on the other side of the hill range, representing 34 000 additional hectares. Approximately 6 700 families are living and working in these areas. The central part of the project area is crossed by a volcanic chain of recent formation that is still active. Altitudes in this region vary between 100 and 1000 m above sea level. The climate is hot with an annual average temperature of 27.4oC (dry tropical forest zone) and the annual rainfall is between 1 100 and 1 560 mm, falling mainly during the rainy season (May-November). During the last three years, this figure has suffered a reduction of 300 mm per year. Around 80% of the soils are of volcanic origin, with corresponding characteristics. The remaining 20% are soils with a high concentration of loam, making them less suitable for the production of annual crops. The land use pattern in the project area is as follows: 35% degraded forests; 31% annual crops (out of which a high percentage is on degraded land); 7% perennial crops; 3% semi-perennial crops; 11 % pastures; and 11 % houses, roads and non-arable land.

Local communities have no historical roots as such in the area, since *haciendas* (plantations) were the predominant systems of production before the 1979 revolution. With the adoption of land reform, former contract workers were mobilized and brought together in cooperatives, most of which collapsed after some time. Therefore, the small farmer is a relatively new phenomenon in this region. Another factor in this connection was the expansion of cotton production in the lowlands between 1954 and 1981, which caused the large-scale out-migration of the local people.

The project is working with some 30 villages *(comarcas)* with a total population of about 1 600 households (12 000 inhabitants). Most of the *comarcas* consist of small hamlets with 5-7 families *(caseríos)*. Land tenure is a very complicated and delicate issue. The political developments of the past 15 years have created a situation of uncertainty concerning ownership and usufruct rights. It is estimated, however, that almost 25% of the families do not own land. Of those that do own land, 30% have less than 5 *manzanas (1.4 manzanas* = 1 ha), 25% between 5 and 10 *manzanas,* 5% between 10 and 20 *manzanas* and 30% more than 20 *manzanas*. Agricultural production systems have contributed to a continuous degradation of natural resources and ecosystems during the past four decades. In particular, the intensification of cotton production (pesticides and chemicals) and the irrational exploitation of marginal lands for permanent agricultural production have caused a significant reduction of the groundwater level, degradation of soils, and overexploitation of natural forests and forest-related resources.

OBJECTIVES OF THE PROJECT

The general objective of the project is to improve the living conditions of the farmers through sustainable and rational management of natural resources and the environment. The immediate objectives for the second phase are to achieve: (1) a replicable system of agroforestry extension based on both farmer participation and institutional participation, which also strengthens the rural extension functions of the concerned governmental and non-governmental institutions; and (2) the active participation of around 3 000 farmers, of whom at least one-quarter are women, who will develop an adequate capacity in planning, management and rational use of the natural resources. Although the immediate objectives of the first phase were not similarly formulated, in practice the project has been working towards these two objectives from the start. During the second phase, the methodological, technical and operational experiences are being put into practice and verified through expansion of its coverage to the other side of the Maribios range, and through establishment of further linkages with other institutions and organizations working in the region and elsewhere in Nicaragua.

APPROACH, METHODS AND TOOLS

The rapid rural appraisal (RRA) constitutes an important component of the methodological approach of the project. A field manual has been produced for the rapid appraisal of rural zones and the diagnosis of farming systems. Field documents illustrate how this manual is used in practice. They show that RRA is being used as a tool for the extension worker to systematically collect some basic information about the rural communities.

Typically, the first part of the exercise is to formulate a general description of the comarca. This information is collected by the extension workers and technicians mainly through structured observation and semi-structured interviews with key informants during a pre-project phase. It allows them to make a first assessment of the "strong and weak" points of the following aspects of the communities: urbanization (physical appearance of the community); infrastructure (roads, health, education, recreation); organization (political committees, development committees, service or production cooperatives); authorities (political, administrative, "traditional"); and past and present projects (successful or unsuccessful, with or without participation). Each of these variables is given a certain weight. By adding them, a total "score" is obtained for the community; this is used as a criterion for the selection of the communities to be targeted by the project.

The next step is to get to know the people and their problems. In the manual, a number of suggestions are given for establishing a viable dialogue with the different groups in the community, referring to basic communication skills and to attitudes such as the ability to be receptive and flexible. A framework of issues to orient the meetings is provided, such as the authority structure, more specific community information or a problem census. The information is obtained by using forms. After the data have been collected at individual level, they are clustered by group (landless, small, medium and large farmers, cooperatives) in order to identify common problems of the different groups and group-specific problem areas. This exercise results in a selective list of the most important problems of the community. At present, however, no explicit reference is made to the importance of a gender-specific problem census.

The following step is to identify those problems that fall within the scope of the objectives and strategy of the project. Meetings with the community are focused on issues related to natural resource management in order to determine the extent of community awareness of problems that might be solved with project support. For that purpose, another list is made of measures for resource conservation that have been or are being taken by the community. The manual suggests doing this exercise at the level of groups, examining the reasons why specific measures have been taken, how, by whom and with what results. On the basis of these group meetings, an initial appraisal is made of possible project support.

Before concrete plans are worked out with individual farmers, an analysis is made of the opportunities and constraints of their farms (*fincas*). This is done by the extension worker and the farmer, based on direct observation (transect walking) and interviews. A number of forms have been designed for these exercises, covering the following areas: general information about the *finca*, the farmer, the owner, etc.; a map of the actual use of the different spatial units (agriculture, pasture and forestry); and a detailed description of the use of the units. For each of the three categories (agriculture, pasture and forestry), special forms are used, recording information about the crops, inputs, credit and investment, efforts for improvement and the monthly labour requirements of each activity.

Next, family off-farm economic activities are recorded, and then a description of the main problems and their causes as experienced by the farmer, including recommendations for actions to be taken in the future. At this point, a map is prepared by the extension worker and the farmer of the recommended land use in view of the land use capacity. Then a farm management plan is worked out, specifying the changes to be introduced. This is followed by the elaboration of a workplan, specifying when activities have to be executed and the required inputs. The management plan and workplan are put into an written agreement between the farmer and the project.

These steps constitute the process of participatory extension. As developed by the project, participatory extension is a continuous, progressive and iterative learning process for the extension worker and the farmer. The rural appraisal is considered the starting point of this process and is aimed at the identification of problems and possible solutions (from the farmer's perspective). The extension activities to orient and support this process are the execution of a participatory appraisal and the promotion of alternatives. In this way, the different phases of participatory extension are defined both from the institutional and farmer's perspective.

Table: Participatory Exbonsiow Approach

Farmer	Extension Worker	Extension Objective
assessment and solutions	participatory appraisal and promotion of alternatives through field visits plenary meetings/workshops	widening horizon of analysis and awareness of possible solutions
decision-making	follow up results previous phase; planning workshops	action plan
execution	training: demonstration, technical assistance, training workshops;	local capacity building
evaluation	evaluation: fields visits and evaluation workshops	validation

RESULTS AND LESSONS LEARNED

The response of farmers has been very positive. In some *comarcas* the project is working with all the families without exception. This situation has contributed to the phenomenon of interest group formation, through which a number of people elaborate their proposals for improved land use management and present them for approval. This is useful because many of the envisaged protection and conservation activities serve common interests. Women, often on their own initiative, have started to prepare management plans for their home vegetable gardens, introducing such activities as the production of fruit and forestry trees, flowers or medicinal plants. They also apply soil conservation and protection measures.

Landless peasants such as the fuelwood collectors of the Cerro Negro (the Black Mountain) constitute another particular group. These groups were very difficult to approach when the project started as they had been always involved in illegal tree cutting and fuelwood collection. The project was seen by these groups as part of MARENA, their "natural enemy." As described by an extension worker:

Marena had a very bad image since it was the institution that persecuted them, and they never benefitted from its work. That was the point, to try to convince these people to listen, to become familiar with the objectives of the project and to realize that they will benefit when they organize themselves...

Now, the majority of the families are participating, not only men but also women. Now that we have started working with the women, the participation of the community has become richer. But it has not been easy because of the bad reputation of MARENA which caused them to see us as inspectors or policemen coming to control those who were robbing wood... they couldn't stand officials of

MARENA, and therefore initially we told them we were working with FAO, not with MARENA. Only gradually did we tell them about MARENA, but now that the work is going fine they have become very close to us...

The positive responses indicate that the project's technical menu responds to the local opportunities and constraints and that the approach helps the farmers take control. This is not surprising: the project responds to the basic problem that most of theses families do not have access to land, to appropriate technologies for land use management or to financial resources to invest in improvements. Irrational cutting of the forest resources is the consequence of the poverty of most of these families, who depend almost entirely on the revenues obtained from cutting and selling fuelwood. This project is strengthening the claiming and negotiating capacity of the individual farmers or groups of farmers. It is providing them with the means to do so effectively, facilitating access to land for agricultural production and tree planting, to technology and to credit.

The credit system has been important for the promotion of sustainable management of natural resources. It started on a very modest basis, and after some years of experimentation and critical review, new options became visible. The system works as follows. The project, through its extension work, has promoted the creation of Municipal Committees for Forestry Credit in the four municipalities of the project area. This committee is composed of the project director, a credit administrator, a representative of the Municipal Council and five to seven representatives elected among the leaders of farmers' groups. At least two of these farmers' representatives are women. The committee appraises farmers' project proposals for improved land use loans, and then selects projects and grants the loans depending on the financial resources available. The committee is also responsible for the loan administration. As can be expected, this system has various kinds of difficulties to cope with. In spite of this, however, the municipalities are showing a marked capacity to improve their performance and the farmers consider these credit facilities their own.

One example where the credit system has proven to be very instrumental and effective is the Association of Fuelwood Collectors of the Cerro Negro. During the first months of 1990, an RRA was conducted in this region and the results indicated that many families depended for their livelihood on cutting and selling fuelwood from natural forests 15-20 km away, using oxcarts for transport. The sandy tracks meant that this journey could take up to eight hours. These families are landless and, in many cases, do not have access to land for agricultural production. There are no off-farm employment opportunities in the region.

A public meeting, organized by the project in collaboration with the leaders of the groups living at the foot of the Cerro Negro, took place at the end of

April 1990. The objective of this meeting was to present and discuss the results of the RRA, to identify priorities and to analyse what to do next. At the end of the meeting, the participants agreed to create an association, and four representatives were selected from the four sectors that had attended: Monte Redondo, Los Urroces, Los Caleros and El Pastal. Together with the project, these four representatives were given the task of preparing the draft internal regulations of the association and a workplan. After a number of revisions, the final Internal Regulations of the Association of Fuelwood Collectors of the Cerro Negro have been approved by the members, stipulating that:

The fuelwood collectors of the sectors of Urroces, Pastal, Caleros and of the camarca Monte Redondo have formed an Association, as has been recorded in the minutes of our meeting, dated April 24, 1990. This Association of Fuelwood Collectors of the Cerro Negro has been recognized by the mayorship of Leon and the Institute of Natural Resources and Environment (IRENA). The objective of the Association is: the improvement of the living conditions of the members through the rational use of the natural resources which are under their responsibility. To achieve this objective, the Association defines an annual workplan which includes a calendar of activities. The workplan, discussed and approved by the members, will complement the regulations of the Association. The Internal Regulations define the rules and norms of the functioning of the Association and is composed of the following points: duration of the Association, its members, representatives, rights and duties of the members and sanctions...

The organization of the Association is based on small groups of 10-15 members. Each group has its own representative or leader who acts as contact person for the extension worker of the project. The group leader is responsible for the internal organization of the work as defined and agreed upon in the annual land use plan of the group. The other level of the organization is composed of the territorial leaders. They are members of the Board of the Association and responsible for implementation and follow-up of the annual workplan. The group leaders are their contact persons in the field and with them ad hoc problems are solved or suggestions for adjustments are discussed.

In effect, the planning is flexible, based on principles established when the Association got the usufruct rights of an area called Alto de la Cruz. When this land was granted, an initial plan was prepared by representatives of the Association, the project and Agrofocsa (the state company) whereby Alto de la Cruz was identified as a reforestation area for the landless and poor farmers. The next step was to assign to each of the interested persons a piece of land of three *manzanas* for agroforestry and possibly two*manzanas* after some time for crop production, grouping together people from the same sector. This has enhanced mutual support among the group members, execution of activities of collective interest such as fire protection and clearing, and sharing of experiences, ideas and materials and equipment. In general, people are convinced that they will benefit from their efforts, but some still have doubts regarding the role of the Forestry Department, as one of the extension workers describes:

Look, these doubts will not disappear completely until the farmers start cutting and will realize that all the product is theirs. Because many of them are convinced that it is theirs, but there is a small percentage still not convinced, in particular the new members who are becoming part of the Association. Because they call you and they tell you "look, explain it to me well: 1 want you to tell me how this thing is. I am new and just starting and I want to know the arrangement." With these words they talk to me, obvious, as they are new they don't realize how it is that this whole thing functions.

Although the project integrated its women's programme as a component to be looked after in all the activities being promoted in the field, women have shown particular interest in improving their home garden systems, establishing their own groups and electing their own group leaders. Meetings to discuss tree-related issues are mainly attended by men. However, both men and women are present in meetings where credit issues are on the agenda. As mentioned before, two women are members of the Credit Committee and recently a women was elected as a member of the Board of the Association. A female extension worker explains what happened:

Because of the problem of land, the need came up to assign them [the women] land in Alto de la Cruz to grow their vegetables because they always join their husband when they go out planting. In the Board of the Association a small area of one-quarter of a manzana was proposed and assigned, but the women had problems with their vegetables: the vegetables were eaten up, there were transport difficulties and theft... When there were elections for candidates for the new Board, 1 suggested to some of them become candidate and to become members of the Board to be able to solve their problems of representativeness. Initially, the women were not interested and were even scared, but gradually they started to like the idea of becoming candidates. When the election took place, one woman was elected and she is now the women's representative.

In the field, vegetable gardening constitutes a potential additional source of family income. Its introduction has an impact on the traditional roles of men and women. One of the consequences of this new activity is that women get the opportunity to go out on their own to participate in training workshops, sometimes with a duration of some days. These workshops have permitted them to work out their own projects and to define the most appropriate way to implement them in view of their many other tasks.

On the other hand, they are well informed about the activities being developed by the men, and they consider these activities very important. This indicates that at household level project activities are discussed, experiences are shared and opinions are expressed.

At project level, the participatory extension approach has been developed gradually. The field experiences of the international staff obtained in other parts of Latin America and elsewhere have proved to be very relevant. Also, experiences obtained elsewhere can be used to develop instruments to follow the process and results in the field (monitoring and evaluation). Regular work meetings with the field staff and intensive supervision and support in the field have been the most effective mechanisms for obtaining regular internal feedback. These experiences have been systematically discussed and analysed and have contributed to the further development and verification of the extension approach. They have strengthened the project's integrated technical menu of options for the sustainable management of natural resources. In-service training of project staff to familiarize them with this approach was a priority during the first years.

The mid-term evaluation mission concluded that the project document for the first phase constituted an inadequate framework for project operations, but that the project had rightly decided to adjust this framework. In particular the immediate objectives and the methodological approach of the project had been poorly formulated in view of the different local interest groups and the changing political situation. Apparently, the project document had been formulated without a pre-project feasibility study. This weak point has been overcome by the rapid rural appraisal exercises at the beginning of the project, which to a large degree determined the future direction of the project activities.

As can be expected under circumstances of political change, the organization and administration of Marena have been subject to persistent adjustments that are still having an impact on the institution. Therefore, it has been extremely difficult to focus the efforts of the project on strengthening Marena's institutional capacity for community forestry. The project strategy in this connection has been to make use of the few opportunities as much as possible, both at the central planning level of Marena and at the level of the different technical divisions. For example, the establishment of the Extension Division of the Forestry Service of Marena in April 1994 has been actively supported by the project, as this could constitute an opportunity to strengthen the extension services. Similarly, the project has supported Marena by participating in the elaboration of new project proposals, introducing basic concepts such as farmers' participation, the integrated technical menu, the participatory approach and gender issues. In addition, the project collaborated actively with the Project Monitoring and Evaluation Unit of the Planning Directorate of Marena, where the forms and procedures developed by the project are now in use. However, the overall impact of the project on the institution at central level is still limited.

The project has established interinstitutional linkages with research, training and administrative institutions, undertaking collective research in the field, providing training facilities for students from universities and technical institutes, and collaborating actively with the four municipalities situated in the project region. As illustrated in the case study, there is a growing interest in the natural environment at the municipal level. The project has been assisting these municipalities in the formation of special committees for issues related to natural resources, such as territorial planning and land use. In addition, municipal tree nurseries were established in order to produce the required seedlings, not only for urban reforestation campaigns, but also to respond to the demand of rural areas.

An important step has been the formation of the Municipal Committees for Forestry Credit. The role of the municipalities is important, since they represent the State as the official owner of public (often marginal) lands. As has been demonstrated in the case of Alto de la Cruz, these lands can constitute a real opportunity to improve the living conditions of rural families and can contribute to sustainable resource management. As a result, the four municipalities in the project area are becoming more involved in issues related to the rural areas. A good example is Leon, where the municipality has created its own Department of Natural Environment. This Department is supporting the project in its efforts to obtain resources from the Ministry of Social Action to help the most disadvantaged sectors of the rural population.

Finally, it is important to mention the role of the project after the eruption of the Cerro Negro volcano, when most of the families had to be evacuated, their houses were destroyed and their crops and animals were lost. The project played a leading role in assessing the damage, providing its logistical resources and participating for six months as an active and full-time member of the Cerro Negro Commission, installed to coordinate the emergency assistance of the different institutions and organizations. This emergency situation also created an opportunity for the project to establish linkages with other ministries, such as Construction and Transport, Communication, and Agriculture and Animal Husbandry.

In spite of the above mentioned initiatives and results, the innovative character of the project and its methodological approach of participatory extension have not yet generated the expected institutional development at central level. Short-term opportunities at local and regional level for institutional strengthening in these programmes have been found by the project through the establishment of farmers' associations and the progressive involvement of local municipalities.

THE BEGNAS TAL RUPA TAL WATERSHED MANAGEMENT PROJECT IN NEPAL

The Begnas Tal Rupa Tal Watershed Management Project (BTRT) is being jointly implemented by the Department of Soil Conservation (DSC) of Nepal and the American non-governmental organization CARE International. The BTRT project started in 1985 and is currently in its second phase. Its working area is the Kaki District in Nepal's Western Development Region. This case study was conducted in 1993.

THE PROJECT AREA.

The project area of 170 km2 is located about 13 km east of Pokhara Municipality and comprises seven Village Development Committees (VDCs). A VDC is an administrative unit consisting of wards, villages and hamlets. The topography of the area is characterized by its location between the Mahabharat range in the south and the Himalayan foothills in the north. It represents a typical mid-hill area of Nepal with dominant north-facing steep slopes and south-facing gentler slopes. The climate varies from subtropical in the low lying areas to subtemperate in the mountain areas. The average annual rainfall is 3 710 mm. Land use patterns indicate that almost 50% of the total area is under cultivation, 30% under forest, 6% under grazing and the remainder covered by lakes, rivers, banks, cliffs and wasteland. The cultivated land is classified into rain-fed upland (*bari*) and lowland *(khet).* Slightly more than half the cultivated land is *bari* land. The dominant farming system combines both crop and livestock activities.

The total population in the area is about 31 000 (1990). The people belong to different ethnic and occupational caste groups and to Hindu, Buddhist and Islamic religions. Brahmin and Chhetri are the dominant castes in this area, followed by Gurungs. Besides these, occupational castes considered to be of lower status such as Kami, Damai and Sarki are also present in some numbers. The majority of the people are engaged in agriculture as their main occupation. The people from the lower castes tend to depend on seasonal paid labour. Only 2% of the population in the area is landless. Over 60% of the people own less 10 *ropani* of land (10 *ropani* = 1 ha); the average landholding is 2*ropani* per person. In general, public services are inadequate or non-existent. Infrastructure is poor and the literacy rate in the area is about 46%.

OBJECTIVES OF THE PROJECT

The development objective of the project is to stabilize the physical environment and increase productivity in the project area through sustainable community management of human and natural resources. The intermediate objectives to be achieved by the end of the project are formulated as follows: (1) 40% of the farm households in the project area adopt soil conservation techniques; (2) the physical environment undergoes rehabilitation at all identified critical soil erosion sites; (3) 40% of farm households in the project area adopt more productive agroforestry practices; (4) productivity is increased on 600 ha of forest in the project area through protection, planting and management; (5) 100 user groups increase their ability to identify, plan and manage their catchments; (6) women, occupational castes and minority groups of the community increase their involvement in sustainable resource management in the project area in order to ensure that all sections of the community participate in and benefit from the project.

According to the project document for the second phase, the strategy of this phase is aimed at training and assisting Community User Groups and Community Development Conservation Committees (CDCCs) to adopt sound land use management practices in order to address decreasing productivity and environmental decline. An integrated approach is envisaged to achieve this goal. The primary components of the strategy are the following: (1) conservation farming aimed at improving farm practices and management for improved soil conservation and increased productivity; (2) community forestry oriented towards community management of forestry resources on private and common land; (3) bio-engineering for the rehabilitation of the physical environment at critical soil erosion sites, together with water management activities; and (4) conservation training and extension in order to facilitate community participation in planning, implementing and maintaining project activities.

APPROACH, METHODS AND TOOLS

Planning for the identification and implementation of development activities in BTRT begins right from the initiation and motivation of the villagers themselves by the BTRT project personnel. The final stage of this process, called "programme development", is the implementation of local project activities and the sharing of the benefits among the participants. In between these two stages are three other stages of programme development in which villagers and BTRT project personnel are involved.

INITIATION AND MOTIVATION

Formation of user groups or CDCCs is a prerequisite for support for the development activities from the BTRT project. Initiatives for bringing the villagers together and forming the user groups are usually taken at the local level by such people as local leaders, school teachers, educated persons or ex-servicemen. These people inform and try to mobilize the villagers. The field staff of the project, and in particular the Women Motivator and Farmer Assistants, have been quite successful in motivating the villagers to conduct development activities through the user group approach. The Women Motivators and Farmer Assistants are recruited from the VDCs where the BTRT field offices are located and are assigned to the field office in their own VDC.

FORMATION OF CDCCS AND USER GROUPS

The villagers at village or ward level, motivated to carry out development activities, come together under the leadership of any of the villagers described above or under the guidance of the BTRT project staff. Meetings of villagers who are potential members of the user groups are held, possibly in the presence of BTRT field staff. The decision to form a user group or, in a broader perspective, a CDCC is submitted to the BTRT field office for necessary information and formalization. Recently, it has become common practice to register these CDCCs under the Chief District Officer as non-governmental organizations.

Most of the CDCCs are involved in more than one activity. Therefore, it is common for most CDCCs to form subcommittees in addition to the executive committee, to look after and execute specific development activities. These subcommittees consist of three to five members. The members are usually chosen in a mass meeting for their initiative, knowledge in the particular field and the area of residence. The CDCC in Bastola Village, Majhthana VDC, Ward no. 6 can be cited as a good example of having undertaken different development activities through specific subcommittees. In addition to the executive committee, four subcommittees have been formed in this CDCC. A construction subcommittee has been established to look after, supervise and monitor the construction of stone wall, checkdams and plantations in Ahale Khahare Khola (stream) area. An agroforestry subcommittee is carrying out agroforestry activities in one hectare of barren land. The agriculture subcommittee is responsible for vegetable and fruit cultivation, and the forest subcommittee is implementing and monitoring community forestry management and protection according to the rules specified in the working plan for the community forests.

PROBLEM IDENTIFICATION, NEEDS ASSESSMENT AND PRIORITIZATION

Usually, formation of CDCCs is initiated to discuss the perceived problems faced by some or all of the villagers in a locality. When meetings are held, different problems, constraints and perceived needs are discussed. These meetings are attended by BTRT project staff, who provide guidance in identifying and explaining opportunities related to resource development. Also, a needs assessment is conducted by the group in a meeting under the guidance of BTRT staff. Priorities for development activities are fixed. These are then submitted to the field office with a request to undertake the prioritized activities.

Activities are planned based on the problems, constraints and needs identified by the CDCC members in the village meeting, or by the CDCC executive committee in consultation with the members. The BTRT encourages communities to use people's participation to formulate their own development activities for their own benefit, using available resources. Not all activities planned by the communities are undertaken by BTRT because the project is limited by the predetermined series of activities targeted in its annual plan, and because of budgetary constraints. Therefore, the BTRT staff orients the

CDCCs to formulate their plans to match its targets and budget. Provision is usually made for the inclusion of CDCC plans in the annual project plan and budget in the coming year if the plans are technically feasible and socially in conformity with the objectives of BTRT.

PROGRAMME FORMULATION AND NEGOTIATION

Prioritized development activities submitted to the field office of BTRT for possible technical and financial support undergo a series of steps before final approval by the project manager. Programmes are formulated after necessary negotiations with the villagers or CDCC members. The five major programmes that are formulated to create awareness of soil erosion, mitigate land degradation and increase productivity of the project area are: (1) land use planning; (2) land productivity conservation; (3) infrastructure protection; (4) natural hazard prevention; and (5) community soil conservation. Negotiations between BTRT and the CDCC members may take place for only some programmes out of the list and for labour contributions through people's participation. The BTRT project, according to its established policy, supplies the technical input, required amount of non-local materials and cash payment to cover the skilled and semi-skilled labour. The people's participation in the form of labour contribution is fixed through the decision of CDCCs.

IMPLEMENTATION OF PROGRAMMES

The implementation of development activities or programmes is a joint effort of the villagers (CDCCs) and the project. The share of effort of any one party depends on the type of activity or programme. For example, the efforts or contributions of the villagers in the management and protection of community forests are much more than in the construction of a drinking water system.

No stepwise, specific printed or audiovisual tools. However, videos and slide shows on interesting rural community development activities are organized from time to time. Usually, these are organized in the initial stages to motivate the rural community and to initiate intervention by the BTRT project and field staff. The project staff also uses flip charts related to conservation farming. This is used more for teaching different steps and techniques of conservation farming than for the different methodological steps. The project also produces annual wall calendars and brochures for distribution to rural communities on such topics as the techniques of conservation farming, growing different cash and fruit crops or livestock health and sanitation. To some extent, these printed materials help in the initial steps taken by the rural communities themselves. The BTRT staff act as facilitators to initiate group discussions on problems and needs. The priority problems and needs assessed by the rural communities in meetings become the basis for planning development activities for the particular group of rural people or the community.

There are no specific guidelines on the number of meetings, working sessions or time planning needed for each of the stages to enable a new user group to be fully operational. The time needed can differ significantly depending on the type of activity, the type of community, the time perspective of expected results and the socio-economic conditions of the participants. Planning of new activities requires more time than planning of activities with which the communities are familiar. All villages are different, and some are more heterogeneous than others. Planning of activities for which different groups will be accountable, and from which all of them are supposed to derive equal benefits, is more time consuming than the planning of activities with a more homogeneous group. In addition, activities that give quick results require less time planning and group meetings as compared to the activities with long-term results. Finally, participatory planning and decision-making are to be considered as time investments of those who are directly involved. It is well known that time availability is limited in the villages, particularly among the poorest. Therefore, mobilization and organization of these groups will take more time than mobilization of the more privileged.

RESULTS AND LESSONS LEARNED

During the second phase, BTRT staff members at the field stations have been successful in promoting a participatory approach and forming CDCCs in the communities. The hiring of Farmer Assistants and Women Motivators from the local communities has increased the confidence of the local people in BTRT project activities. The involvement of most of the CDCCs in implementing participatory activities at the local level seems to confirm that the communities consider the project as their own. The people have realized the dramatic situation they may have to face in the near future if the existing forest resources are not properly protected and managed and new tree plantings are not initiated on common lands. Many CDCCs are thus effectively protecting and managing forest resources and using forest products on a sustainable basis. There have been important changes in the local communities' technical and administrative capacity to manage and benefit from local forest resources.

Several forest user committees, working under the CDCCs as well as independently, have prepared workplans involving the participation of their members, including women, the poor and the low castes. They have demonstrated technical capacity for management and benefit sharing in the establishment and management of community forest nurseries, as well as in silvicultural operations such as pruning, thinning and harvesting of forest products by rotating among different patches or strips of forest. The sustainable administration of forest production through management and benefit sharing among user group members involves ensuring protection by watchmen or members themselves, and obeyance of rules and regulations specified in the management plan. It also includes management of the group's funds, raised from contributions, subsidies from BTRT and sale of forest products. The forest user committees have gained the required administrative capacity for these kinds of responsibilities.

The CDCCs have proven to be an adequate organizational structure, permitting the elaboration of a global framework for planning development in which a number of wards or villages participate. At the same time, the CDCCs delegate ongoing planning of specific activities to the different groups. In other words, at CDCC level a kind of development policy plan is prepared and approved (identifying the required institutional linkages with line agencies), while at the level of the different committees further detailed plans for implementation are prepared. The workplans prepared by the villagers or CDCC members are submitted to the concerned Forest Area Office and District Forest Office for necessary action. Forest Office actions are geared towards approval of the workplans and handover of the community forest to the CDCC or user group.

The importance of using local knowledge in the elaboration of community forestry management plans has been demonstrated by villagers belonging to different CDCCs. Their knowledge of forestry resources and their organizational and managerial skills in protecting and managing forests for sustainable use were demonstrated while preparing the Community Forestry Plans of their village or ward.

In order to strengthen local capacity, training is considered an important part of BTRT project activities. Training is provided to build knowledge of different aspects of human and natural resource management. The managerial skills acquired through training are then used to plan development activities for the future. Technical training related to income generating activities has greatly contributed to the strengthening of planning capacity at individual as well as CDCC levels. During the training, selected farmers are requested to prepare sketch maps of their respective households to plan conservation activities. They also prepare crop calendars. This provides them with opportunities to learn by doing the activities themselves. These farmers then act as promoters in the community to disseminate the techniques of conservation farming to the other villagers.

The socio-cultural context at local level can limit the ability of participatory planning to empower disadvantaged groups. Although most of the CDCCs comprise villagers of differing socio-economic status, educational levels and ethnic groups, they tend to be dominated by the local elite. Literate villagers tend to show supremacy over illiterate members and influence decision-making. It is not uncommon, therefore, that participatory planning is limited to needs assessment and subsequent participation in implementation through labour contribution. Decision-making on priorities and activities to be undertaken is in the hands of the more influential members of the CDCCs. In particular, the dominant position of the artisan class seems to be a widespread phenomenon. This, of course, is not conducive to planning that responds to the needs of different interest groups at local level. Therefore, there is every chance of arousing the suspicion, among the poor and the low castes, that participatory planning only means favouring the desires of the artisan or elite group. The poor, the low castes and women are not proportionally represented in the participatory planning process. Since most of the low caste members are daily wage labourers, it is very difficult for them to participate in the planning process, and thus their role in participatory planning is very marginal.

The target-oriented development programmes of line agencies, including BTRT, set back participatory planning. Most of these agencies (and the project) have annual targets that are to be achieved within the particular fiscal year. These target-oriented programmes may be partially based on the needs assessment of the villagers (CDCCs) in the previous year, since the CDCCs submit their programmes for inclusion in the next year's target and budget. As the programmes of the agencies are target-oriented, they are often in a rush to implement the programmes within the allotted time frame. Thus, the scope of participatory planning in decision-making and implementation is somewhat restricted.

On the other hand, the consolidation of different user groups into CDCCs for their better management has reduced overlapping of these groups in the community. Participatory planning of development activities is done through a series of general meetings of members of CDCCs, of the executive committee or of sub-committees for specific activities. The attendance of the members at the general meetings has been satisfactory for most of the CDCCs. Opportunities have been provided for women and the poor from lower castes to participate in different committees. Moreover, the meetings of executive committees and subcommittees of several CDCCs are held open for attendance by all interested CDCC members, to allow better coordination and participation in the planning process.

THE PREVINOBA PROJECT IN SENEGAL

The Village Reforestation Project in the Northwest of the Groundnut Belt *(Projet de reboisement villageois dans le nord-ouest du bassin arachidier - PREVINOBA),* Tivaouane, Senegal, started in 1986 for a period of three years. Its second phase had a duration of five years and was concluded in 1994. The project is in the district*(Département)* of Tivaouane, Thiès Region, which is part of the agro-ecological zone known as the "groundnut belt". It is implemented by the Department of Water, Forests, Hunting and Soil Conservation of the Ministry of Environment and Protection of Nature. It is financed by the Government of the Netherlands, and supported by technical assistance from

FAO. The project is one of nine projects that constitute FAO's Programme of Forestry Development Assistance to the Government of Senegal. Technical coordination between the projects of this programme is the responsibility of the Rural Forestry Development Support Project *(Appui au programme de développement de la foresterie rurale)*.

THE PROJECT AREA

The project area is approximately 2 5001 with a rural population of roughly 210 000 people, living in 907 small villages, which constitute 13 Rural Municipalities*(Communautés rurales)*. The main ethnic groups are the Wolof (80%), Peul (9%) and Sérère (8%). The majority is muslim (95%), illiterate (90% of the women and 80% of the men) and young (60%).

The climate in the north is sahelian and in the south sudano-sahelian. During the dry season from November to July a hot, dry wind blows (the harmattan), while the monsoon blows during the rainy season (mid-July to mid-October). Precipitation is low and poorly distributed in time and space. Average rainfall during 1982 and 1991 was between 315 and 350 mm annually. Topographically, the region is flat, except in the southwest. The soils are poor and strongly affected by wind erosion. Agriculture is predominant, extensive, rain-fed and traditionally based on a yearly rotation of groundnuts, millet, cowpeas and fallow. In general, productivity is decreasing because of soil degradation. Livestock husbandry is practised in combination with agriculture. In addition to livestock in and around the compounds, cattle are kept semi-sedentarily around the villages. Furthermore, the project area plays an important role in the transhumance (seasonal migration of cattle herds) from the northern pastoral region to the agricultural zone of the south. Forest and tree resources are very scarce in the region. Leaves, fruits and other products from trees and shrubs are collected for human and animal food and for the production of handicrafts. Women and children are responsible for the collection of fuelwood.

Demographic pressure (annual population growth is estimated at 3%) is generating a rapid growth in the demand for agricultural, livestock and forestry products. Extensive land use, combined with unstable climatic conditions, is one of the main factors contributing to a growing pressure on the existing natural resources, deteriorating the living conditions of the population and creating a generalized process of environmental degradation. As a consequence, seasonal migration is a widespread phenomenon.

OBJECTIVES OF THE PROJECT

The general objective of the project is to contribute to the battle against desertification through the improvement of the natural environment and the living conditions of the rural population. The mid-term objectives are: (1) to promote the large-scale participation of the population in forestry activities in order to increase their impact on the protection of the environment; (2) to restore the forestry cover for local self-sufficiency in forestry products based on sustainable output and ensuring the enrichment of the soils; and (3) to increase the financial means of the farmers as a result of incomes generated by silvicultural activities. The immediate objectives are oriented towards: (1) the consolidation of the local capacity for the promotion of rural forestry in terms of motivation, technical know-how and economic resources; (2) integrated village land use management, comprising the integration of forestry activities into agriculture and livestock husbandry and the elaboration of an integrated plan for the management of natural resources; and (3) the institutional strengthening of the forestry service.

Project activities to achieve these immediate objectives are reflected in its internal organization: a training and extension division for the elaboration of approaches, methods and tools for training and forestry extension at institutional and community level; a management and silviculture division, responsible for the development and verification of technical proposals; and a monitoring and evaluation unit. Externally, close interinstitutional links have been developed between the project and other governmental and non-governmental technical services at different levels in the region (agriculture, livestock, education, planning and development, etc.).

APPROACH, METHODS AND TOOLS

The methodological approach has not been developed in isolation but through dialogue with similar community forestry projects in Senegal, other Sahelian countries and elsewhere. Instead of pressuring local communities to participate in project activities through incentives (putting the sustainability of these activities at risk), the approach of this project is to create the conditions for a permanent dialogue between the local population and the "development agents". The point of departure is to support the local people in taking their development into their own hands according to the principles of self-help: the implementation of their own projects through analysis of the situation, determination of priorities, selection of actions to be undertaken, and mobilization of local knowledge and means.

The approach aims to develop an iterative process of identification, planning, implementation, evaluation, and back to identification, etc. In the end, this. will result in the accountability of the beneficiaries for their projects. Based on the annual planning of activities, the villagers progressively take charge of these activities through the combination of their own knowledge and skills and the application of new technologies. The approach strengthens their capacity for appraisal, problem identification and analysis, organization, training, implementation and monitoring and evaluation. It brings together efforts and knowledge as well as promoting the sharing of responsibilities and a mutual commitment of the different parties involved. In addition, the approach seeks to strengthen the coordination and Collaboration between the different governmental and non-governmental agencies working in the same area in order to identify their complementarity and to implement or support mutually agreed activities.

A distinction is made between two categories of actors. The first category is the principal actors (the villagers), who initiate actions and decide to implement them for their own benefit, either at community level, or at the level of the specific interest group (e.g. youth clubs, women's groups), or at individual level. In the second category are the support actors (development agents) who provide their political, technical, educational or organizational support for planning and implementation of activities. These include administrative and local authorities, technical/educational project staff, peasant associations and NGOs.

Methods and tools developed by the Research and Support Group for Peasant Self-help (GRAAP - *Groupe de recherche et d'appui pour l'autopromotion paysanne)* have been adapted and improved. Many of these methods and tools have been used in the field, such as theatre, cassettes, village maps, intervillage visits, etc. In addition, particularly during the planning phase, PRA methods and tools are frequently used, such as historical profiles, transect walking and listing of intervening factors.

At regional or zone level, the first step is to inform the different authority levels about the project, to explain its methodology and to present its staff. These contacts are maintained during project implementation, providing regular feedback and strengthening institutional support and collaboration. The next step is a general appraisal of the socio-cultural, economic and ecological characteristics of the region and the development of criteria for the selection of villages to work with. This general appraisal is supported with more specific environmental profiles prepared by the forestry staff. On the basis of the results of this preparatory work, an action plan is prepared, which will constitute an important tool for the orientation of the project staff.

Based on the appraisal studies, target villages are selected for direct project support. In each village, workshop meetings are conducted by the project staff with the villagers. At these meetings, villagers are asked to analyse their natural environment on the basis of their own observations and experiences, discussing the role they can play in the battle against desertification and degradation of their environment.

These exercises are aimed at the identification of needs, opportunities and constraints. A series of educational support materials, produced by GRAAP, are used for these workshops. The role of the project staff is to orient and facilitate these workshops and to promote the evolution of this process into a self-sustaining activity. These workshops are organized in public places and have been attended by both old and young people of both sexes. The following step for the villages is the prioritization and selection of the forestry activities they will undertake. This process is supported by the project staff, who provide technical assistance in such areas as species selection, tree production and management techniques. Initially, these activities are carried out on an experimental and educational basis.

The next step is the organization and programming of activities, aimed at strengthening the local capacity to assume full responsibility for their implementation. Villagers adapt the activities to their specific needs and conditions and integrate them into their agricultural production systems. In most cases, existing local organizations assume the coordinating responsibility, delegating specific tasks to forestry committees. The project policy is not to work with blueprint organizational proposals but to promote design by the villagers themselves of the most adequate organizational structure, according to their own customs and traditions.

Farmers' training is an important component of the project. In PREVINOBA, farmers' training is conceived in terms of the exchange of experiences between the farmers and the project. During the first phase of the project, theoretical and practical training for contact farmers from different villages took place at project offices. The idea was to achieve a multiplier effect upon their return to their villages. Results were disappointing, so this training method was modified in 1992 and decentralized to village level, thereby also making it more accessible to women.

The project incorporates systematic monitoring, which permits the different actors not only to supervise and control implementation of the activities but also to identify specific aspects to be strengthened, adjusted or modified. With technical support from the project, the village forestry committees usually supervise the project activities carried out at family and community level. In addition, field visits by the project team, administrative authorities and local representatives are organized in order to strengthen the political and institutional commitment to these local level initiatives for forestry development.

The final step is evaluation. A distinction is made between ongoing evaluation, self-evaluation and global evaluation. The ongoing evaluation is annual, retrospective and guided by the local forestry committee. Its main emphasis is on technical aspects of tree production and management. The self-evaluation of project implementation by the village takes place annually during village meetings. Specific materials, based on the GRAAP approach, have been developed to support and orient this process of self-evaluation and to use the results as inputs for planning. A global evaluation of the technical packages and results, village participation and the project methodology is carried out annually, and all actors directly involved in the project take part. The results of these exercises are used as internal discussion points for corrective actions and as an agenda for further dialogue during meetings with other parties involved.

RESULTS AND LESSONS LEARNED

The approach of the project contains important components designed to achieve a real strengthening of local accountability for sustainable community forestry development. In general, very important conditions are being met in the field: motivation and interest, technical knowledge and skills, strong local organizations, rights and equitable benefit sharing. Overall, the experience of the Previnoba project indicates that the participatory approach leads to a progressive accountability of the villages and appropriation of the project by the participants. There is an active participation of the villagers in forestry activities, and in particular of women, in spite of their heavy daily workload. Investments are made by the villages themselves with their own resources to finance the fencing of village woodlots and to purchase new materials. More and more village organizations have adopted measures such as sanction systems for the protection of the environment.

There is a common understanding of the project objectives and approach among the different parties involved. At village level this understanding reveals itself through a significant change of attitude towards external support, which has come to be considered as something temporary. Village land use management *(gestion des terroirs villageois)* has proven to be an appropriate framework for designing project interventions using the participatory approach. It has taken at least five years, however, to develop the methods and tools of this approach on the basis of practical field experience, and to make the different parties involved familiar with their use. These years ofCollaboration and partnership between the project and the villages have resulted in a strengthening of village capacity for diagnosis, organization, implementation and evaluation. In addition, new technologies have been learned, with regard not only to forestry and related activities but also to developing skills for improving existing land use management systems.

The village land use management plan contains the signed contracts between the village and the project, the action programme and a draft management plan. New working and exchange relations within the community and between the community and the outside world have been defined. It has been strongly emphasized in the planning phase that it is :up to the villagers to implement what they have planned. The role of the project is to help the villages during the planning phase and to provide them in due time with the necessary support, such as training and technical and organizational advice.

At institutional level, an increasing number of governmental and non-governmental agencies are providing support to project-related activities through specific services that are beyond the capacity and mandate of the project or the forestry department. These services are delivered for the implementation of microprojects, such as health centres, functional adult literacy courses, small-scale irrigation or grain mills. These microprojects are identified and designed in the context of the village action plans promoted by the project. For their implementation, Previnoba assumes the role of catalyst and facilitator, mobilizing its institutional network.

The project has been able to establish close relations with the "Multifunction Centres for Rural Development" *(Centres d'expansion rurale polyvalents),* administrative authorities and local representatives. This has had a positive impact on the use of the participatory planning approach in village land use management. Interinstitutional coordination and collaboration are extremely useful, if not indispensable, for effective participatory planning and the mobilization of external support for the village plan implementation. As demonstrated in Previnoba, the establishment and consolidation of interinstitutional collaborative networks requires the project to provide specific inputs and attention, and to promote this activity systematically. On the other hand, the resources available from the project and the collaborating institutions are too limited to respond effectively to the increasing claiming capacity of the target villages. In order to "democratize" the delivery of external support, some kind of interface is needed between villages and the institutions, such as intervillage peasant associations. Such associations could also play an important role in ensuring that regional or departmental resource management planning exercises take the village plans into consideration.

THE COMMUNITY FORESTRY PROJECT IN POTOSI, BOLIVIA

This project, located in the northern Andean Highlands of the Department of Potosi in southwestern Bolivia, started in 1991 for a period of five years. The National Secretary of Natural Resources and Environment of the Ministry of Sustainable Development and Environment is responsible for its execution, with technical assistance from FAO and 'international fund from the Dutch Government.

The project fits into the framework of the National Forestry Action Plan of the Bolivian Government. For its formulation, lessons learned from a similar project in Peru have constituted important guiding principles. These lessons were related particularly to the technical component, in such areas as the promotion of indigenous tree species, the conceptualization of community forestry extension and the importance of local planning.

THE PROJECT AREA

The Department of Potosi is composed of two regions, divided by the north-south Lipez mountain chain. The western part, at an altitude of 4 000 m, is flat, very dry and famous for its impressive salt lakes *(salares).* The population density is very low as the natural resources are extremely limited. Agriculture consists mainly of potato and sorghum cultivation, but extensive raising of llamas and alpacas plays an important role in the household economies. The natural vegetation is limited to indigenous grasses and shrubs. On the eastern side of the chain of the Lipez mountains the situation is very different, with altitudes varying between 2 500 and 3 900 m and various ecological zones. This permits more diversified livestock activity and agriculture, as well as a diversity of tree species.

In this environment of contrasts, the natural resources are limited and deteriorating. Poor soils, scarcity of water, high altitudes and corresponding climatological adversities (such as ice-winds and hail storms), combined with socio-economic factors like demographic pressure, decreasing agricultural production and productivity, and inadequate support services are seriously affecting the sustainability of natural resource use and, hence, the living conditions of rural families.

The project works in the northeastern part of the Department of Potosi with approximately 140 peasant communities scattered over the provinces of Chayanta, Quijaro, Cornelio Saavedra, Linares, Tomas Frias and Chichas North. The case study was carried out in peasant communities in Chayanta, a province with an area of about 4 800 km2, a population of 130 000 persons and an average density of 27 persons per km2. The population is *q'echua* speaking and of different ethnic origins. The peasant community in this region is a small organizational unit, which is part of a more complex traditional structure. The families, grouped together in small or big *ranchos,* are the basic unit of the organizational structure. These *ranchos* are sometimes called "patrilocal groups".

A number of these groups together constitute a *cabilde.* The next level is made up of various cabildos and is called the *ayllu menor* or sullka *ayllu* and constitutes a socio-political unit with direct authority over territorial issues. Anthropological studies indicate that the *Ayllu* system is weakening, although it is still an important factor in the project area because it constitutes the historical framework of socio-political and economic conflicts between communities.

Adult illiteracy is high, particularly among women, and enrolment rates at primary level are still low because of structural constraints. There is usually only one school teacher for the first six grades, without any support, equipment or teaching materials. Similarly, health services are poor and hardly accessible because of poor infrastructure. Finally, this is a region with a very high rate of seasonal out-migration (77%) among the adult male population, mainly during June, July and August. Permanent migration is estimated at 20%. Seasonal migration of women is very limited as they take care of the household and the animals during off-season.

OBJECTIVES OF THE PROJECT

The development objective of the project is to contribute to improving the living standards of the peasants of the Bolivian Highlands. This should be done through the integration of sustainable forestry activities into existing production systems, in order to satisfy the need for forestry products, increase agricultural and livestock production and preserve natural resources. Since mid-term, the project's national-level objectives have been the adoption of a national forestry development strategy, which includes the application of a community forestry methodology for the Bolivian Highlands and the budgeting of the necessary resources. At community level, the mid-term objective is to increase the availability of fuelwood, construction wood, fodder, fruits and other forestry products.

The immediate objectives are: (1) the integration of tree planting management into agricultural and livestock land use systems in order to get benefits from the trees, improve the output of the production systems and conserve and protect soils and water; (2) the verification of the extension and training methodology and the community forestry technical menu in order to develop an approach suited to the Bolivian Highlands; and (3) the development of the institutional capacity to promote community forestry approaches within governmental and non-governmental organizations in the Department of Potosi, and to contribute to the formulation and elaboration of departmental forestry development policies and planning.

APPROACH, METHODS AND TOOLS

The methodological approach can be summarized as follows. The project promotes a technical menu called "Community Forestry Development" at village level. This technical menu consists of tree production, planting and management and the commercialization of forestry products. It is oriented towards agroforestry, in order to integrate forestry and tree activities within agriculture and livestock production systems. Extension activities (promotion, training, research, monitoring and evaluation) are oriented towards establishing a dialogue with the local communities on the basis of this technical menu. As soon as the local communities have decided to start forestry activities, the extension worker starts supporting them in the -preparation of their "Community Forestry Plans". A clear distinction must be made between Community Forestry*Development,* which is an institutional proposal, and the Community Forestry *Plan* of the communities, which is an adaptation of the institutional proposal on the basis of local needs and priorities determined by the local communities. The approach can be visualized as follows.

In this approach, the extension worker assumes the role of promoter, facilitator and trainer, supporting and orienting the local communities in the planning, implementation and evaluation of their forestry development. This methodological approach can best be described as "participatory extension for community forestry": it is flexible, process-oriented and based on partnership. There is no predetermined technical package, nor a detailed field manual with rigid instructions on what to do. Instead, much emphasis is given to pre- and in-service institutional training of the extension staff in order to develop and strengthen their appreciation of the basic criteria for participatory extension. A proper understanding of the project objectives and methodology is of paramount importance.

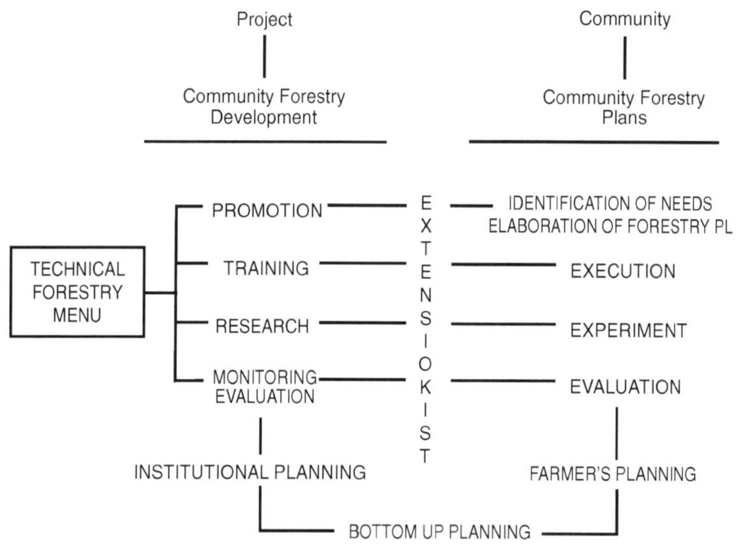

Fig. The community forestry approach

Rapid rural appraisal methods and tools are integrated into this extension approach. They are not used exclusively or in particular for planning purposes in preparing the Community Forestry Plans but are seen as more general tools of participatory extension. They enable the extension worker to better analyse and understand local realities and dynamics. This understanding of the local reality (production system, agricultural calendar, local politics, power and conflicts, the role of women, land tenure, etc.) constitutes the strategic framework in which to identify, plan and execute activities. In other words, it permits the project to identify constraints and opportunities for intervention. RRA tools such as transect walks, diagrams, mapping, interview techniques and drawings are taught as part of the basic extension skills training programme.

In general, linkages are established with the communities as follows. During the first months, the extension worker familiarizes him- or herself with the local reality, assessing constraints and opportunities for intervention on the basis of discussions and meetings with local authorities and selected local population groups. His or her role during this first phase also involves informing the local community about project objectives and methodology. This is usually done at community meetings, under the chairmanship of the community president. It is during these meetings that the decision is taken whether to start forestry activities and how to organize the preparation of the Community Forestry Plan. In most cases a working group, called a forestry committee, is selected by the farmers to assume this responsibility and to act as the counterpart of the extension worker.

The members of these groups are called "forestry promoters" (*promotores forestales*). Since there is such a high amount of seasonal migration of the male population, most of the members of these groups are women. They are not paid by the project, because these responsabilities are perceived as special social duties for the benefit of the community. The members are compensated by being freed from., other communal work. As these committees are supposed to replace the extension worker after some years, regular training opportunities are provided to their members by the project. The training at group and at community level is focused on the local realities, experiences and knowledge. Its methodology is based on the principles of practice, dialogue and reflection. Concretely, this means that local knowledge of sites, species and management is identified, discussed and incorporated when designing the Community Forestry Plan. When implementing its Plan, the community trains itself through practice and generates learning experiences, which are shared with others. When evaluating a tree production cycle or a planting activity, the community reflects on the results achieved and the difficulties encountered, seeking ways to improve the results next time. When preparing the next productive cycle, the lessons learned from previous implementation experiences are used and further deepened, for example by making adjustments to the forestry calendar.

RESULTS AND LESSONS LEARNED

In many cases, project participants stated that the project has contributed to a strengthening of the internal organization of the *ranchos*. For example, in the case of the community of Uma Jila, it was reported that "before the extension worker came to this community, no regular meetings were held" and that "the project has unified the population more than ever before". This process of internal strengthening is the result of a number of factors. The local communities in this region are very well aware of the multiple benefits of forestry activities for the improvement of their household economies. These activities do not compete with other work to be done, as they do not require a permanent or large-scale mobilization of labour. "The work is easy and we work only a few hours; we never work the whole day with the trees," as one of the respondents said. The time factor is particularly important in the Andean system, because almost all available time has to be invested in this very complex system of agriculture and live-stock production, leaving little space for other productive activities.

Practical training in new technologies has also proved to be important: "Formerly, we didn't have this system of production and planting of trees. We have learned now how to do it ourselves and we really like it." Although indigenous tree production technologies seem to be limited mainly to natural regeneration, there is a general knowledge and understanding of the importance of forests and trees for soil conservation and for improving the productivity of the land. In addition, a custom has developed among the farmers to experiment with tree species when returning home after their frequent "interecological" commercial travelling in the region. This custom also helps to explain why the project is being received with real interest by the farmers.

A final important factor in this context relates to the organizational activities of the project. As explained, the project actively promotes local forestry committees as mechanisms for articulating community decisions concerning forestry activities. The functioning of these committees in relation to the community has not been dictated by the project but has been defined by the communities themselves: "We do the organizing by ourselves, and the planning with German, the extension worker. We keep our records to see who is missing and who is working and that way we keep control." In practice, these committees function as a management unit through which the community organizes itself on the basis of a programme of activities, defined with the support of the project. These committees have developed their own mechanisms for the division of work, which fit into the traditional structures and systems. The division of labour in forestry activities is done according to the labour type. As in agriculture, only a few of the activities are done exclusively by women or by men; most of the work is shared between both genders, depending on the time of the year (because of the seasonal migration of men).

Traditional mechanisms are used by the local communities for the organization of forestry work. In most cases, each member of the forestry committee has a small working group of families under his or her authority, with specific, complementary responsibilities for the implementation of the Community Forestry Plan. This system of organization of work reflects the traditional system of the *faena*, or communal work done by small family groups in rotation which permits the community and the families to rationalize and economize the allocation of labour in turn, facilitates the development of an important participatory potential within the community, and explains why families indeed are participating in forestry activities and consider the Community Forestry Plan their own.

Although the above description clearly displays the elements of strengthening (organization), enabling (training) and empowering (decision-making) of local communities, some additional observations should be made in this context. There were several instances where the project interventions were limited to one sector or secondary *rancho* of a primary *rancho*. As these two levels are considered parts of the same patrilocal unit with its own socio-political mandate, negative repercussions might occur if the processes at secondary *rancho* level are further consolidated without including or compensating superior levels of community organization. This depends on the balance of power between the different levels. It is also possible that certain secondary *ranchos* might be in an increasingly independent position.

The issue of those who do not participate in the community forestry activities, their perceptions and their experiences, is to be' placed within this framework of organizational levels and customary relationships within local communities. At the level of the *rancho,* participation in community forestry activities is determined by the residential location of the family groups in relation to the community nursery. Families living nearby will participate in the project, while those of the same community who are living in another place (secondary *rancho)* are practically excluded. As one farmer stated:

... So, we decided to start in the mountains first. We have worked two days, all of us, constructing the nursery and the fences. Then we also prepared the seed beds and when the seedlings already were growing, they got annoyed with us because we didn't show up one day. They said that we were lazy and then they moved the nursery to another place, even farther away in the mountains. Since then, we do not participate any more. We hope to have our own nursery one day, though we don't dare ask the project to help us. But we want to have the nursery, with or without them.

There is no doubt that the geographical distance plays a role, since time availability is a structural constraint. In this case, certain other factors could have intervened as well. The decision of where to construct the community nursery depends, among other things, on technical and economic criteria such as availability of water, land, construction materials and accessibility. Its location therefore tends to be linked to those parts of the communities that are relatively better off.

The forestry and agricultural calendars constitute the framework for programming of activities, and it should be respected in order to minimize risks of tree production and planting failures. The farmers are well aware of this. Experience has shown that local communities cannot invest much time in preparatory activities. The attitude in general is: "Let's start when the time has come and find out if it works." Therefore, one or two months after the extension worker has started to work with the local community, the first annual Community Forestry Plan will be prepared. As soon as this plan has been approved by the community, it will become an important frame of reference for the extension worker's own monthly workplan.

The case study shows that local forestry planning capacity has been strengthened significantly after a few years of activity. Through practical experience, local communities have improved their ability to develop their plans on the basis of local constraints and opportunities. Similarly, the project has strengthened its own capacity to respond more effectively to the Community Forestry Plans as the project staff has developed a better understanding of local realities. The project has been able to adjust its own annual planning procedures. Annual inputs, activities and planned outputs or results are based, within the framework of the project Document, on the profiles of the community forestry plans.

The project has signed a number of agreements of Collaboration with governmental and non-governmental organizations that are promoting rural development in the project area. The aim is to institutionalize the methodological approach and technical menu of the project, and, in particular, to develop and verify agroforestry systems. In addition, the project has developed a network of departmental institutions with which specific activities are developed. The project also supports a large number of governmental and non-governmental institutions in their efforts to initiate forestry projects and activities in communities where they are working. This support is provided through training of their field staff in community forestry methodologies, provision of inputs such as seeds and planting materials and technical follow-up visits in the field. The participatory approach of the project and the research results obtained so far (such as those regarding customary organizational structures) have proven to be highly relevant for most of the institutions working in this region.

In this context, it is worth noting that the present Government of Bolivia is giving high priority to decentralization and regionalization. The development plans and strategies currently being developed are oriented toward the most deprived sections of the population and put emphasis on direct participation of the population, improvement of the natural environment and sustainable development. Therefore, the objectives, methodology and strategy of the project fit very well into the current policy framework of the Government.

THE MALAKAND/DIR SOCIAL FORESTRY PROJECT IN PAKISTAN

The Malakand/Dir Social Forestry Project is being implemented by the Forestry Department of the North West Frontier Province (NWFP) in Pakistan, and funded by the Dutch Government. Technical assistance is provided by DHV Consultants in the Netherlands and EDC in Pakistan. The project started in 1987 in the provincially administered tribal area known as Malakand Agency. At the start of its second phase, its coverage was extended to the Dir District.

THE PROJECT AREA

In Malakand Agency about 50% of the land area is arable. The remainder is made up of hills too steep to farm. Almost all arable land is privately owned.

More than half of the households are landless and depend heavily on agricultural wage labour for their livelihood. Among the landowners, 32% have less than 1 ha of land. The hillsides are generally owned by communities and sometimes by sections within the communities. About 73% of the people have ownership rights to the hillsides through these groups. However, except in the rare cases where some form of management exists, the hills are open to free access by all. The majority of the villages have access to these hillsides. In some of these, the gujars (livestock herders) and landless constitute the dominant group. These people rely heavily on the hillsides to meet their fodder and fuelwood needs. The areas of project intervention are dominated by either small landowners, farmers or tenants and non-farming landlords.

In Dir District, only about 10% of the area is arable. Here, too, hillsides make up a large part of the land mass and usually are held jointly by the communities. Hillside use is the same as in Malakand Agency. The people draw on them heavily to meet their needs for timber, fodder and fuel. Fodder is very scarce, and is often imported from other districts, especially for the lean period in winter. As compared to Malakand Agency, Dir is better endowed with forestry resources, though they are unevenly distributed. Whereas the northern mountains have a preponderance of forests, the lower areas are devoid of them. The coniferous forests in the upper reaches of the hillsides (outside the project area) are officially state-owned, although they are also covered by customary rights systems of the local people. Oak forests, which occur all along the different valleys, are disappearing steadily because of uncontrolled use and the ever rising demand for fuelwood.

All villages in the project area in Malakand have an elementary school for boys, and 65% have an elementary school for, girls. Secondary school facilities are few for boys and almost absent for girls. Basic services of health, water supply and electricity are present in most of the villages (53%, 63% and 82% respectively). In Dir District, literacy is very low (7%), especially among women. Public services are generally lacking.

Ethnicity, religion and gender play a fundamental role in the socio-cultural, economic and political power structure of the villages. The Pukthun values of power and female segregation (*purdah*) are very important in the context of the project. The management of commonly owned areas depends on the willingness of people to decide upon obligations for controlled use. However, this is often complicated by power conflicts, a common feature in Pathan society. Moreover, because of the *purdah* system, men deliberately ignore women's role in the use and management of trees, shrubs and grasses, since women are supposed to stay at home. Under these circumstances, projects that promote participatory approaches and try to bring the different groups together, talking about equity and benefits for all (including women), face a difficult task. Religion and politics play an important role in people's lives. Religious leaders are among the most influential members of the society and people's faith in them is very strong. Nearly all men are associated with one or another political party, and these associations are mostly used to further personal interests.

OBJECTIVES OF THE PROJECT

The development goal of the project is to "contribute to raising the standard of living in Malakand Agency and Dir District by improving the productivity and use of the hillsides and marginal farmlands". The project objectives are (1) to restore a suitable vegetation to the denuded hillsides and marginal farmlands in order to create a sustainable, ecologically and economically improved living environment; (2) to further develop an extension approach for these field activities; and (3) to foster institutionalization of this extension approach at local level and within the NWFP Forestry Department. Although these objectives have been maintained during the years, the emphasis changed in methods for achieving them soon after project inception in 1987. The initial exclusive emphasis on establishment of forest plantations on denuded hillsides was changed to include other components, such as range management, training, extension and women's activities.

APPROACH, METHODS AND TOOLS

From its second phase onwards, the Malakand project has gradually developed an approach it calls "Village Land Use Planning" (VLUP). This approach can best be described as a structured participatory planning and implementation process. It is a blend of RRA techniques, awareness raising, participatory planning and programming, social organization, implementation of land use interventions and monitoring and evaluation. The approach is based on principles that more or less coincide with the assumptions of participatory planning as outlined in the conceptual framework. Key concepts in this approach are participation, social organization, control, distribution of benefits and responsibilities, integrated approach and gender specificity. The VLUP approach has been incorporated in a field manual, which is being further developed and tested. The seven steps of VLUP, as defined in mid-1993. It is interesting to quote some of the guiding principles for users of the manual as they indicate how this approach is perceived.

You are a social forester. This means your role is to help villagers to restore and/or maintain vegetation on hillsides and marginal farmlands in such a way that the land is productive and remains so in the future. You can help them in their planning of optimal land use. Villagers are the owners and/or users of the land, so they are responsible and take decisions on its management. You advise and support them.

In order to be able to help the villagers you first have to understand clearly their present land use, the role of different user and owner groups in this present use and their main needs, constraints and opportunities. It also helps them to think about and formulate how they want to develop their areas in the future. The villagers provide this information and this helps them to become more aware of their present problems as well as possible solutions. Through this form of cooperation a relationship of trust and understanding is gradually established between villagers and the Project.

The role of the Forest Development staff and the villagers in the VLUP process differs. During data collection you take the initiative by collecting all relevant data, analysing them and discussing them with the villagers, while the villagers provide us with information, list their problems and possible solutions and discuss and adjust the findings. However, during social organization and the development of management plans, the villagers are the main responsible actors, supported by you.

The objective of VLUP is to assist the local population in the-development of a management plan to sustainably increase the productivity of vegetation (trees, shrubs and grasses) on privately or commonly owned hillsides and farmlands. The outcome of this planning process is a village land use plan based on (1) an assessment of socio-economic and biophysical constraints and opportunities in the village, (2) the needs and desires of land users, and (3) the services that the project can provide, summarized in what is called the "social forestry menu". This menu is developed for three types of land use: natural vegetation, vegetation established by the Forestry Department and agricultural lands. For each, potential project activities during the establishment, maintenance and the harvesting period have been identified. These technical interventions are complemented with supporting activities such as organization, training and awareness raising. As in the Bolivian case, the formulation of the local plan is not seen as an entirely open-ended process, being based instead on what the project can deliver as inputs and services, and on local constraints, needs and opportunities.

Explicit attention is being paid to gender issues, both by promoting women's activities and in particular by trying to make the VLUP approach more gender specific. This is done by the directly involving a women's team during the VLUP process, incorporating gender analysis techniques, and organizing the planning process in such a way that the results of the activities of the women have to be discussed with the men. However, the project has encountered serious difficulties in constituting a women's team and integrating gender issues in the day-to-day planning and implementation of activities, mainly because of cultural factors (the *purdah* system).

The planning process is implemented by the villagers together with an interdisciplinary team of outsiders, consisting of a Range Forest Officer, a Forester and Forest Guard, a Social Organizer, a female Programme Officer and a female Forest Extensionist. Experience has demonstrated that the process, up to the implementation of the first plans, takes around 20 days per village, spread over a period of two to three months, depending on the local conditions. Broadly speaking, the following phases can be distinguished during the process: (1) preparation; (2) data collection; (3) analysis of village land use; (4) social organization; (5) development of a general village management plan; (6) development of management plans for specific land use units; and (7) implementation and monitoring of the management plans.

During the preparation phase, basic information is collected in the village and at the office by the VLUP team. The methodology for data collection and processing is based on RRA techniques. Only information that is specifically needed for drafting a general village development plan is collected. Data collection activities encompass field observations, updating of the village map, informal interviews focusing on key issues in social forestry, user group meetings to complete a problem census and an analysis of hillside management, and use of key informants. During data processing, information is exchanged and cross-checked among the men and women. Processing is done with the aid of pre-defined forms. These include a description of key issues and results of the problem census for each user/interest group, ownership relations, local institutions and organizations, a fodder calendar and data on the role of women in land management. Information on land use and ownership is visualized in the map. The village is subdivided into management units based on criteria of ownership and use. Finally the data are presented and discussed with the villagers, resulting in adjustments and identification of further data collection needs.

During this phase, data collection and processing is done by the project in Collaboration with all the villagers in general, not with a specific group. Because village social structure is highly stratified, any village working group collaborating with the project at this stage would be dominated by the local elite. This might be counterproductive for the project, which seeks opportunities to establish relationships with the other groups as well (other lineage groups, women and non-owners such as tenants and settled nomads).

The next step is the formation of Village Development Committees (VDCs), comprising representatives from the different owner-lineages. Whenever the circumstances in the villages permit, the project also promotes involvement of representatives of non-owners. The findings of the case study indicate that this has not always been successful. However, while the composition of the VDCs is an important factor, its profile does not necessarily constitute a rigid framework for further planning and action.

The VDC approves the village development plan as a broad outline, based on an analysis of the problem census and what is called a "goal statement exercise". In this exercise, the villagers define their needs for hillside products (fodder, fuel and construction material from grasses, shrubs or trees), the location where they will produce them and the consequences for actual land use management.

Next, the VDC and the project discuss the formation of a management committee for each management unit. Management committees are composed of owners and users of a specific area, the management unit. A management unit can be, for example, a side valley or a hill of a village, which is owned by one or more lineages and used by tenants living in or near it for grazing and cutting.

After approval of this operational set up, the management committees start working with the project. Walking transects are made and discussions held in the management units to make an inventory of the present vegetation, management practices, regulations for land use and needs and options for change. A management proposal is worked out, indicating the needed products, the location where they can be produced, activities required to produce the outputs, required inputs, timing and distribution of rights (benefits) and obligations (costs) among interested groups and the project or Forestry Department. In this way, local land use management projects are defined and presented for approval to the VDC and the project. If approved, an agreement is signed between the VDC/management committee and the project/Forestry Department in which the rights and obligations of both parties are specified.

Once the plans have been approved, implementation starts and each of the parties involved assumes its responsibilities. The project staff continues visiting the villages in order to identify problems during implementation and to provide training of committee members. An annual joint evaluation is envisaged, covering the results so far and reviewing the applicability of the plan. The plans are not considered blueprints, but are seen rather as indicative and flexible instruments to stimulate conscious decision-making about the management of an area.

RESULTS AND LESSONS LEARNED

Conflicts of interest and power at village level are one of the major constraints faced by the project. These conflicts occur not only between owners and non-owners, but also between groups of owners, as in the case of a village called Totakan. In this village, the project (before the development of the VLUP system) approached the landowners, who, of course, constitute the most powerful group. They agreed with the project to reforest some of their village communal area, which was partially commonly managed by all the three lineage groups *(khels)* and partially subdivided among them.

At the same time, the project told them that it would help in a development scheme, also within the village. The three *khels* came up with a list and then out of the list selected the construction of a water canal, which was to be jointly funded by the project and the village, the project being the major contributor. The canal was to benefit all the three lineage sections *(kandai)*. The chapter of the Mubarik and Dadi *khel* were completed, but then money ran out before the canal could reach the chapter of the Ismail*khel.* This has generated conflicts between the three *khels,* which have been further deepened as a result of disputes over the protection of the communal area under reforestation. As the four-year agreement with the project has been completed, the project has withdrawn its support, leaving the area open to intruders. According to the other two *khels,* the Ismail *khel* wants to be part of any decisions that are made about the areas belonging to the individual sections, such as the appointment of watchmen, which the others do not accept.

The heads of the sections want to take decisions regarding their respective sections with no interference from other *khels,* even though they are all part of the same VDC.

The landless, tenants and livestock herders *(gujars)* were not approached for any of the activities. They first became aware of them when the reforestation areas were closed off. They believed that the project was there for the benefit of the owners only.

However, although initially upset over the closure of the area, the *gujars* saw the benefit later on in the form of good quality grasses, which had been scarce in these nearby areas. Some of them did not mind paying for it but suggested that for the two monsoon months of July and August, the areas should be open for free grass collection by those who could not afford to buy it, and then closed off again. They preferred to have a controlled system implemented in the areas rather than being completely closed off.

As we have seen, because of internal conflicts among the owner groups, their reforestation project has failed and the area is left open without a controlled management system. But it is interesting to note that the exclusion of the group of non-owners does not mean that these people do not follow what is happening. On the contrary, they make up their minds and, as demonstrated in this case, can come up with their own proposals and suggestions. During the first phase of the project, many such important lessons were learned, constituting the basis for the design of the VLUP methodology. This approach helps adapt project interventions to divergent (and sometimes conflicting) interests at the local level, as demonstrated in the following examples, where the implementation of the approach is under way.

When conducting the VLUP exercise in 1993 in a village called Jabbar, the project proposed a division of the village into 42 land use units. The villagers, through the VLUP exercise, changed this to only seven units. The project staff, which had not sufficiently understood the village social system and use of the area, realized its mistake and agreed with the VDC proposal. It is interesting to note that members of all six lineage groups of the village have ownership rights in every unit. According to them, this makes protection very easy because each of the six groups has an interest in every unit. Their elders had thought up this system to keep intruders out and protect their investments jointly. The VDC decided which units were to be treated as priority, which the project accepted.

In one of the selected units the project proposed a bigger area for planting, which the VDC did not accept. They said that they were planning a canal on one part of the area and that it would be pointless to plant trees there as they would have to be taken out later on. The VDC also curtailed the planting proposal of the project in another chapter as that was used by the main village for grazing. Another reason for selecting relatively small areas for planting was that they want to be practical. It would take a long time to establish new trees on large areas and they preferred to see the results before expanding the planting area. It should be done a little at a time, as the farmers put it. The project suggested planting eucalyptus, but the villagers did not accept because they had experience of its extremely poor survival rate in heavy snowfall areas. Therefore, the villagers suggested other species they already knew, which the project accepted.

On the other hand, the project has been able to introduce some innovations, such as in the traditional system of fines *(nagha).* Before, whoever caught the offenders was rewarded with the *nagha* amount for his diligence. Now the *nagha* money goes into the village fund, which the project helped set up. An interesting point is that the *nagha* for the women offenders had been fixed by the villagers at twice the amount imposed on men. The argument was that women, who did not know how to lop trees, were destroyers of the forests, so that heavier penalties would mean that they would abstain from going into protected areas and breaking the rules.

The project suggested that the men use a uniform system for both men and women without distinction and that it would train the women in lopping trees. The men eventually agreed. The project spoke to the women about this issue, but they did not think they were doing any harm.

The women were not yet fully involved in or informed about the project and its activities. Some information relevant to the whole village reaches the women through the village loudspeakers but men, in general, do not discuss project issues with them.

One of the constraints mentioned by the villagers is that they feel the project is moving too slowly. After six months to a year they have not gone further than meetings. As farmers are generally action-oriented and want to see results,. expressions of waning interest appear quickly. The project on the other hand, keen to avoid mistakes of the past, prefers to practise great caution. Another point mentioned by the villagers is that since they are farmers, they do not have much time to devote to meetings without disturbing their work and, hence, their livelihood. The timing of the meetings was also mentioned as a constraint, since they sometimes took place during heavy workload hours when the villagers are busy in the fields. The project is well aware of these constraints. A schedule for the VLUP exercise has been defined and supporting materials, such as forms, have been produced in order to ensure that the process indeed generates the expected outputs in the shortest possible time.

The National Forest Policy of 1991 and the Forestry Sector Master Plan constitute the framework of strategic planning of the Forestry Department. Although people's participation is considered as an important component, a proven framework for strategic planning of social forestry is still lacking. The experience of the project shows that people's participation should be given a central role, and also that the Department should integrate its various programmes of watershed, hill forest, range management and farm forestry, not hesitating to combine several into a single project.

In this context, it is interesting to mention the network of extension services established some years ago in order to facilitate the exchange of different project field experiences in the region. During its last meeting in April 1994, some 40 participants of the NWFP extension coordination network met for an expert consultation on village land use planning. Representatives from other projects and officials of the Forestry Department discussed the applicability of the VLUP approach in their own working areas, reviewed options for further standardization and worked out a plan of action for the coming period. The quality of the comments of the participants at this meeting and the keynote address of the Chief Conservator of the Forestry Department indicate that the institution is gradually creating more and more opportunities for community forestry.

On the other hand, it became clear that before this approach can be applied on a wider scale, the Forestry Department would need to re-examine its mandate and policies. The Department needs to formulate long-term strategies and goals, determining the allocation of national and international resources and defining the role of the private sector (including local communities) in conjunction with its own. Only when these factors are clear will it be possible to determine whether a larger-scale application of the social forestry approach can contribute to those long-term goals or not.

At institutional level, planning takes place according to a prescribed standard governmental procedure of drafting, scrutiny and approval of all kinds of project Documents. It is at this level that serious constraints exist concerning the planning process (top-down, output-oriented, blueprint approach). As has been mentioned before, the project faced these constraints during its first phase. However, it turned out to be possible to overcome some of these constraints by drafting more flexible and open-ended annual working plans and organizing monthly strategic meetings. In addition, before drafting the project document for the second phase, a detailed and systematic analysis was made of the lessons learned during the first phase.

This method, in which the institution takes stock of experiences, is important for strengthening the learning capacity of the project. It is also an important tool for generating more institutional support for corrective measures. It is gradually becoming clear at institutional level that the social forestry approach comprises a participatory planning process of the negotiations with and between the villagers, whose final outcome can never be planned beforehand. The annual plans will have to allow for this, for example by only specifying how many VLUPs will be carried out and maybe in which villages, leaving flexibility in the setting and achievement of implementation targets. In other words: the process can be planned but not the outcome.

However, it takes time and experimentation to establish organizational structures that facilitate decentralized planning. This requires delegation of authority, participatory leadership skills at different levels of the organization, strong motivation and commitment and smooth communication. In other words, adequate management of social forestry programmes requires a participatory management style within the organization: the lessons learned in the field have to be systematically fed back into the organization so that appropriate decision-making can take place. Therefore, control of progress and staff performance is important. Monitoring the quality of performance of extension workers is not easy, however, since one must follow the quality of the process as well as the physical outputs.

The division of work and responsibilities in the Forestry Department is laid out in the service rules. In general, the Forestry Department staff has successfully taken up social forestry tasks on a pilot basis. These new tasks have not yet been reflected in the service rules, however. At institutional level, the position of "extension worker" does not exist. So far, the project has contracted "social organizers" to assume these tasks. The question is whether special extension positions should be created within the Forestry Department and what extension tasks can be carried out by officers in currently existing positions (such as Forest Guards). The project experiences have demonstrated that extension skills can be acquired by personnel in existing staff positions. Besides, the combination of technical and extension skills in a single position increases the institutional commitment and support to social forestry. Job specialization at field level, on the other hand, would mean that forestry technicians would keep on working only with trees and the extension staff only with people.

The Malakand experience demonstrates that in spite of many institutional constraints, the social forestry approach is receiving more and more attention and priority at institutional level. Currently, an action plan is being implemented by a number of projects and programmes in order to develop common denominators based on lessons learned from the VLUP approach. The goal is to define a minimum level of standardization, which will facilitate the institutionalization of the approach. But, as indicated above, it is not just a question of defining a standardized approach. The organizational implications must be worked on as well. The Malakand project defines its role in this connection basically in terms of: (1) human resource planning (number, levels and skills required); (2) systems development (communication and information management); and (3) extension and management training programmes. These three components constitute instruments to generate the managerial and organizational innovations in the Forestry Department, which are necessary to conduct social forestry programmes.

3

Interregional Project for Participatory Upland Conservation and Development

This project started in 1991 with the aim of promoting people's participation in the conservation and development of upland catchments. It is financed by the Italian Government and executed by FAO. After completion of the first phase at the end of 1993, the interregional project was extended for another period of three years. In the national field projects, emphasis is given to the adaptation and application of participatory methods for the promotion of an integrated approach to watershed management. Direct support is given to projects in Pakistan, Nepal, Rwanda, Burundi and Bolivia.

The development objective of this interregional project is the active involvement of local communities in the management and development of upland catchments in accordance with the social, economic and production system requirements of the rural communities concerned. The immediate objectives of the interregional project and the individual field projects are: (1) the installation of five integrated upland conservation and development projects in the selected countries incorporating the participatory approach; (2) the coordination of upland catchment management systems in the five target countries, ensuring mutual strengthening of design, planning, implementation, monitoring and evaluation of methods and tools; and (3) contribution to information dissemination and transfer of approaches, methods and techniques on participatory management of upland catchments.

The project approach is process-oriented and focused on local capacity building. Project workplans are based on the outcome of the participatory planning process. Interinstitutional networking and linkages are considered important instruments for broadening the scope of technical support available for implementation of local plans with the local communities. In addition, this networking is crucial because sustainable management of watersheds also depends on services of a "public works" nature from the government.

In each of these field projects, the first three to four months were reserved for assessment, restitution and planning with the local population. To facilitate this participatory approach, tools of PRA and RRA were selected and tested in action. On the basis of the results of this initial PRA/RRA period, a workplan for immediate implementation was prepared by the local population together with the project team. Implementation of activities started in most cases by the end of 1992.

The interregional project was designed with an initial pilot phase of two years in order to develop and verify the methodological approach and tools. Therefore, during these first two years, a special emphasis was given to the exchange between the five field projects of experiences undergone and lessons learned. To that end, the five project teams met in Rome for an internal technical review meeting at the conclusion of the pilot phase.

THE PUCD PROJECT IN FOREST

THE PROJECT AREA

In Nepal, the project is working in the Bhusunde Khola Watershed (BKW), located in Ghorka District in the Western Development Region. It has an area of 44 km2 with a steep topography. It is a typical mid-hill area of Nepal with north-facing steep slopes and south-facing gentler slopes. The climate varies from subtropical in the low lying areas (around 450 m) to subtemperate in the upper parts of the watershed (around 1 500 m). The area has a population of approximately 20 000 people. Brahmins, Chhetries and Gurungs represent the major ethnic groups, but ethnic and occupational caste groups such as Kumal, Kami, Damai and Sarki also inhabit the area in small numbers. Most of the villages and settlements are inhabited by mixed ethnic and occupational castes except for some homogeneous settlements of Gurungs, Brahmins and Kumals. Population pressure and economic hardship have resulted in migration to the Terai and other areas over the past several decades. This migration continues.

As small farmers, the people depend on subsistence agriculture. The average landholding is less than one hectare. Most of the area in Bhusunde watershed (65%) is under cultivation. The valley floor and the bottom slopes are usually under irrigated rice cultivation, while dryland crops are cultivated on the upper slopes of the mountains. Livestock is an integral part of the farming system. Traditionally, animals are grazed on community land and forest: this grazing land is very scarce, so the pressure of animals on land is very high.

Households are clustered into small hamlets or villages (*tols*) scattered within "wards", the lowest level of government administration. In this area, government administration is based on four Village Development Committees (VDCs), each one made up of nine wards. VDC members (Chairperson, Vice Chairperson and Ward Representatives) meet once or twice each month. They regulate all development activities in the VDC. There are no women Ward Representatives.

It is common for households within *tols* to be linked by patrilineal kinship ties. The most important unit of social organization and economic life is the individual farm household (*ghar* or *pariwar*). At this level, significant decisions regarding land use and farming practices are made, influencing both privately owned resources and common lands. This process of decision-making is democratic, consensual and egalitarian, with women members and even children participating in household discussions, which are aimed at reaching consensus. In public meetings, where consensus is also sought, women are absent. Although women play active roles in farm decision-making, their status is inferior to that of men in many other respects. This is particularly so among the high caste groups, where women in general have far less autonomy, authority and power than men both outside and inside the home. However, education and new economic opportunities for women are changing this traditional picture of gender inequality among high castes. Among middle and lower caste groups, a greater social and religious equality between the sexes has always existed.

Infrastructure in the area is minimal. There are no roads, health clinics or post offices, nor are there adequate water systems. The trails or farm roads are difficult to travel in the hilly areas. The most visible infrastructural feature in the area is the large number of schools. On the other hand, a number of development organizations are active in this region The Gorkha Development Project (with German bilateral aid) works mainly throught VDCs and the government ministry offices in Gorkha District. International non-governmental organizations (NGOs) such as Save the Children, CARE and Worldview International, as well as local NGOs (Drabya Shah Community Forestry Preservation and Management, Sarbodaya Society Building Association, Community Development and Research) provide valuable opportunities for linkages with the project.

APPROACH, METHODS AND TOOLS

In this project, participatory rural appraisal is considered the first step in a larger participatory process that will continue throughout the life of the project. The initial PRA activities were specifically focused on directly involving villagers in the planning that guided implementation of the activities through the first year. The project uses participatory assessment at six separate times, giving inputs at various points along a chain of stages linking the farmers of the project area to the implementation of their activities.

APPRAISAL

At stage one, a rapid field reconnaissance was carried out over the entire project area as the initial step of the planning phase. Contacts were made in the field with the villagers in each VDC area in order to familiarize them with the project and its objectives, to introduce the VDC members to the project field team and to discuss and record major issues related to soil conservation and management. For this purpose, maps of VDC areas were prepared for further discussion and analysis at VDC level. These maps served as reference for identification of the villages that were in greatest need of watershed conservation and management activities. On the basis of the results obtained, pilot villages were selected for follow-up actions. Village meetings were held and local priorities for project activities were identified. By the end of these meetings, a long list of activities was obtained for each area. These village meetings were positive and informal, without going through the official VDC structure. They focused attention on specific activity selection rather quickly, without a prior, structured process of problem identification or an analysis of the physical and social conditions of the communities.

Next, there was a second series of field visits for the purpose of narrowing down the long lists of priorities for project activities. This time, a record was kept of persons attending the general meetings, as was a list of the priorities decided upon. After these general meetings, one member of the project team went on "site tour" with a small group of villagers to see and discuss each site (gully, landslide, trail, forest). These "site tours" provided a good opportunity to discuss informally many aspects of potential project activities. Other members of the project team occasionally remained in the main village area to conduct semi-structured interviews with women. Towards the end of these field trips, more structured assessment activities were conducted in two villages on the basis of the results of mapping exercises for the natural resources. These exercises were videotaped, as was a general priority-narrowing meeting with villagers and project personnel.

These initial assessment tools (general meetings, semi-structured interviews, site tours and mapping) were already familiar activities to villagers, with the exception of mapping. This allowed for flexibility and informality, which put villagers at ease and stimulated open discussion and debate. This was enhanced by the fact that these meetings were arranged in village communities rather than through the VDC/Ward structures. On the other hand, the timing of the second stage during the rice-harvesting season was not convenient. In the case of village women, interviews were held after (instead of before) the general village meeting when important decisions had already been made.

RESTITUTION

During the stage of restitution of the results of the assessment of priority issues, meetings were held with the villagers and videos of previous meetings and slides of critical sites in the project area were shown to them. During this phase, three major sessions were conducted. First, a meeting was arranged in one of the villages. However, transport of video equipment proved to be so difficult that the planned activities had to be dropped. For the second session, farmers from each of the remaining villages were invited to attend a meeting at the base camp of the project. Along with 10 male farmers, two women (both from the same village) attended this meeting.

Project activities were reviewed site by site, then an agricultural calendar was prepared for the assessment of time availability of both men and women for project implementation. This exercise was conducted as a first step towards planning the implementation of the identified activities, trying to match labour needs for project implementation with local labour needs for agricultural tasks. The day after this meeting, a final session was held at the base camp with VDC chairs and vice-chairs in order to inform them officially of project activities and methodology. The following development activities and resource management measures were confirmed with the village representatives: water source protection, trail improvement, irrigation channel improvement, gully and landslide control, degraded land improvement and income generating activities.

PLANNING AND ORGANIZATION

The planning stage is conducted mainly through village meetings to draft a workplan for the selected priority activities using forms prepared by the project. These workplans are presented by the village and the project to the VDC to which the particular village belongs. During the next phase, beneficiaries of the planned activities are identified and user groups are formed. The executive or subcommittees of user groups usually include members representing different villages, since many of the planned activities (such as trail improvement, gully and landslide control, water source protection) respond to the needs of several villages. At the same time, the technical and economic aspects of the proposed activities are elaborated by the project, resulting in a more detailed contract proposal for Collaboration between the user group and the project. This proposal specifies the distribution of costs and labour between both parties, payments to be made in instalments on the basis of performance, the raising of revolving funds, and so on.

IMPLEMENTATION

So far, almost all planned activities have been implemented by 22 user groups. The project has provided the required material, financial and training inputs. The user groups assumed their responsibility for the organization and mobilization of the labour inputs. Support from other line agencies has been sporadic since the activities selected were those that would remain as much as possible within the mandate of the government counterpart agency, the Department of Soil Conservation and Watershed Management.

RESULTS AND LESSONS LEARNED

One of the major constraints faced by the project since its initiation has been the insufficient number of field staff and poorly timed transfer of international staff to and from the project. Initial training for project staff was not sufficient to develop the necessary conceptual orientation and analysis of participatory approaches; nor was it adequate in terms of practical training in the effective use of PRA tools in the field. Moreover, very poor infrastructural facilities in the field resulted in transportation and communication bottle-necks that impeded effective coordination between the project and the villages. Because of these and other circumstances, field staff preferred to remain in their offices rather than spend more time in the field and stay at the base camp.

At village level, previous negative experiences with government agencies and development projects had created an attitude of scepticism among the villagers. The people of the project area have been heavily conditioned by the previous "top-down" style of development projects, and they have established their own adaptive attitudes of suspicion, mistrust and pursuit of individual gain. Under these circumstances, it is important for a project to show that its approach is innovative. To promote this innovative approach effectively in the field, the project staff has to have the right skills and attitudes and a proper understanding of participatory approaches. As mentioned, the project faced serious constraints in this respect. Moreover, the project had to demonstrate its credibility as a serious partner, meaning that activities should produce rapid results.

Participatory planning, however, takes time, requiring careful assessment of proposed activities with the different interest groups before implementation can be initiated. This might easily result in decreasing interest in the project among the villagers, especially among the less privileged. In this case, the process of participatory appraisal and planning of participatory was speeded up. Activities were selected without a community environmental assessment exercise or problem identification and analysis. Together with these constraints, the potential opportunities for improved resource management in the area include a strong local awareness of and concern with problems of environmental degradation. In addition, villagers are very able and apparently willing to organize themselves into viable user groups. A strong tradition of democratic discussion and debate and group decision-making through consensus is also an asset. Finally, the recent political changes in Nepal have encouraged people to express their interests more openly and to pursue their rights to control their natural resources.

Most of the planned activities have been implemented, and the user groups have demonstrated their technical and administrative capacity to carry out the activities as agreed upon with the project. However, most of the villagers consider the project-supported activities not as their own initiatives but rather as ad hoc external initiatives to which they contribute. This perception is further reinforced by small but important details. For example, in order to assess critical areas of the watershed in which to focus project activities, a base map was prepared by the project instead of the villagers. The villagers indicated critical areas with coloured paper markers, which they could have done without any support from the project team. After the meeting, the map was removed by the team for reproduction, instead of remaining as property of the VDC.

Under the responsibility of the user group committees, labour and time are mobilized for specific activities, such as trail improvement. Once the work has been finished, maintenance and repair activities become necessary that do not necessarily require the large-scale mobilization of labour. Therefore, although most of the activities were identified as short-term solutions for specific problems, they should gradually be placed within the context of an integrated approach to participatory management and conservation of natural resources. The results achieved so far should be used as inputs for new priority activities, in order to develop a coherent sequencing of project development.

This might also have consequences for the organizational set-up for local project planning and implementation. Thus far, single-activity user groups have been formed. In some villages this has led to a proliferation or duplication of these groups, creating confusion and problems of coordination and administration.

Organizational structures need to be promoted for planning and implementation of an integrated and coherent *programme* of interrelated activities.

This case study has demonstrated that sufficiently trained field staff is a precondition for the effective promotion of participatory approaches in the field. Training and preparation of project staff should be focused not only on practical skills but also on conceptual, methodological and attitudinal issues. The practical field experiences should be used systematically as inputs for further capacity building of the project staff.

Only limited baseline data about the local communities were collected, and particular attention was not paid to specific interest groups. Unless special meetings are held with disadvantaged groups such as the poor or women to discuss and analyse their problems and opportunities, it is difficult to elaborate strategies to facilitate a higher degree of participation for them. It is difficult to counter the influence of local artisans and the elite in planning and implementation. Particular emphasis should be given to the elaboration of strategies to ensure that women are involved in the assessment, planning and implementation phases. Women are not members of the VDCs and traditionally do not become involved in local group meetings. They are, however, key actors with respect to forest resource use, and they are strongly affected by the consequences of poor upland conservation, such as degraded trails, landslides and poor water sources.

Furthermore, little systematic attention has been given to local knowledge systems with regard to management of natural resources. Of course, during the public meetings, individual interviews, site visits, planning meetings and implementation of the activities local knowledge and skills have been expressed or used by the villagers. However, the technical design of some of the selected activities, for example, was prepared mainly by the project staff or external advisers.

In practice, the participation of most of the male villagers is limited to the stages of appraisal, restitution (to a certain extent) and implementation, and to a lesser extent to the elaboration of specific plans. However, the project and its participatory approach aim at encouraging local people to come together in consultation with the project, to determine activities, discuss their feasibility and define the responsibilities of the different actors. This process should be seen as a learning experience for the local community and for the project, and that takes time. Although it seems interesting to invite village representatives to the base camp to attend a three-day planning meeting, this reduces the planning exercise from a village-based learning experience almost to that of an individual. Broad-based village participation or consultation for planning is fundamental. This helps the local people to understand more clearly what their "participation" in "planning" means in terms of their power to make decisions.

Finally, the case study has shown that it is very important for community members to feel that some progress is being made. In the case of the Quetta case in Pakistan, some of the important moments during the process. In addition, a contract was signed with a local NGO to provide specific services to some of the villages. In the Bhusunde Khola watershed the services of a number of NGOs could have been mobilized in order to undertake short-term interventions.

The initial period of time allocated for the participatory assessment and planning phase of the project was too short in view of the size and population of the watershed. The availability and professional experience of national and international project staff was a bottleneck.

THE PUCD PROJECT IN PAKISTAN

THE PROJECT AREA

In Pakistan, the project is being executed through the Balochistan Forest and Wildlife Department of the Ministry of Agriculture. The project area is the Kanak Valley, Mastung District, Balochistan, southwest of Quetta. It is an area of about 40 000 ha with a population of about 20 000 living in 40 villages. Its climate is semi-arid with an average precipitation of 170 mm. Within this area, the 8 000 ha subwatershed of Noza has been selected to start project activities.

The population of this watershed belongs to the Brahui ethnic group, composed of more than a dozen tribes, which are divided in clans, sections, subsections, lineages and sublineages. Each tribe is ruled by a *Sardar*, the chief of the tribe. Usually the village is a small community that coincides with a segment of a lineage or with some extended families. Thus, all the families of a village usually have strong kinship bonds. Each village has a leader or chief. Decisions are taken on behalf of the village by the chief and an informal village council. This council is composed of the elders or old wise men who represent the interests of the villagers. Women are excluded from this decision-making body. In Brahui society, the status and position of women is very low and, because of the control of men over their behaviour and movements, they have very little direct access to life outside the village.

An estimated 6% of the land is used for rain-fed agriculture, 2% for irrigated orchards, 1 % for vegetable production and the remaining 90% left for grazing animals in the so-called *fan* areas. The use and ownership of uncultivated land is usually governed by traditional land tenure systems and used as communal property. This kind of land is very often degraded through overgrazing and soil erosion. Most of the *fan* area and a certain portion of land around the villages fall into this category.

Land used for agricultural purposes is divided among all the families by the village chief according to the needs of each family. In addition to this system, there are written laws and regulations that give the property rights to land based on public registers. These two systems overlap and either or both may be used according to the circumstances. Furthermore, tenancy is a very common form of land use in the project area. An estimated one-third of the farmers are tenants while two-thirds are owners or holders of traditional use rights. Most of the land worked by the tenants belongs to absentee landowners living outside the Noza project area. In the most common tenancy arrangement, labour is provided by the tenant while all other inputs are provided by the landowner. Then, the landowners receive two-thirds of the total output and the tenant retains one-third.

Water, because of its scarcity and the low rainfall levels, is the most important natural resource in the area. The most significant cash crop, apples, could not be produced without irrigation from tubewells. In the 14 villages of the project area there are 80 tubewells. On irrigated land worked by tenants output is divided as follows: one-seventh to the landowners, two-sevenths to the tenant and four-sevenths to the well owner, the person(s) who has invested the capital for digging the well. On irrigated land worked by the owner, four-sevenths of the output goes to the well owner and the remainder is retained by the landowner.

Educational facilities are very poor and as a result about 90% of the population over 10 years is illiterate. The literacy rate for girls and women is only 1% as there are no schools for girls in this region. Similarly, primary health care facilities are very limited, in particular for maternal and child health care. As a result, health is a critical issue for women in the project area.

APPROACH, METHODS AND TOOLS

APPRAISAL

The project started with preparatory activities for the execution of an initial participatory assessment and planning phase, which involved the rural population in the elaboration of the project workplan. For that purpose, in a limited number of villages, the methods and tools of PRA were tested. Prior to this, secondary data were collected and contacts with other relevant organizations were established. At the end of this preparatory phase, the project was presented to the project area Union Council, which is the local representation of the Provincial Government of Balochistan.

During appraisal, the following tools were used: group meetings, timeline exercises, map building exercises, semi-structured interviews, ranking, rating and sorting exercises, community environmental assessment (transect walks) and strengths, weaknesses, opportunities and limitations (SWOL) analysis.

The timeline exercise was used during group meetings as an instrument to encourage discussion of present problems and issues, and explore their relation to historical events. The drawing of village maps proved to be a very successful activity to understand how the villagers see their village. On the other hand, the activity as such is easily monopolized by those who know how to use the drawing materials. Although both tools are supposed to be instruments to orient further discussions, the general impression is that the villagers considered these activities to be something for the project, and not for themselves: they provide the project with information it needs to determine the activities to be implemented.

The transect walk usually took place after the timeline and map building exercises, and was used as a means to verify and complement the information. These field visits with farmers were very useful in obtaining a better idea of the complex water management systems. Villagers showed interest in the transect walk because it gave them the opportunity to illustrate their problems in the field. However, the objective of these field visits should be clearly explained as they might also be perceived by the farmers as a commitment by the project to solve individual problems.

In the case of the women's programme, similar tools were used but different challenges had to be faced. Group meetings are new for these women, since they have not had previous contact with other projects nor with health or social welfare workers. The project team had to help women to learn how to conduct meetings (speaking one by one and listening to each other). In addition, since women do not have much authority over children, toys were included in the toolbox in order to keep the children relatively quiet. After two months of regular group meetings it was possible to hold productive sessions in relative peace.

In every group meeting, one project team member acts as the "observer" and records the meeting. This has been very useful as it constituted a good in-service training opportunity for the staff in disciplined listening. The observer's notes are discussed by the team and used as inputs for the planning for the next meeting. As the women are illiterate, tape recorders were used to record group discussions and decisions. The tapes are replayed for the village women to reinforce group discussions and to illustrate the process. Moreover, although photographing women is culturally sensitive in the project area, project photo albums have been introduced in all the villages. A technique employed by the team for strengthening village organization and group building among the women is to remove all the photos from the album and ask the women to arrange them on the floor in sequence. Spatially, women are more accustomed to working on the floor than sitting and viewing a flip chart. The women then discuss the sequence of activities done by the group and while doing this they remember the process and can see their own progress.

The timeline exercise was conducted by women in two villages. Some older women, married into the family of the village chief, were the appointed "speakers" for women and they outlined the history of the village with younger women listening and occasionally giving comments. The timing of events is established mainly through association with marriages, deaths and births in the village, or with natural calamities such as floods or epidemics. For these women, the exercise seemed to be one of listing all the negative events in the past ten years of their lives. Initially, the map building exercise created some difficulties because the women were very shy about using drawing materials and paper. One of the women said: "Oh, we are illiterate. How can we possibly make anything on paper?" But once they started drawing they had few problems. The project team was hesitant to suggest a transect walk because it was not known how women moved about the village, but the idea surfaced naturally when the women were anxious to show the project team the village after drawing the map. Because residents of these villages are all related, women are free to move within the village. but they use certain routes.

Finally, daily time profile exercises were included as a tool for the participatory appraisal phase. For this exercise, use was made of cards of different size with simple drawings of women performing specific activities. Women select a drawing that indicates what they do at a certain time of the day and the size of drawing selected suggests roughly how much time is spent on the activity. This exercise was used as a tool of holding semi-structured interviews with key women informants. In the early phase of the PRA it was found, however, that women were reluctant to allow project team members to hold private interviews. There are feelings of jealousy in the group and women think that if project staff talk to a woman individually then this particular woman might gain something from the project that others won't get. A similar point was observed in the case of the visits to the individual farms of the men. Therefore, the team decided to conduct this exercise with one or two women in a group setting so that all women could see what the exercise involved. Then women were asked to volunteer to do the exercise with the project team in their own homes, which proved to work quite well.

RESTITUTION AND PLANNING

On the basis of the results of the assessment phase, the project has been able to get a better perception of the main issue in the sustainable management of natural resources. In the past, the production system comprised subsistence agriculture (rain-fed and irrigated) on the plain areas and livestock husbandry in the poorer grasslands of the *fan* (grazing) area on the slopes of the mountains. Traditional *karezes* (hand-dug underground irrigation tunnels) provided water to irrigate the fields for vegetable and fruit production.

Increased population pressure, the introduction of the motor pump, the low price of energy, the availability of technology for digging tubewells and the increasing Market for cash crop production have led to rapid expansion of irrigated agriculture. Tubewells provide increasingly large and unregulated amounts of water to agricultural fields, resulting in a lowering of the level of the water-table by some 0.8 m each year. Furthermore, there is a great waste of water. Once pumped to the surface, water is "stored" in ground reservoirs and channelled above ground, mostly through unlined canals to the fields. Nearly 30% of the water pumped to the surface is lost through infiltration and evaporation. Another problem is related to the degradation of the *fan* area grasslands. This common property land used by transhumant herders has become overgrazed and of very limited utility. No trees are left and what cannot be grazed is cut by farmers and nomads to meet their fuel needs. As a result, infiltration of rainwater has decreased significantly, to the point where the traditional *karezes* are drying up, triggering increased well digging.

In view of this analysis and the desired actions mentioned by the villages, the project has been able to distinguish three fields of action as a general framework: (1) increase the infiltration of rainwater by reducing runoff; (2) improve on-farm water harvesting techniques and water management; and (3) improve water-use regulations. The next step was to review and discuss this framework with the villages and identify and agree upon priority actions that would fit within this framework. In practice, this meant making a more thorough cause-effect analysis of the issues mentioned by the villagers, in order to arrive at a feasible plan of action for each village. For that purpose, posters were prepared and presented to the villages in order to visualize the "water issue".

Since the main problems are water-related and most of the dug wells and tubewells are the private property of a small number of powerful people, it was difficult to visualize a comprehensive strategy within reach of the majority.

People know that the excessive number of wells is a key factor in lowering the water-table, but they feel they cannot do much about it. This is partly true. In spite of restrictive regulations, it is not too difficult for contractors to get an official permit to install a new tubewell. As a consequence, their number is still increasing and the situation can best be described in terms of "mining of water."

However, the farmers depend for their income on wage work done on tubewell irrigated lands. Hence, measures that would affect the tubewells might affect their job opportunities as well. Therefore, it was decided to follow both a short-term and a long-term strategy. In particular, the short-term strategy was very important, since a follow-up phase of the project was not yet guaranteed. For the short term, the project and the villages agreed to implement activities that would optimize efficient use of irrigation water by reducing waste due to infiltration and evaporation, such as the construction of underground cement pipelines from the tubewell to the reservoir, cementing of channels and reservoirs, establishment of nurseries for the production of seedlings far the *fan* area (fuelwood and fodder) and for the orchards (fruit trees), repairing of dikes and field levelling and rehabilitation of experimental plots in the *fan* areas.

In the case of the women, poultry raising was agreed upon in most of the villages as an income generating activity for which support could be expected from the project. The assessment phase encouraged a broad identification of problems and needs. Although it was possible for project staff to guide women to select activities that the project is capable of supporting, the assessment had raised their expectations. While they expressed their needs for fuel and fodder, their priorities, aside from income generating activities, concerned the need for health services and education. Therefore, the project contacted government line agencies and NGOs to provide their services in these fields.

The restitution and planning phase has been a crucial moment for the elaboration of the project workplan and the mobilization and allocation of project resources and services. In addition, this phase resulted in a very dynamic process of negotiation between the villages and the project concerning the activities as proposed by both of them. In some cases, village proposals have not been supported by the project, such as the construction of a school or a tubewell. Some project proposals, such as rehabilitation of degraded fan areas, were agreed upon by the villages if other villages would do the same.

Once the activities had been selected, the project started to assist the villages to plan and undertake their implementation. For that purpose, Village Associations were established, both for men and for women. The Village Associations are seen as vehicles for the planning, organization and implementation of an activity being undertaken in Collaboration with the project. The strategy of the project is to assist the villagers in understanding and respecting certain rules and procedures applied to the support provided by the project. The role of the project is to provide technical assistance, advice and some physical inputs to selected activities while the villagers are responsible for organizing and implementing the activities agreed upon. Since most of the Village Associations have been established recently, it is too early to comment upon their functioning.

RESULTS AND LESSONS LEARNED

It has proved to be difficult to achieve a clear understanding among the villagers of what the participatory approach means in practice. In this region, near the Afghan border, many projects are delivering relief to Afghan refugees. It is understandable, therefore, that the villagers should assume that outsiders are always the "givers", bringing free inputs to poor people. It appears that this attitude prevails irrespective of a project's methodology. It is an attitude that constantly needs to be addressed by the project team. In addition, there is also the attitude expressed by many women that "we are poor and illiterate therefore whatever is decided or whatever happens, we will be grateful". It is common for the villagers to consider themselves too poor to undertake action or not intelligent enough to assume responsibilities.

Participatory approaches aim at creating opportunities for different interest groups to express their priority needs and problems. In the Kanak Valley it was difficult and almost impossible to involve the different interest groups in the appraisal phase. First, it took more time than expected to contract female project staff to start fieldwork with the women in the villages. There are almost no Brahuispeaking female professionals and the competition in the donor community to contract these scarce human resources is very strong. Because of these limitations, field-work with the women started long after the project had initiated its activities in the villages. Second, the appraisal exercises were conducted with small groups, mainly composed of representatives of the local elite. In spite of the efforts of the project team to propose to the village heads to invite more people to attend the meetings, the results have not been fully satisfactory. An important factor in this context is the role and powerful position of the village chief. He feels that he represents the villagers, so from his point of view there is no need to invite other villagers except close relatives. Moreover, the timing of the appraisal exercises during winter was not appropriate (although it could not be postponed). Many villagers work as day labourers, so that meetings cannot be held before 3 pm, and even then many people have not yet returned. Formal meetings in the evening are not possible, at least in the winter, because of the failing light and the low temperatures. Another factor is that many people in the project area spend the winter in the lower parts of Balochistan, especially the livestock owners (who wish to feed their animals and to look for wage labour) and day labourers. Even the elders, who play an important role in decision-making, often leave the area in winter in search of warmth, or for religious activities. Finally, in particular at the beginning of the period of work in the fields, some villages did not appear to be interested because the project could not give a clear answer when asked what activities would be executed. It seems to be that this "lack of clarity" has been interpreted as lack of openness, which has created some distrust. On the other hand it should be kept in mind that the participatory appraisal exercises require significant investments from the participants in terms of time, patience and understanding. The appraisal tools as such do not enhance participation of the local population: people will not join the meetings just because they like the exercises. In particular the less privileged groups usually assume a wait-and-see attitude to decide whether or not these activities are of interest to them.

The language issue has been an important constraint, both within the project and between project and villages. In particular at project level, it turned out to be difficult and sometimes impossible to translate some of the basic concepts for which no proper equivalents seem to exist. In all training sessions for the national field staff, translation into Urdu was needed, which affects the quality of these events. Moreover, this situation made it impossible, in particular for the international staff, to use specific situations or group dynamics experienced in the field as references for practical field staff support in *situ*.

The methods, techniques and tools used, worked well in general. Effective use has been made of the "toolbox", which proved to be very useful. The approach was new for the villages as well as for the national project staff. Therefore, in particular for the field staff, intensive in-service training and follow-up support in the field was needed. For both groups, this way of working with each other was an interesting experience that was gradually internalized. However, appraisal exercises have to be carefully explained in terms of objectives, methods and expected results. In order to reorient the general understanding among the villages that these exercises are conducted for the benefit of the project (which, to a certain extent, is true), it is important to develop feedback instruments as much as possible. The photo album, as used in the women's programme, is a good example. In general, visualization of the different steps and the progress made seems to be an effective way of recording the process. This kind of visual recording provides also the means to monitor the process, by understanding the extent to which the issues are understood among the parties involved and whether the process is moving in the right direction.

It has been mentioned that meetings and discussions are easily monopolized by the representatives of the local elite groups. Because of this situation, many villagers do not attend the meetings or keep silent. Under these conditions, the field staff has to act with a certain diplomacy, trying to create conditions that might permit a greater number of people to participate. It has been demonstrated in the Kanak Valley that individual exercises, such as drawing, are effective tools to stimulate each individual to express his or her perceptions, no matter whether they know how to manage the drawing materials. However, the experiences demonstrate that the PRA approach, which is aimed at general participation, does not easily lend itself to traditional hierarchical social groups such as those existing in the project area. In this context, the project women's team has concluded that in some villages more emphasis needs to be put on group building and training to increase individual self-confidence and participation before moving to the identification and planning for activities.

The PRA was conceptualized as an initial stage of the project, aimed at the generation of the project's workplan for the time left until the completion of its (first) two years. In practice the PRA did more than that. The PRA tools generated information that proved to be relevant for setting the agenda on both sides. At the same time, they stimulated a process of mutual confidence building as a result of the intensive interaction between the villages and the project. Because of frustrating past experiences with the Forestry Department and projects, this confidence building is a fundamental step for participatory approaches to be effective. Interpersonal communication skills of the field staff and their ability to listen and to learn are priority areas for their training and support. This has to be done systematically, for example through special task assignments to record the meetings with the villages and to review the notes critically afterwards as a group.

Restitution of the results of the assessment phase needs to be carefully prepared, implemented and evaluated. The experiences in the Kanak Valley demonstrate that it is convenient to invite other organizations or departments to attend these meetings with the villages when delivery of their services is being considered. Feasibility of village proposals has to be discussed with the villages and technical and organizational aspects should be elaborated with them. A striking example has been the proposal of women to start a commercial poultry farm. The practical consequences of having a commercial poultry farm were elaborated with inputs from the technical support staff in group discussions. Then it turned out that the idea was imposed by the men and that the women had never considered all the steps and the time involved in successfully operating such a farm. Probably, the men had imposed this idea anticipating that in practice they would run the farm themselves. Other cases have also shown that proposals should be carefully reviewed and discussed. Specific information on crucial aspects, such as ownership of land or water sources (wells) should be in order to prevent decisions being made on the basis of incorrect or incomplete information.

The establishment of Village Associations constitutes an important first step towards strengthening local capacity for the planning, implementation and monitoring of specific activities. This institutional strengthening at local level is still in its initial stage and needs to be further supported by the project through training and regular follow-up visits. The small size of the village populations and the fact that most of the families are related to each other seem to be contributing to the effective functioning of the Associations. On the other hand, there are significant differences within and between villages with regard to availability of and access to resources such as land, water and livestock. Therefore, the Village Associations will probably not succeed in mobilizing the village population in general unless opportunities are created to propose activities that respond to the interests of specific groups. Although the project does not have the means to change the existing power structure within villages or Village Associations, the field staff should still endeavour to ensure the inclusion of all interested villagers and to encourage full consultation when decisions are taken. The project should also promote equitable arrangements for sharing responsibilities and benefits related to the activities supported by the project.

THE PUCD PROJECT IN RWANDA

THE PROJECT AREA

In Rwanda, the PUCD project is working in three sectors of the *commune* (Municipality) of Runyanya, Province of Butare, in the south of the country. The Municipality is the executing agency. It is an area of about 35 km2, with a population of 13 000, giving a density of 370 people per km2. The three administrative sectors are Kibingo, Karama and Buhoro. Each sector is composed of *cellules* ("cells", similar to subcounties), which generally include a number of *collines* ("hills"), the lowest level of organization for administrative purposes. Traditionally, the *colline* constitutes a social unit of organisation, control and solidarity based on extended family links and interests, under the leadership of a Council of Elders. The social and physical *collines* do not necessarily coincide: a physical "hill" can include more than one social *colline* and vice versa. Therefore, the physical division of a watershed can have consequences for the *colline as* a social unit, with one part of an extended family "belonging" to one subwatershed and another part to another subwatershed. The main ethnic groups are Hutu and Tutsi. The Batwa constitute a small minority and are a disadvantaged group.

The climate is temperate with an average temperature of 20oC, four seasons and an annual rainfall that varies between 1 000 and 1 400 mm. The *collines* are a characteristic feature of the landscape with an altitude of around 1 850 m. In general, the soils are degraded and poor. Subsistence agriculture is predominant, practised on small landholdings. Around 80% of the farmers have less than one hectare.

Officially, all land belongs to the State, but traditional usufruct rights are usually respected. In the irrigated lowland areas, however, a process of concentration of land-holdings in the hands of a few families is under way. Because more and more land is being brought under agricultural production, grazing lands are disappearing. As a consequence, the number of cattle is decreasing rapidly, resulting in diminishing supplies of organic fertilizer available for agriculture. Because of demographic pressure and lack of off-farm employment opportunities, land is being overexploited for agricultural production and the average size of landholdings is becoming smaller. The combined effects of rising population, hilly topography, poor quality of the soils and climatological irregularities have resulted in a serious degradation of the natural resources.

APPROACH, METHODS AND TOOLS

Starting in July 1992, the project conducted a participatory appraisal with the local population. This was an iterative process of problem analysis, planning, programming and implementation of priority actions, followed by planning of more complex activities for the short and mid-term. A detailed project workplan was elaborated and finalized on the basis of actions selected and planned by the population. The process can be described as follows.

Appraisal phase

This phase included preparatory activities including getting acquainted with the local environment and selecting 10 representative "pilot-*collines*". In August a four-day training session on the participatory approach was conducted for project staff. As in the case of Nepal, this workshop was attended by representatives from other projects and organizations working in this region, so that the objectives and methodology of this project could be explained to a wider public.

After this workshop, in collaboration with two local NGOs, two multidisciplinary teams conducted fieldwork in the selected area at *colline* level, sub-*colline* level and farm level. The meetings at *colline* level were announced and introduced by the government representatives of the respective Sectors of the Municipality of Runyinya and were attended by numerous people, both men and women, of varying ages. More structured appraisal exercises were conducted at sub-*colline* level and farm level. Several PRA tools were used, including semi-structured interviews, the timeline exercise, the agricultural calendar, and rating, ranking and sorting of agricultural crops. Meetings were videotaped. About 40% of the participants at the meetings were women. This fieldwork period took almost one month. During the appraisal phase, people were invited to express their needs and to propose actions. Because of the relatively long history of development assistance projects operating in the region, the first reaction of most people was: "What will the project be doing for us?" They were generally quite surprised when asked what they felt the project should do. Most people wanted the project to carry out activities to generate employment opportunities and income.

Restitution phase

This phase took 2-3 weeks, was completed by the end of October and was less elaborate than the appraisal phase, mainly because this phase coincided with an agricultural peak period. Because of this, the groups attending the meetings were smaller. The meetings started with a presentation of the objectives, followed by the video that was made of the appraisal meeting. After the video presentation, people were invited to make comments. When environmental issues were discussed, these points were further illustrated with the projection of slides of relevant local sites and situations. This first part of the restitution phase was concluded with a presentation of a summary overview of the issues raised. On the basis of this overview, the people indicated what they considered most important. Those actions that everybody agreed were priority actions were kept as "definitive". This resulted in a list of identified priorities, which was still very long, ranging from agriculture and animal husbandry to water, infrastructure, crafts, extension and training, health, and education. On the basis of this list, three programmes were then formulated by the project: soil conservation and soil fertility improvement, income generation and infrastructure.

Out of the activities identified, so-called "spark actions" *(actions étin-celles)* were selected. These are actions that the people consider to be urgent and of common interest, for which they are prepared to collaborate collectively and that can be supported by the project in the very short term. After having selected these "spark actions", a local *"antenne"* (usually a local leader) was selected for each of the *collines as* a liaison between the project and the *colline* population, and for feedback of the results of the meetings to the local population.

The restitution phase was terminated with an internal evaluation workshop of two days, in which the project team discussed and analysed the results and worked out a first draft workplan. In addition to the project team, the Mayor of the Municipality of Runyinya, some of his technical and field staff and two farmers' representatives participated in this workshop. The workshop was focused on evaluating the results of the appraisal and restitution phase and elaborating strategies to provide adequate support to plan and implement the priority actions. In particular, training needs of the project staff and the farmers were discussed, as was the organizational setup.

Planning and organization

In order to strengthen the cohesiveness and the commitment of the local population, it was decided to start the planning phase with the "spark actions". For that purpose, training was organized in November combining technical aspects of the "spark actions" with methodological aspects of participatory planning. Subsequently, for the planning of these "spark actions" at field level, core groups of four persons were elected to support the local spokesperson, forming a development committee for each of the *collines*and responsible for the supervision of all the planned actions. This core group, however, would not touch the executive responsibility of each of the specific target groups. These core groups should become a dynamic unit for the promotion of local empowerment, integrated development of the *colline* and sustainable management of its natural resources. The core groups attended a four-day planning workshop in February 1993 to discuss and analyse the programmes for each of the *collines.* As a final preparatory step for the implementation phase, a workshop was held in March for the *antennes* and the project team to develop common criteria for self-evaluation, including indicators, phases, methods and tools.

Implementation

A total of about 150 groups, involving approximately 1 700 members, have initiated their respective projects. These comprise the three programmes mentioned above: a programme for soil conservation and soil fertility improvement, a programme of income generating activities and a programme for infrastructure improvement. Within the first programme, different projects are carried out, such as tree nurseries, hillside stabilization, planting of fodder grasses or shrubs, stall feeding for manure production, genetic improvement, erosion control and use of agricultural inputs. The target groups of each of the projects sometimes overlap. The organizational setup, as well as the mechanisms and procedures for external support, depend on the specific activity and the resources available. In some cases, existing *équipes agricoles* (agricultural teams) were reactivated by their members, and in other cases new groups were formed. Most of the activities are externally supported, both by the project and by the Municipality. In general, the groups themselves define their internal rules and regulations without project interference. In specific cases, such as genetic improvement, agricultural inputs and credit for livestock, more detailed agreements are made between the parties involved in order to ensure equal opportunities for those who meet the criteria as the project support is provided on a rotative basis.

The income generating programme includes projects such as the bakery for a girl scout group, a restaurant, a grain mill project, livestock (pigs and goats), local beer production and small shops. In general, these income generating projects have required more careful assessment of feasibility. In the case of the "Abunzubumwe" women's group, for example, the initial idea of the group was to start a chicken project. After a study tour to similar projects outside the project area, the women changed their minds and proposed a goat raising project as feeding of these animals would be less problematic and the products (milk/meat and manure) would respond to their immediate needs of improved diet and soil improvement.

As in the case of the income generating projects, the infrastructural projects (roads, bridges, management of water sources) have to be carefully and critically assessed, including from a technical point of view, because their implementation requires large-scale mobilization of labour and sometimes high financial investments. On the other hand, particularly in the case of the water sources projects, it was found that in general the organization of project management was established by the local people almost spontaneously, and that in most cases rules and regulations had been clearly defined. The conclusion might be that the more an activity responds to real and vital needs of the majority of the local population, the more spontaneously the people take action and organize themselves.

The activities carried out so far have led to a number of results. Without any doubt, the capacity of the population to give direction to its own development process has increased. Although still incipient, there is an increased level of farmers' organization. Production and conservation programmes have been started, and physical works have been implemented. Methods and tools for planning and implementation have been tested and are being used locally.

RESULTS AND LESSONS LEARNED

One of the major constraints encountered in this project is the contradiction between the long-term and short-term perspectives: possibly because of the generalized poverty in the region, the local population is inclined to give priority to actions geared towards short-term results. The "spark actions" are supported by the project in order to respond to this short-term orientation and to strengthen its credibility as a serious partner. It also attempts to create some space at local level to develop a long-term programme of activities for the sustainable management of natural resources. However, this long-term perspective cannot be consolidated when the pilot phase of the project has a duration of only two years and a follow-up phase has yet to be negotiated with the donor country.

The participatory approach is a new concept in Rwanda. As a consequence, a fundamental reorientation of attitudes, expectations and behaviour patterns, is needed, both at local and institutional level. In particular during the initial stage, the project had to deal with traditional compensation expectations of "core groups" and "key persons" at local level because of the opportunity cost of their time investments in the project. This factor is closely related with the socio-economic and cultural reality of the region: in general, organizational links between groups of families are very weak also because of the dispersed settlement patterns, and there is almost no indigenous tradition of farmer organization for the pursuit of common interests. In addition, the poor infrastructural facilities and the fact that animal traction is unknown constitute important time-consuming factors for most families, in particular for women, in satisfying basic needs such as water, health and marketing of cash crops.

The case study indicates that local communities are gradually perceiving the project as their own. The most important instrument in this context has been the supportive role of the project in training and the provision of equipment and materials for the implementation of priority activities identified and agreed upon through dialogue. Local communities are more and more capable of analysing their problems and constraints, determining their priorities, taking decisions and mobilizing their own resources for the implementation of their own projects. An open dialogue is active between the local communities and the project staff, manifesting itself during appraisal, planning and evaluation meetings. In particular, it has proven to be very useful to review and analyse the process and results obtained together with the administrative authorities, farmer representatives and the project team.

During all phases of the project, the political authorities of the Municipality participated in the meetings with the local communities. A number of administrative and technical issues have been dealt with and possible solutions envisaged. In the case of the swamp areas of Buhoro, for example, conflicts between different groups were officially brought to the attention of the administrative authorities. As a result, the poorer minority Batwa tribe recovered swamp areas from which they had been excluded. Similar interventions took place with regard to water rights: in most cases where water management and administration was identified as a priority action, the water sources were "private property". In Karama, where a location was needed for the construction of a bakery, the administrative authorities provided the necessary support. Many other examples exist of direct and effective negotiation between local communities and the administrative authorities. In particular the Mayor of the Municipality played a key role in this process of facilitating political support.

One of the instruments of participatory planning is the promotion of local self-organization. The initial strategy of promoting core groups and local project spokespersons at*colline* level has not yet led to the expected results. In view of the low level of farmer organization and the individualistic orientation, much time is still needed for the development and consolidation of appropriate organizational structures of farmers at *colline* level. These structures were proposed by the project as a experiment in establishing regular links between the project and the *colline* and to deliver its services as efficiently and effectively possible. Aware of the experimental nature of this organizational setup, the project has followed the functioning of these structures closely. Certain difficulties appeared, not only with regard to the functioning of these structures (abuse and monopolization of power) but also with regard to the perception and understanding of the local communities of the tasks and responsibilities of those who had been elected by them. Therefore, the policy of the project has been reoriented towards supporting agricultural groups and other functional groups. By the end of 1993, some 150 of these groups had been recorded.

At the time of the case study, it was found that, to a certain degree, local knowledge had been integrated in the proposals for action. In particular some of the appraisal tools such as the timeline exercise, the elaboration of the agricultural calendar and the rating, ranking and sorting of agricultural crops constituted effective instruments for that purpose. The results of these exercises have been important inputs into the analysis of the current situation, to determine priorities, to propose solutions and to plan activities. However, it is difficult to determine whether local technical knowledge is being integrated or just "common knowledge". Therefore, it is felt that more systematic and targeted efforts are needed to identify local knowledge systems and to assess their potential for further adaptation of local project planning and implementation.

The results of local capacity strengthening for self-development are modest but promising. However, some critical points should be kept in mind. The participatory approach is a slow process and it takes time to develop and consolidate the necessary conditions to be able to be effective. It is very important not to overestimate the capacity of the local population to participate in project activities and to assume additional tasks and responsibilities. Therefore, the rhythm and the evolution of the local groups should be carefully followed, supported and respected. One should not expect these groups to have developed a perfect internal organization in the short term. The activities undertaken by the groups and the results obtained should be reflected upon by the groups and the project team as learning experiences that might further strengthen their capacity and accountability. As much as possible, these experiences should be shared with similar groups in the region or elsewhere.

However, it is also important to keep in mind the institutional capacity of the project and other organizations to support and follow up local initiatives adequately. This is not only in terms of time but also in terms of technical and methodological capacity of the staff. Interinstitutional networking and linkages require time investments for promotion, support and follow-up actions. The experiences in Rwanda demonstrate that progress has been made, particularly at the level of the Municipality of Runyinya. On the other hand, because of the very limited previous experience with participatory approaches and the institutional environment of the region, progress has been limited by a chronic lack of sufficient and sufficiently qualified personnel. The participatory approach requires not only intensive work in the field but also a systematic sharing and feedback of field experiences among the project staff and collaborating organizations in order to strengthen commitment and skills. The project experiences in this respect demonstrate that the institutional framework might constitute a more limiting factor for the promotion of participatory approaches than socio-economic constraints at local level.

THE PROJECT AREA

In Burundi, the PUCD project is working in the Rwaba watershed, particularly in the Sector of Nyamirinzi of the *commune* of Vugizo, Makamba Province, in the south of the country. The project area of 5 500 ha covers four *collines* with ten *sous-collines* ("subhills"), constituting five subwatersheds. The *commune* is an administrative public institution with an internal structure based on a division between geographical zones and sectors *(collines)* composed of *cellules* or*sous-collines.* The *colline* is the lowest level of organization for administrative purposes.

The project is embedded within the institutional structure of the *Sociéty régionale de développement du Buragane* (SRD - the Regional Development Society of Buragane) in the Ministry of Agriculture. Implementation of the project is shared between FAO and the SRD. The Director of the SRD is also the national Director of the project. The SRD is the most important development organization in the region. Traditionally, its extension work has been based on the principles of "Training & Visit", but recently a process of reorientation has started. In particular the Director of the SRD perceives this project as a good opportunity to further develop participatory approaches of the SRD. Technical support for training and communication is provided by a local NGO, *Conseil pour l'éducation et le développement* (COPED - the Council for Education and Development).

The project area has a population of around 5 000, composed of Hutu and Tutsi ethnic groups. Population density is approximately 100 persons per km2. Houses are scattered on the hillsides, with no clustered village structure. The *colline* represents not only a geographical reality but, in the case of Burundi, can also be considered as a social unit, based on functional socio-economic linkages between individual families. However, there are no farmers' organizations. The most important organizational units are the extended family (the *rugo),* and below it the household group (the *intongo'),* which is the production unit responsible for the management of the agricultural plots and fields belonging to an individual and his nuclear family.

The climate is tropical/temperate with a rainy season of eight months and a dry season of four months. The *collines* are a characteristic feature of the landscape with altitudes of around 1 500 m. In general, the soils are degraded and poor. Subsistence agriculture (or slightly above subsistence) is predominant, practised on small farms with an average size of one hectare. Market-oriented crop production will increase with the opening of new roads, now under construction. As in Rwanda, more and more land is being cultivated and grazing lands are disappearing. As a consequence, the number of cattle is decreasing and with it the amount of organic fertilizer available for agriculture and, hence, production. The gradual impoverishment of the subsistence economy is the consequence of a combination of interrelated factors, such as the overexploitation of the soils, the disappearance of fallow lands, the fragmentation of landholdings and the cultivation of marginal and fragile lands, which are easily affected by erosion.

APPROACH, METHODS AND TOOLS

The project started with a first workshop of two days for the project staff to elaborate the conceptual and methodological framework of the participatory approach. This workshop was part of a training programme for project and institutional staff that was designed to guarantee-opportunities for staff development based on field experiences. Thus, during the project, regular workshops were held, for example, to evaluate the results of the appraisal phase, to analyse and discuss priority needs and solutions as preparation for the restitution phase and for planning and programming purposes.

Appraisal phase

Appraisal activities were carried out in the four *collines.* Because of farmers' previous experiences with more top-down approaches, it was important to take the time to explain the participatory approach and methodology and to establish a dialogue between farmers and project staff. The following aspects were important for the planning of this phase: (1) there are no villages in Burundi, but instead people live in houses scattered on the hillsides; (2) there are almost no indigenous organizations and the existing organizational structures have been established by the State, the political party, the SRD and, to a certain extent, the Church; and (3) because of the socio-political situation people are not prepared to attend meetings unless they are organized by the respective authorities. Therefore, public authorities at different levels were fully briefed on the objectives and methodologies and the meetings were officially announced by them.

The appraisal phase took 15 days. One meeting was held at the level of each of the four *collines* with the head of the *colline* and some elders to talk about the history, evolution and daily life in general. Subsequently, meetings were conducted at the level of each of the ten *sous-collines* (subhills) with the respective heads, some heads of family groups and women, to talk about daily life, social stratification and organization, problems and opportunities, existing infrastructure, and so on. The meetings were conducted using semi-structured interviews for which a form had been prepared. At farm level, meetings were held to interview individuals on their farmland about issues like their farming system, household economy and division of labour. In addition, numerous informal encounters took place with groups of women, youth, artisans, etc. Group and individual interview techniques were the main tools used during most of the meetings, for which specific forms were prepared with guidelines. In the case of meetings with small and more homogeneous groups, some additional tools such as drawing and mapping were used. Most of the meetings were videotaped.

Despite the fact that the appraisal phase was conducted under difficult conditions (lack of infrastructure, rainy season, time pressure), and although the results were far from complete, some important points emerged. Unexpectedly, population pressure appeared to be much lower than in other parts of the province and country and, consequently, problems of land availability and decrease in soil fertility were not as serious as elsewhere. It was found that the *sous-colline* was the most appropriate level on which to concentrate efforts and support for strengthening local capacities. In addition, a tentative list could be developed of priority problems including drinking water availability, road construction, erosion control, sanitary facilities, pest control and schools, representing environmental, social and infrastructural issues.

Restitution phase

After finishing the appraisal fieldwork, a three-day workshop was held to develop a first synthesis of the main issues formulated by the farmers. An outline was also prepared for a video programme to be used for restitution purposes afterwards. In addition, to prepare the field staff to conduct restitution meetings, practical exercises were conducted with the field staff on how to proceed with a problem analysis and find solutions using the results of the appraisal phase.

Restitution of the results of the appraisal phase took place during meetings at *colline* level with large numbers of participants(200-300), because no functional groups had been formed and no time was left to visit each of the 10 *sous-collines.* It was therefore decided to use video as the principal tool, not for a systematic restitution of the results but in order to provoke reactions and to stimulate a debate. The original idea was to visualize the complexity of the problems identified earlier by the people and their analysis of the situation, and then to motivate the people to take action and to organize themselves. Although the video was certainly not an exceptional product, it worked extremely well, in particular because it illustrated a number of issues of common interest in the region, and a large number of people attended the presentation.

Although there were some doubts beforehand about the possible negative effect of their presence, a number of government authorities were invited in order to strengthen their political support for the participatory approach. Their presence proved to be a positive factor, in that it stimulated the farmers to share their ideas and opinions. This, in turn, was a very important learning experience for these provincial and municipal authorities, who greatly appreciated it. In retrospect, it seems to have been a crucial and positive turning point in the development of institutional opportunities for the promotion of participatory approaches in the field. After each meeting, *sous-colline*-based groups were formed and working sessions were held, supported by project staff. During these sessions, the preliminary list of priority activities was reviewed and agreed upon and an agenda was prepared for a next meeting to discuss their work programme. In some cases special meetings with women were organized in view of the fact that during the large meetings their interventions were rather limited.

Planning phase

The restitution phase, follow-up actions were discussed in small groups at *sous-colline* level. These groups were asked to review and analyse their priority actions and to discuss the most appropriate organizational forms for the implementation of the activities. In some cases, considerable progress had been made by the people towards the planning meeting with the project team, such as preparing an overview of the available material, financial and human resources for the implementation of their project. In other cases the process took more time, and more support from the project staff was needed. Often, this depends on the basis of group formation and on individual qualities in particular.

During the planning meetings, the problem-tree method was used to elaborate upon the identified priority activities and to discuss the complexities involved. It was emphasized that this meeting was a first step in an iterative planning process of evaluation, programming and implementation. Only those priority actions were selected around which groups had been or would be formed. In some cases, groups would undertake more than one activity; in other cases, groups were formed to undertake one activity. For the groups involved, these activities were gradually considered projects.

Consequently, the support from the project staff was more and more focused on the different phases of preparation and planning of the different local project ideas of the various groups. These phases included: meetings to discuss the project idea; identification of activities needed to overcome initial handicaps; identification of similar projects elsewhere in the country; visits to groups or individuals already involved in similar projects to incorporate their knowledge in their own proposals; restitution by those who visited other places upon return to their community; decision-making by the group and approval of the proposal by the project staff; and training for the specific project activities by the field staff, other farmers or other agencies.

Implementation

At the time of the case study, approximately 130 families, organized in 21 groups, were involved in the preparation or implementation of their own project activities. These projects cover the following fields: water source construction and management, erosion control and soil fertility improvement, improved agricultural production, development of cattle, goat and poultry raising and the promotion of new activities in production, processing, recreation and social communication. These microprojects have been prepared and designed by the groups themselves with additional support from the project. This support has been provided with the objective of strengthening capacities of the groups involved in terms of analysis, planning, management of the resources in their environment, self-organization, mobilization of their own financial, human and material resources, economic and financial management and self-evaluation.

The size of the groups varied from 5 to 24 persons, depending on the type of microproject. Most of these groups have established their own rules and regulations and their own internal organization with clearly defined responsibilities, tasks and sanctions. Although still incipient, other organizations in the region are collaborating with the implementation of the locally based microprojects. For example, UNICEF and the public administration authorities of the region are providing financial and technical support for the projects of water source construction and management, which have been identified as priority activities in the 10 *sous-collines* covered by the project.

RESULTS AND LESSONS LEARNED

The remnants of top-down approaches have been one of the principal initial constraints for the implementation of the participatory approach under the project. At institutional level, this legacy was particularly visible in the attitudes and behaviour patterns of the field staff assigned to the project. In spite of the attention paid to their training, progress in improving their interpersonal communication skills in the field has been very slow. One of the constraining factors in this respect has been the language problem, as in the case of Pakistan. International staff members do not speak the local language. Therefore, they do not follow the dynamics of the interaction between field staff and local population. These field situations should have been systematically used by the international staff as learning opportunities for the local field staff.

At community level, people were used to doing what they were told to do. Hence, there were initially expectations that did not coincide with the project approach. Much time had to be invested in explaining how the project would operate, building up its credibility as a serious partner. The scattered settlement pattern of the rural population, in combination with poor infrastructure, has been a further complicating factor for smooth communication and coordination. At project level, one of the principal constraints has been the limited institutional capacity to provide adequate support to the different groups with the technical, economic and social appraisal and planning of their microprojects, and to initiate concrete field activities without too much delay.

The case study has shown a reappearance of social dynamics within the communities, characterized by an increased awareness of their own capabilities, and of their existing resources and potential, and by the start of spontaneous collective initiatives.

Ikibiri, the traditional system of solidarity and collective action, is being taken up again by many groups. This is happening in spite of bad experiences with the cooperative movement that was promoted in the past in the region. It seems that the decision of the project to concentrate its support on *sous-colline* level has been an important factor in this context. The emphasis that has been put on organization during the planning of the microprojects, without imposing rules and regulations, has contributed significantly to strengthen the self-confidence of the groups.

It has been rather difficult to develop and promote a coherent technical menu. The project objective of sustainable management of natural resources by the local people cannot be achieved unless farmers perceive concrete benefits in terms of production and income. The production and income components usually reflect the immediate needs. Therefore, in order to ensure a more coherent menu of project options, linkages should be sought between activities identified to respond to immediate needs, and activities for natural resource conservation and management, in order to use the first type of activity as a starter for the second type.

Because the national staff lacked previous experience with participatory approaches, project take-off has been difficult. In particular during this period much attention should be paid to the exchange of field experiences and the supervision of the project field staff. On the basis of their own practical field experiences, field staff members develop a better understanding of their role and functions in promoting a participatory process at local level. On the other hand, the SRD took keen interest in the participatory approach, as could be learned from the fact that special staff meetings were organized to discuss the consequences of the participatory approach for the functioning of their institution.

Relatively little use has been made of the different appraisal tools. In order to arrive at a more comprehensive and complete appraisal of the local situation, different tools should be used for the different settings. They have to be used creatively and should be adapted to the local situation. This requires testing and verification on a pilot basis. The case study has demonstrated that adequate time planning and management is equally important, and that the available human and time resources should not be overestimated. When semi-structured interviews have to be conducted, forms or written guidelines should not be prepared by the technical staff, since in most cases they will be used by the field staff as questionnaires. Technical and field staff should jointly discuss and identify the issues to be raised. Restitution of the results of the appraisal phase constitutes a fundamental step towards planning and should be done systematically at the proper levels without mixing different objectives (such as to strengthen political commitment and to further analyse priority activities).

Large numbers of people attended the restitution meetings. The follow-up meetings, however, took place with small groups that were formed around specific activities. Most of the members of these groups belong to the better-off farmers who have the resources to respond to the project. In order to prevent this situation, the different interest groups at local level should be identified carefully during the appraisal phase and their priority activities should be discussed further with each of them separately. One cannot expect that these disadvantaged groups will benefit automatically from the project. Additional and carefully targeted project intervention strategies are required to reach these groups.

There is no doubt that local knowledge and skills have been mobilized and integrated within the identification, planning and organization of the microprojects, in particular during the appraisal phase of needs, constraints and opportunities. However, it is difficult to indicate exactly which elements have been integrated within which activities and how this was done. Apparently this process has followed a more or less "natural" course of sharing of information, knowledge and skills between the local people and project staff. The case study has shown that the project team and the institutions involved are very much aware of the farmers' logic, analytical capacity, creativity, initiatives and knowledge of the environment. On the other hand, technical matters related to implementation of the microprojects have been dealt with mainly on the basis of institutional know-how.

4

The Evolution to Participatory Assessment, Monitoring and Evaluation in Community Forestry

The evolution of community forestry over the past decades has taken place in a number of progressive stages. Each stage has built on the cumulative knowledge and lessons of the past.

In the first stage, outsiders gathered as much information as they could about communities, in order to provide the best solutions that were available. The monitoring and evaluation was done by outsiders, and focused mainly on whether the solutions had worked or not. While there were many successes, there were difficulties in determining whether the solutions addressed the real needs of the communties.

In the next stage, outsiders were encouraged to listen to local people. Participant observation and other social science methods were used so that outsiders could better understand what it was the communities percieved as their needs and priorities. Based on this information, solutions were sought. The monitoring and evaluation throughout this stage was done mainly by outsiders, but local perceptions were included.

Throughout this stage, many lessons were learned, and with these lessons came the realization that people, in many instances, understood and could articulate their needs and a range of solutions. it was also found that people had a wealth of indigenous knowledge and skills that could be combined with outsider's knowledge to accomplish together what neither could do alone.

We are now entering a new stage in Community Forestry, the stage in which local (insider) knowledge is combined with outsider knowledge. Participatory Assessment, Monitoring and Evaluation (PANE) offers a new way of thinking about assessment, monitoring and evaluation. It is based on the premise that it is the communities which are, 'ultimately, the final evaluators of project success or failure. Sustainability depends, to a large part, on communities' ability to analyse, judge, and explain to others the value of various options. Their analytical skills should thus be supported and/or strengthened in order for them to ask and answer their own questions. Their communicative skills can be improved so that they can present their evaluations in terms extensionists, research centres, and policy makers can understand.

PAME blends an approach, techniques and tools to assist communities in assessing, monitoring and evaluating the value of the project to themselves. An important spin-off benefit to this is that the very presence and practice of PAME contributes to the learning experiences of both the project staff and community members, and assists in achieving the development objectives of self-help and sustainability.

PARTICPATORY ASSESSMENT, MONITORING AND EVALUATION AND COMMMITY FORESTRY

This document is directed to community forestry projects, where management decisions and project activity benefits are retained by the community (either individually or communally).

The community can be in any country, and encompass any social, economic or cultural group. What may be common to all communities is that they want and need either inputs, resources or a new perspective in order to change, improve, manage, rehabilitate, or more usefully and equitably process the forest and tree resources around them.

THE BENEFITS OF PARTICIPATORY ASSESSMENT, MONITORING AND EVALUATION

Pame can have benefits for both "insiders" and "outsiders". Both require information to guide them in making wise decisions to ensure that their activities are successful. Both require information that is:

Timely	Accurate
Relevant	Useable
Understandable	Cost-effective

For the "outsiders" some of the benefits of PAME are: they can learn from communities what their needs are, and how to better serve these needs; they can understand the constraints faced by communities in satisfying their needs; they can use PAME as an entry point to a non-participatory project and perhaps establish the basis and justification for future participation; they can receive information from communities if communities choose to share it; they can discover relevant research questions inspired by communities' questions; they can see whether project objectives address the real needs and priorities of communities; and they can have a window for evaluating participation.

For the "insiders" some of the benefits of PAME are: they can know clearly what the project offers; they can have the opportunity to learn different kinds of analytical skills in their process of problem identification/analysis and information gathering; they can get new perspectives on old problems; they can learn new ways to judge whether their efforts are worthwhile enough to continue; they can learn new ways to articulate their needs to outsiders and to better understand outsider's information; and they can activate, control and, in effect, "own" the information.

Both "insiders" and "outsiders" benefit from PAME, the goals of sustainability and self-help are encouraged, and as a result, the chance for a long-term positive impact is increased. In addition, projects are more likely to be successful because relevant, useful information is available to facilitate decision making and mediate between conflicting goals and priorities.

THE FOCUS OF PARTICIPATORY ASSESSMENT, MONITORING AND EVALUATION

The primary focus of PAME is on the information needs of the communities, while the secondary focus is on the information needs of the project. This prioritization ensures that people are not merely collecting information that the outsiders need to monitor and evaluate. It also ensures that the information is relevant to the development problem.

In order to guarantee this focus, it is best that field staff have, or actively seek, the support and understanding of those above them in the project hierarchy: the project and programme management; the national government; and the donors.

The kinds of information received directly from communities is valid, legitimate, and important. It gives a rich understanding, reflects the community reality, and is an important contribution to higher level decision-makers.

FIELD WORKERS AS FACILITATORS OF PARTICIPATORY ASSESSMENT, MONITORING AND EVALUATION

PAME is designed for use by people at the community level although it can be facilitated by project field staff. In some instances, especially if the project has not had a great deal of experience in participatory methods, it may be necessary to use the services of an outside consultant experienced in PAME. The consultant can facilitate PAME and train field staff in PAME methods at the same time.

Forestry project field staff may come from an extension, forestry or general background and work with a large or small non-government organization, a national forest service or a large multinational organization such as the United Nations.

Whoever they are, field staff are the facilitators of PAME. They are guided by the community, helping to: support and encourage community creativity and participation, focus the problem solving, analytical and evaluative abilities of the community and interpret information from outside specialists.

A good facilitator will respect the knowledge and creativity of people, and view them as equal partners in the development process. Participatory skills can be developed through field worker training in sensitization and self-awareness. Some excellent manuals for participatory training are available. These manuals emphasize the need to develop characteristics such as: the ability to lead but not direct, flexibility, open-mindedness, a non-judgemental approach, honesty, awareness, and concern for the problems of the rural poor.

Effective PAME facilitators will have a broad understanding of the basic concepts of PAME, and the kinds of methods and information gathering tools available to foster participation. They will resist imposing ideas or "convincing" people, instead offering a range of options for a particular situation. They must be willing to look at ways to adapt and develop ideas.

PARTICIPATORY ASSESSMENT, MONITORING AND EVALUATION

Most projects go through very definite PHASES: project concept and design, planning, site selection and entry into the community, implementation, evaluation, and, exit from the community. Each of these phases offers an opportunity to include communities in the decision-making process.

Some projects already include the community in all phases of project decision-making; some include the community in some phases; and some have not yet taken the opportunity to include the community at all. Although it is ideal to have beneficiary participation from the beginning, any phase can be an entry point for PAME.

The benefits of PAME can be realized at any project stage. Even if it is only the final evaluation that is done by beneficiaries, going through the process of a participatory evaluation can strongly influence future projects in the community. If, for example, the entry point for PAME is an Evaluation Event two years after the project has been operational, PAME can redirect or modify project activities so that they are more likely to result in success.

LINKING THE APPROACH, WITH THE TECHNIQUES AND THE TOOLS

PAME will vary according to a number of factors: specific community information needs, community cultural, political and social conditions, local resource availablity, or local access to other resources. Because of this variation, there is no one way to go about doing PAME. But the field experiences of those who have experimented with PAME are beginning to provide lessons that help in the development of a conceptual framework.

Participatory Assessment, Monitoring and Evaluation is designed so that the approach, the techniques and the tools all fit together to compliment, link and interact with each other in an iterative process.

DESCRIPTION AND PURPOSE OF COMMUNITY SELECTION BY OUTSIDERS

Unfortunately, projects are often "stuck" with an identified, pre-determined "solution" to a "problem" long before the community is consulted. Most projects are funded for a specific purpose, be it forestry, health, water, or education. So in many ways the "site selection," in terms of country, area, and focus, the "problem" and the "solution," have been done in advance.

It would be ideal to have "blank slate" projects. And while some agencies are moving towards this by including community members on outsider appraisal or assessment missions, or offering several activities under one "umbrella" project (Health, Water, Forestry, Education), most projects start with some proscriptions, "givens". For example, field staff often have to choose specific communities in which to work. There are often many potential communities from which to choose, but the project is limited by having the financial and human resources to work with only a few. How can field staff decide which communities to work with? The purpose of a community site selection by outsiders is to obtain information on which to base these kinds of decisions.

METHODS FOR COMITY SELECTION

Some projects have found that developing a list of criteria can be helpful for community selection. These criteria are often a list of characteristics which are thought to be necessary for project success. Criteria can be organized under the following headings:

PROBLEM IDENTIFICATION

Does the community have, or see itself as having the same problems and the same order of priorities that the project does?

It is important to identify the communities which need the services the project and its resources can provide. Observation, use of government records and existing studies, and tours of potential sites are probably the best information gathering techniques. A round table "community selection" discussion by field staff and selected community members, based on the information which is gathered, can help to establish appropriate criteria for site selection. Quite often decisions will be based on informed common sense.

PHYSICAL POTENTIAL

Assessing the physical potential of a community will depend on the project's range of possible activities. It is important that the basic conditions for meeting objectives either exist or have the potential to exist in the community.

For example, it would be unrealistic to initiate a community woodlot in a community that does not have any communal or unused land, or to introduce alleycropping in an area that is not experiencing soil infertility.

Ask the question:

"*What factors must be present in the community in order to accomplish the proposed activities?*"

Some of the factors that may have to be examined are:

- Land availability and land and tree tenure
- Water availability
- Labour availability
- Access (roads and transport) to community

PROJECT CONSTRAINTS

Pre-defined projects have many constraints. They are often limited to specific goals and specific areas in which they can undertake activities. They are limited by legal frameworks of national forest policies. Can people cut the forest they plant? Can they sell charcoal they make? They are limited by the number of staff and budget made available to them. And they may also be limited by factors such as transportation, and access to materials. It must be very clear to field staff what can and cannot be done by the project so that they are able to relay the message clearly to the communities with whom they are going to work.

Answering the following kinds of questions may help:

"*What project/regional characteristics will limit possible success?*"

(For example, lack of trained staff, national forest policies, legal constraints regarding land).

or "*What can we realistically provide to communities?*"

COMMUNITY ORGANIZATIONS

It is generally believed that community organizations are the key to successful community forestry projects. Community organizations are defined as collections of people who have reason to work together to accomplish a goal.

If the project is going to be channeled through a community organization, the potential for existing or new community organizations must be assessed. If the project is dealing with individual farmers, assessment of community organizations may not be required.

However, if resource use will be changed by the project, if neighbors will have to keep their animals off a farmer's property even after crops are harvested in order to protect tree seedlings, community discussions and general agreement supported by informal and formal leaders will be needed. There may already be organizations functioning in the community that can take on an extra set of activities, or organizations that can be strengthened and supported to take on new roles.

If an existing organization is going to be used, look at who controls it and whether the leadership has the desired qualities (concern for equitable distribution of benefits and the best interests of the community). Examine the time and leadership resources the organization has available. Consider the pros and cons associated with giving the organization extra responsibilities. This may help to decide if an existing organization is capable of handling extra responsibilities.

In one area in Kenya, women's groups, which were traditionally organized along kinship lines to support funeral rituals, were used for training and group extension to promote nurseries and tree planting. In Korea, Mother's Clubs turned to nursery production to earn funds for their other activities. Experience shows, however, that it is often difficult for an informal group organized for one set of objectives to take on a completely different type of responsibility.

Setting up a new organization which mirrors an existing organization is another alternative which has sometimes been successful. An agroforestry project in Sudan modeled the new nursery committees on the water committees which had been in existence for decades.

By the time the Community Selection has been done, the project staff will have a better sense of:

1. What they can and cannot offer communities.
2. What community resources will be required to implement the project. In community forestry this is especially important, because a great deal of the input from the community may be required in the form of land, labour, risk, and time.
3. The outsider's role, if a contract with the community is to be negotiated.

COMMUNITY PROBLEM ANALYSIS

DESCRIPTION AND PURPOSE OF COMMUNITY PROBLEM ANALYSIS

A community is a complex arrangement of people with kinship, political, economic, religious and social ties to one another and other communities. Depending on the nature of these relationships, communities can be cohesive or divided. Ties among community members are often generational, and deeply entrenched, as are the ways in which a community deals with crisis or problems. While the methods that are used to address problems under normal conditions may be effective, these indigenous problem solving methods may break down when social structures have eroded or when new, unprecedented problems present themselves.

Community Problem Analysis (CPA) builds on pre-existing community problem solving methods, laws and structures to help community members identify, analyse and find solutions to their problems. It uses these same structures to facilitate negotiations between community, outside interest, and/ or user groups. Often, through the assistance of an outsider, the communities can probe and explore new approaches to problem solving. The new perspectives which are introduced can increase the likelihood of new solutions.

The purposes of CPA in the context of community forestry projects are:

- To provide a community forum for focused problem analysis, identification of needs and priorities, and development of possible solutions.
- To build up trust and partnership for project activities.
- To provide information and begin to build the basis for negotiations between user/interest groups.
- To provide baseline information against which change can be measured.

To establish community objectives, strategies and plans.

THE TIME TO DO COMMUNITY PROBLEM ANALYSIS

While CPA is most often done at the first (design) phase of a project, before implementation, it can be used in other phases. Many of the methods and tools can be used during project implementation. Here are a few examples of times that this method can be used.

During The Project:	In the middle of a project (which has not been "fully" participatory) it is noticed that there is a problem. Community enthusiasm has died down and volunteer labour is not sufficient to keep the project going. Targets are not being met. CPA is useful at this point to discover what the problems are, and to redirect future activities, targets and/or strategies.
During An Evaluation:	During a mid-project or final project evaluation, it is recognised that there is ample quantitative information available, but very little information about whether the project has met the real needs of the community. CPA can provide qualitative, retrospective information, and help to direct future activities. In this way, CPA encourages community participation, iimproves project design and results in more sustainable projects.
During A Crisis:	CPA can also be used to help resolve a crisis. The crisis may be the result of community conflicts that were not recognized when the project began, or unanticipated conflicts that have resulted from project activities. CPA provides analytical methods and tools to assist in conflict resolution.

GUIDELINES FOR FACILITATORS OF COMMUNITY PROBLEM ANALYSIS

Because CPA builds on local community analytical skills, and existing community structures, facilitators may have to vary the method (and the tools) to fit the specific community.

While some communities will analyse their problems without outside assistance, an outsider perspective can often aid the development of new solutions. Depending on the effectiveness of pre-existing community analytical and communication skills, a facilitator may take a major or a very small role.

Recognized community leaders or groups can lead the discussions, or new leaders may emerge during the problem identification process. And while CPA tools can facilitate the process, the community can also call upon its own pre-existing resources to solve the problem at hand.

Some guidelines for project field staff in the facilitating role are:

1. Develop sensitivity and listening skills. Respect and support the existing community skills and yet know when to introduce appropriate methods (and tools) to strengthen these local skills. Listen to stories telling how problems have been dealt with in the past as this can deepen understanding of existing community analytical processes.
2. Use key informants who can describe the power structure of the community. Working relationships with local leaders can make or break a project, especially when the poorer strata of the community are the prospective beneficiaries. Although the primary beneficiary group may be identified as the poorer group, experience shows that usually local leaders must also benefit. Benefits can be political, economic and/or social.
3. In group discussions, have community members describe the way the community has made decisions in the past. How effective has this method been? Can it be improved upon? How?
4. Clearly and honestly present the project's development objectives and inputs, and the inputs expected from the community.
5. If necessary, suggest tools which are likely to facilitate community problem analysis. Be aware of the uses and benefits of PAME tools.
6. Facilitate community identification of problems by determining their capacity and their needs, and having them set their own objectives. This will enable both field staff and the community to better judge if the project and community objectives are compatible and therefore likely to be achievable.
7. Help the community negotiate when there are conflicting interest groups within (or outside) the community. If the project wants to help the most disadvantaged, negotiation with the community may be necessary in order to reach this beneficiary group.

METHODS FOR COMMUNITY PROBLEM ANALYSIS

In CPA, the community must answer the following kinds of questions:

"Do we need what the project offers?"

"Do we want what the project offers?"

"Do we have the capacity to achieve what the project proposes?"

It may be useful to establish a framework for analysis using the same categories outsiders use to select communities.

PROBLEM IDENTIFICATION

Community problem identification increases the probability that the right problem is being addressed by both parties. Identification helps define the community's interest in problems which in turn, gives the community a vested interest in finding a workable solution. Some of the questions that can be addressed are:

"Do we have the "problem"?"

"Is this problem a high priority?"

"Does this project offer the best solution to our problem?"

There are many tools which facilitate and focus discussion and assist the community's problem identification.

PHYSICAL POTENTIAL

It is important for the community to discuss and ascertain whether the necessary conditions for project activities exist or can be created.

The community can explore the question:

"Do we have the conditions necessary to carry out the project (sufficient land and water, etc.)?"

The relevant physical attributes of the area can be listed, and ways of overcoming constraints can be discussed by the community.

COMMUNITY CONSTRAINTS

Many political or social conditions can limit community members' ability to achieve stated objectives. It is important to identify what can, or cannot be changed. Access to land or to tree products, power structures operating within the community, or labour availability can sometimes be community constraints.

Discussions surrounding the constraints may be very sensitive, especially if community leaders are operating to the disadvantage of some community members. There may be fear of sanctions if sensitive constraints are voiced. Finding ways to raise and recognize these issues is important. Sensitive constraints can be recognized, but do not have to be challenged.

COMMUNITY ORGANIZATION

It is also important for the community to analyse the potential of existing or possible new organizations. The following question may be helpful:

"Do we have (or can we build) an organization that can carry out this project?"

Listing all the existing formal and informal community organizations and examining each organization's resources and potential to take on extra responsibilities may be useful at this point. If a new committee or organization is proposed, it can perhaps be built to mirror an existing, successful community organization.

When community members have examined their Needs, their Physical Potential, the possible Constraints, and existing or potential Organizations that could carry the project, they will be better able to clearly articulate their Objectives, and decide if their objectives will mesh with Project Objectives.

COMMUNITIES SETTING PROJECT OBJECTIVES.

If community members have gone through the CPA process, and decided that they would like to work with the project, they will probably already have a good idea of theproject objectives. It may now be useful to translate these into community objectives and/or beneficiary group(s) objectives, to ensure that the selected objectives are "aligned", and understandable to all concerned.

For example, the following objectives may be established by the different groups:

Project Objectives: .	To increase fuelwood availability to landless
Objectives:	To limit effects of encroaching desert and soil erosion by wind
Beneficiary	To increase availability of fodder for livestock
Objectives:	To maintain/upgrade fuelwood source on common lands and ensure access to this resource

Negotiation and contracts are useful not only because they help' to spell out responsibilities, but also because they facilitate construction of clear agreements between groups with competing objectives.

In the preceding example of objectives by different groups, negotiations might result in a contract which allows landless to plant coppicing fodder/ fuelwood species on common lands adjacent to private farm lands (thus providing the benefits of shelterbelts); to collect and sell fodder produced in these windbreaks; and to selectively cut shelterbelts, therefore maintaining the shelterbelts while also meeting their own fuelwood needs. It is not unlikely that many objectives can be met if they are all recognized and creatively negotiated.

When the Community Problem Analysis has been done, the community, beneficiary group and project staff will know:

1. Whether they can work together as the solutions the project offers are what the community needs and wants.
2. Groups' responsibilities, possibly spelled out in a contract.
3. That community and project objectives are aligned.

5

Valuing The Forest and its Uses: The Available Techniques and their Usefulness in Practice

Once the interested groups and their value perspectives have been identified within the relevant decision context, then attention can turn to the actual economic valuation process.

From earlier discussion, we recall that economic values start with the fundamental concept of a consumer's *willingness to pay* (wtp) for a particular good or service at a given time, in a given place, or a producer/supplier's *willingness to accept* (wta) payment for parting with a good or service, in the case of a supplier. There has been a remarkable growth in the academic economics literature dealing with valuation of environmental services and nonmarket goods associated with forests, and particularly tropical forests and wetlands. However, there are few examples of application of conceptually sound methods on the ground (LEEC forthcoming).

This is not due to a lack of conceptual and theoretical approaches, but due to a lack of data on production functions, a lack of adequate agreement on value tradeoff criteria against which values have to be measured, and a lack of resources to apply many of the time consuming, complex methods developed. Sometimes, of course, it is because there is no need for complex analysis to derive sufficient information to make a decision.

The overall focus in this paper is on the constraints more than the methods of valuation. The latter topic is covered in great detail and abundance in the literature.

THE TECHNIQUES FOR ESTIMATING MEASURES OF ECONOMIC VALUE

The general categories of economic value measures commonly used and more specific examples of different techniques and their applications. A key point here is that in any given analysis a number of different techniques may be used.

USING DIRECT MARKET PRICES FOR GOODS AND SERVICES

Market or exchange values are established through the exchange of goods and/or services in the marketplace, i.e., an interaction of producer values (supply) and consumer values (demand). If a transaction is carried out using some form of commonly accepted currency, we speak of the value established in the market as the market price. If the transaction is carried by some form of barter or exchange without the use of currency, we speak of the value established in the market as a market exchange value.

This method involves direct observation of market exchanges (or uses available records of past market exchanges) to determine the value in exchange of particular goods or service. It assumes that the value of the goods or services exchanged in a market is at least equal to the market exchange rate, although they may be higher.

Table. Valuation Approaches in Relation to Type of Forest Product (Good or Service)

Techniques Involving:	*Examples*
Direct Market Price Technique	This is used to value all market priced goods and services from the forest, unless we believe it does not adequately reflect wtp. The most common cases when the market prices do not are when there exist effective minimum prices or price ceilings on goods and/or services.
Indirect Market Price Techniques (Value Inferred From Other Market Prices):	
Residual values	*stumpage value for timber is derived by looking at market prices for finished lumber and subtracting out costs from stump through processing to lumber sale
Value of production increases	*increased market value of crop production over what it would have been without the windbreak provides a proxy minimum gross value for the windbreak. From that we subtract associated costs to arrive at net value.
Surrogate prices	*the value of fuelwood in a new market is estimated on the basis of the value of an alternative fuel, e.g., kerosene, in that market, after adjusting for calorific value of the two fuels
Opportunity cost	*the *minimum* value of a wilderness park is estimated on the basis of market priced value of the goods and/or services forgone
Replacement cost or cost avoided	*the *maximum* value of a watershed management program focused only on containing sediment in a downstream reservoir is made equal to the alternative market cost of dredging the reservoir of the additional sediment that would occur without the watershed management program

Hedonic pricing	*the market value differences for similar forest properties are used to reflect the value of some environmental service or cost that varies across the properties
Travel cost	*differences in market priced costs of trips by different users to a reserve are used to value nature-based tourism based on differences in use rates in relation to differences in trip costs
Nonmarket Price Techniques (value inferred from surveys of wtp):	
Contingent valuation	*value of a certain wildlife population is inferred from a survey of environmentalists' wtp to save the population

USING INDIRECT MARKET PRICE TECHNIQUES

In some cases, it is possible to use market prices for one good or service to infer values for other goods and services.

a. *Residual or derived prices.* - This method estimates the value of particular goods or services from the prices of goods or services established later in the production-distribution process. (For example, the value of forest products at the farm gate may be estimated by subtracting the cost of transporting the products from the farm to a market where the prices or exchange values are known.) It assumes that the value of the good or service at the farm gate is at least equal to the residual value left after subtracting further production, transportation, and distribution costs from market prices. For some goods and services, there may be a sequence of several market exchanges as the good or service moves from the forest to the final consumer. The value of the product produced at each stage may be in part a residual of the value at the next stage, and all of these intermediate market values may ultimately depend upon the market established for the final product.
b. *Value of production increases.* The increased market value of production of goods and services with and without the change or activity being valued can sometimes be used to value that activity or change. For example, a windbreak can increase crop values behind it; and those increased values can be taken as a proxy measure of the minimum value of the benefits from the windbreak (there may also be others, such as fodder, shade for cattle, and so forth).
c. *Surrogate prices.* - This method estimates the value of a particular good or service from the known values or prices of substitute or comparable goods and services under comparable conditions. It assumes that the value of a particular good or service can be closely approximated by the prices of similar goods and services established

under similar conditions. Thus, the economic value of gathered fuelwood could, in principle, be estimated as equivalent to the cost of the quantity of an alternative purchased fuel, such as kerosene, which would provide the same cooking or space heat. However, in all cases of surrogate prices caution needs to be applied.

d. *Opportunity cost.* - This method estimates the value of opportunities foregone to provide a particular good or service. It assumes that the value is at least equal to the value of the best alternative foregone to obtain the desired good or service. If dung is to be used as fuel, for instance, the opportunity cost could be the increases in crop yields foregone by using that dung for fuel instead of as a means to condition soils.
e. *Replacement cost or cost avoided.* - This method assumes that a good or service produced one way cannot have a economic benefit value higher than the cost of producing the same good or service in another way. Similarly, a good or service that helps to avoid other costs cannot have an economic value higher than the alternative cost avoided. Thus, the value of a hectare of forest that is fixing carbon cannot be higher than the cost of some other means of fixing the same amount of carbon.
f. *Hedonic methods.* - This method estimates values from known values of other goods and services that are technically related to the good or service to be valued. It assumes that the value of a good or service can be estimated from a technical relationship (for example, housing values may decline the closer you get to a loud noise source such as an airport).
g. *Travel cost.* - This method recognizes that for some goods or services the consumer may have to incur substantial costs (in time or money), to obtain the particular good or service. For example, a recreation experience may involve considerable travel expenses; and gathering free fuelwood may require a considerable amount of time.

It assumes that the value to the consumer is at least equal to the travel costs the consumer is willing to incur to obtain the desired good or service.

USING NONMARKET PRICE TECHNIQUES

In cases where there are no market prices that satisfactorily can be used as proxies or direct measures of value, economists resort to surveys and other similar tools to try to estimate consumers' wtp for goods and services. The most notable of these approaches is:

Contingent valuation. - This method is used to estimate the consumer's wtp for a specified good or service or to accept compensation for receiving an undesired good or service. In practice it is usually derived from the responses of potential consumers to a hypothetical exchange situation. The method assumes that the consumer's expressed wtp in a hypothetical situation is a measure of the value to the consumer in an actual situation. It is particularly difficult to apply meaningfully when, like with many functions of the tropical forest, the respondent is being asked to express a value for something that has no established monetary market value, such as cleaner water, which might become available in a hypothetical set of circumstances, such as reduction in upstream harvesting activities.

The techniques mentioned above provide a broad array of tools for assessing the economic values associated with forests and their various uses. Any or all of these approaches may be needed to adequately assess the multiple values involved in any one situation. In applying these approaches, many complicating factors can enter the picture.

VALUING FOREST GOODS AND SERVICES IN PRACTICE

Though the burgeoning literature on the subject may give the impression of considerable recent activity in actual applications, in practice the number is still very limited. As mentioned, most writing still focuses on methodology, hypothetical applications, reviews of other work, or partial applications. The lessons that can be learned from this limited experience are summarized below by looking at their applicability to different forest outputs, since realistic application in terms of total forest value does not exist.

VALUING MARKETED GOODS AND SERVICES

Since this category, by definition, involves establishment of market prices, they can be used as a first approximation to value the goods and services involved.

If market prices are attached to goods and services, and if they are considered valid measures of value of outputs from the alternatives being compared, then differences in points of view on forest values do not matter. The forest preservationist, the logger, the recreationist, the cattle rancher, or road engineer who wants to clear the forest all face the same set of market prices. Of course, the point is that market prices may not reflect all of society's costs and benefits associated with production of the outputs.

It is only worth the time and effort to value things if the values are going to be used effectively to accomplish something. Market prices are useful because producers and consumers in a market create them together, and then generally abide by them when they want to sell or buy something in that market. Thus, by definition they are useful to both producers and consumers. It does not matter how esoteric the use or purpose may be for a resource, good, or service. So long as there is a market, the market value defines the value in exchange, although not necessarily the value in use to any given individual.

Market prices often reflect conditions that are unique to a particular narrow situation (e.g., a monopoly or monopsony situation) and not necessarily the broader, free interaction of suppliers of goods and services and the general population of buyers. This is particularly a problem in trying to assess the likely movement of markets and market prices over time in a dynamically changing forest situation.

From the private interest point of view, subsidies act to reduce the cost side of the picture or to increase the benefit side. Thus they affect the values attached to benefits and costs by those who are subsidized. From the public point of view, a subsidy is merely a transfer of resources from one use to another. But to the individual receiving the subsidy, the result is an increase in net benefits.

Forest clearing for agricultural expansion (whether commercial or subsistence), hydropower development, and other activities often involve significant government subsidies that can cloud the valuation picture, if only market prices are used as measures of value. Subsidies are common for most groups that have an interest in the forest - commercial loggers, those involved in rubber tapping and other extractive activities, and environmental groups.

Taxes need to be considered in a similar light. Taxes represent a cost in the equation of the private parties interested in the forest, whether such taxes are in the form of stumpage or concession fees, income taxes, export taxes, or any other kind of tax. They reduce the net economic value of the forest or forest land use to the potential user. From the public point of view, a tax is merely a transfer of control over given resources from one person or group to another. It is not treated as a cost or return in social economics, but merely as a "transfer payment."

The public manager needs to take subsidies and taxes into account when using market prices as a measure of values of costs and benefits associated with forest uses. Discussion of how to account for subsidies and taxes is provided in the companion volume.

Timber markets and market prices. Nearly all timber is marketed, and therefore it has *market prices* attached to it. Market prices are usually available for roundwood delivered at the processing plant or point of export. Costs of harvesting, extraction, and transport have to be deducted to arrive at a *residual price* for standing timber in the forest. Total values are derived by applying these unit prices to the estimated quantities that could be harvested as sustainable annual flows of timber from the available standing stock.

Valuation of timber should take account of the variation in market values from species to species, and the variation in residual values with location and topography. However, this usually requires more detailed and accurate information than available. Values are also likely to change over time, possibly quite sharply, as technological advances and changing supply/demand balances allow previously unused species to be brought into commercial use. Periodic revisions of the values will therefore usually be required.

The prices prevailing in a country may distort true market values if taxes, subsidies or quantitative restrictions exist. For example, an embargo on log exports, to encourage local processing, could depress local log prices below world market levels. The calculation should then be made using the latter. A more fundamental concern about market prices - even world market prices - as a basis for valuing tropical timber is that they reflect costs of harvesting existing forests rather than the costs of establishing a replacement resource. They, therefore, undervalue tropical timber in terms of *costs of production.*

The calculation of *residual values* of standing timber may have to take account not just of the direct costs of harvesting, extraction, and transport, but also of *indirect costs* stemming from logging damage. If the latter results, for example, in adding sediment loads to nearby rivers in a way that adversely affects water supplies and fish catches, this should be reflected in the costs of timber production.

Marketed nontimber forest products. The term marketed nontimber forest products is used here to describe a variety of physical goods other than timber that are derived from forests that are traded or sold - such as fruits, medicinal plants, fibers, and canes, etc. For those products and quantities produced for sale, the valuation can be based on *market prices,* and follows closely the procedure described for timber.

However, it is likely to be considerably more difficult to apply this approach to nontimber forest products because of the nature of the markets, involved. Only a few of these products, such as rattan, enter world trade in quantities and at prices that are reasonably well documented. Most are traded locally, in markets that largely escape formal recording mechanisms, so that data on quantities and prices are not readily available. Market prices often reflect conditions that are unique to a particular narrow situation. The prices obtained in that part of segmented markets in which people presently purchase a particular good do not necessarily reflect the value that a broader consumer population would be prepared to pay. Substantial expansion in production of many products would create imbalances and a fall in prices below levels that would be profitable.

The attention directed recently to the potential for tropical nontimber forest products in modern sector markets, has tended to obscure the fact that in the more heavily populated parts of the high forest zones in the tropics, such as the coastal belt in West Africa and central India, huge quantities of nontimber forest products presently pass through local market systems. Many forest products used by rural populations involve some form of preparation or processing, die greater part of it by a multitude of small enterprises also located in the rural sector. When rural people migrate to urban centers they continue to use some forest foods, medicines, and products, so that trade in the latter increases. Valuation of the tropical forests, therefore, needs to take account of these actual trade flows. However, its existence almost exclusively within the *informal* sector means that such trade largely escapes formal monitoring and recording, so that it escapes attention and is not well recorded or understood. Scattered market price information can be misleading.

With improvements in rural infrastructure, the markets for many forest products are penetrated by low cost factory-made alternatives from the urban industrial sector. Though some product lines, such as woodworking and handicrafts, tend to have the potential to upgrade and become more competitive, most do not. Many forest-based activities are thus of low value, vulnerable to competition or deterioration in their raw material costs, and offer only a fragile and weak basis for livelihoods. They are likely to collapse or be abandoned in favor of those that offer greater income security and prospect for growth. All these factors have implications in terms of the use of market prices as indicators of value over time.

Though some products exhibit well-established supply and use patterns, many are more ephemeral. Most are low value goods, and sensitive to price and transport costs, thus affecting projections of market expansion and price response. Products such as fruits are perishable and so are marketable only locally. The seasonal nature of supply of many products can result in supply/demand imbalances and a collapse in prices at certain times. The ease of entry into many forest-based activities similarly frequently leads to excessive capacity and output, with corresponding market price impacts. The implication is that one cannot readily extrapolate from point studies and/or pilot scale experiences.

Many of these factors also affect the potential for expansion of tropical forest products into modern sector markets. Access to markets and transport infrastructure limit the locations that could probably place products on the market competitively. Modern sector markets require a level of product or output quality and quality control, which often cannot be achieved with production from an unmanaged resource and processing in small, unmechanized enterprises. Valuation is also hampered by uncertainty about basic input-output relationships for tropical forests.

VALUING FOREST PRODUCTS FOR SUBSISTENCE USE

People acquire many goods, such as fruits, fuelwood, and poles, not through the market but by gathering or producing them themselves. Values for these products need to be arrived at indirectly through the use of *surrogate prices.* A number of alternate approaches may be possible, as is illustrated by the three different bases for valuing fuelwood outlined below:

- By reference to the price of purchased fuelwood, or other purchased fuels such as charcoal or kerosene. This can present difficulties because the different fuels have to be expressed in the same delivered energy terms to compare them. Also, the approach is likely to overvalue subsistence supplies if the users would not purchase fuel if they could not gather fuelwood (i.e., if they would adopt an alternative such as switching to other gatherable fuels).

- By reference to the value of other locally available gatherable fuels - i.e., crop residues and dried dung. As these do not have market values they have to be valued in terms of the*opportunity cost.* The alternative use for dung usually is assumed to be as soil conditioner, and its value in this use is calculated in terms of increased crop yields foregone by diverting it to use as fuel. This approach is valid only if people actually work dung into the soil if they do not burn it, and recent research has suggested that this is less widespread than has been assumed, because farmers find the impact on crop yields is not sufficiently great to justify the labor input involved.
- By reference to the opportunity cost of the time that household members spend gathering fuel from further away. This approach rests on being able to accurately identify what part of the time spent, say, in walking to and from the household's outer fields, and gathering fuelwood *en route,* is attributable to the latter - and what alternate activity the gatherer could have engaged in if not gathering fuel.

The different approaches can produce quite different values in any given situation, which further complicates the task of valuation.

Other subsistence goods can be considerably more difficult to value. Most foods from the forest complement other parts of the diet; for example, providing essential vitamins or proteins. It is, therefore, difficult to separate out their effect. If that were possible it would probably have to be expressed in nutritional or health terms rather than as economic values.

One approach attempting to estimate subsistence values lost with the loss of forest is that of *relocation costs* that would be incurred in moving the population concerned elsewhere. But as it is much more than just their subsistence supplies that they lose in such a case, these costs reflect other values as well. The poor database on nontimber forest product resources, occurrence, productivity, and use apply equally to their subsistence uses - as do the uncertainties about the dynamics of change over time.

VALUING AESTHETIC AND ENVIRONMENTAL SERVICES

The valuation methods discussed earlier, including, for example, hedonic methods, have also been used with various services derived from the forest, although the credibility of these valuation exercises is less than for nonmarketed goods for subsistence consumption. *Recreational use.* The assessment of recreational values for forest areas requires a wtp approach. The *travel cost* and *contingent valuation* methods have both been used in developed countries. A limitation of the first method is that it captures only part of the value to the user. The weakness of the second method is the assumption that people's stated assessment of what they would be willing to pay accurately reflects what they would actually spend to enjoy that recreational experience. There has been almost no experience to date of trying to apply either method to recreational use in tropical forest areas.

Watershed effects. The impacts of change in forest cover on watershed functions can encompass erosion of soil cover, altered downstream water flows, flooding and sedimentation, and consequent damage to agriculture, fisheries, dam storage, and power generation. In principle, many of these effects can be valued in terms of *effects on production* or of *preventive expenditure* methods, e.g., in terms of loss in crop yields due to damage from sedimentation, flooding, or dry season water shortages on downstream agriculture, or the costs of building flood prevention structures to prevent such damage.

In practice, the difficulties, and costs, of tracing and quantifying such complex chains of cause and effect confine valuation exercises to investigating costs and benefits only to the point where decisions can be made about a course of action. In most cases this has meant focusing on effects in the upland areas near the area where the forest cover is to be disturbed. While this is an appropriate strategy to pursue in project appraisal, it evidently provides a less than complete picture of all the costs and benefits associated with watershed effects.

Biodiversity. Conservation of biological diversity is of value because it contributes to increased resiliency of ecosystems, ecosystem stability, improved habitat, and the prevention of loss of genetic material that could be of value in the future. The impetus to ensure conservation of this diversity can arise at a number of different levels - concern to avoid reduction in genetic diversity within a particular species, the loss of a given species, damage or destruction of an entire ecosystem, or degradation of a major biome.

At the species level a *hedonic* approach has been used to establish the value of conserving the gene pool of major agricultural crops. The value can be arrived at by reference to the value of that part of the species range that is presently used commercially, the value of improvements in the properties of that crop already achieved through breeding, and the costs incurred in collection and maintenance of the gene pool used in that breeding. This approach has not been attempted yet for forest tree species.

A large part of the earth's gene resources exists in the plant and animal populations of the tropical forests. Thus, considerable attention has been paid to the possibility of putting values on presently unused species that might prove to have commercial value sometime in the future, e.g., as a source of medical products to combat some new disease or to attack existing health problems more effectively. Though examples of important medical products based on wild forest species have been well documented, it is impossible to assign *ex ante* values to properties or products that have not yet been identified. Furthermore, as potentially useful products acquire significant value only after commercial processes to produce them in a controlled agricultural or industrial environment have been developed, questions arise about what part of that eventual value to attribute to their origins in the forest.

This issue tends to reinforce the *existence value* of tropical forests - the value that people place on their continued existence independent of the values of particular uses. The task of assessing such values is approached through various means of assessing wtp Because of the global values associated with uniquely rich tropical systems involved, this task is as much concerned with assessing what other, wealthier, countries are prepared to contribute to maintaining the tropical forests of importance to the conservation of biodiversity as it is about their existence values within the countries of the tropical forest belt. Any attempts to arrive at such values at present would be highly speculative.

Other ecological effects. In principle, the value of tropical forests in terms of microclimate, climate, and the atmosphere could be assessed through the effects on production (or the preventative expenditure costs) resulting from climatic and atmospheric changes associated with alterations in the extent or composition of the tropical forests. In practice, the relationships between forest change and atmospheric change are as yet imperfectly understood, so this can be attempted only in rather speculative terms.

The clearing and burning of large areas of forest clearly release substantial amounts of carbon dioxide into the atmosphere. But there are other major sources of carbon dioxide, and it is not clear what share of the total output is due to harvesting or burning of tropical forests. Similarly, there are a variety of ways in which carbon dioxide emissions could be curbed or reduced. The value of retaining or managing tropical forests as a carbon store would need to be compared with the efficiency of alternate forms of carbon capture or storage (which could include replacing the forest with carbon dioxide-absorbing plantations or crops, or establishing compensatory fast-growing plantations elsewhere) - and with the values foregone by not exploiting other of the forests' values, such as timber. The fact that the likely impact of rising carbon dioxide levels on different parts of the world is not clearly understood yet further complicates the task of placing values on carbon capture and storage.

Similarly, it is known that transpiration from tropical forests accounts for a substantial part of the recycling of moisture back into the atmosphere; but empirical evidence as to the impact of disruption of this flow through forest removal is limited and inconclusive. However, more local and immediate effects of forest removal may be measured, in much the same way as the effects on watershed functions can be. A falloff in crop yields on adjacent lands, for example, could be assessed in terms of the costs of compensatory inputs of fertilizer, or of the investment in windbreaks that prove necessary to offset the loss of the protection previously afforded by the forest.

IDENTIFYING INTERESTED GROUPS THEIR VALUE PERSPECTIVES

Different groups are affected by a proposed change in forest use in different ways. The affected groups are what we call "interested groups." If the change takes place, some interested groups will perceive negative values (costs) from the change; others will perceive positive values (benefits). Some interested groups will experience both, with the balance determining whether a group falls on the net cost or net benefit side of the equation.

The scale of a proposed change also decides to some extent which groups are included as interested groups. For example, a minute change in a small, remote area may not draw interest from national environmental groups, while a major change of exactly the same nature would do so. Interested groups are not decided by output measures so much as input/technology considerations. For example, we may be looking at changes that would add some 10,000 m^3 of lumber to the national economy.

If it is produced by thousands of small, independent pitsawers, we see one set of interested groups. If it is produced through a large, modern mill, we have another set of interested groups.

As a first step, we have to identify the various interested groups involved or affected by a proposed change and then define their various value perspectives that need to be reconciled in the decision process. To what extent are the various perspectives complementary? To what extent do they conflict?

As an example of typical forest interested groups, assume that it is proposed to open a forest area for logging. Obvious interested groups would include the proposed loggers, the indigenous populations that live in the forest areas, the citizens of the country or province that owns the forest, various environmental groups, and possibly the consumers of timber products, if the increased logging resulted in lower prices for consumers.

The value perspectives of these various interested groups vary along a continuum. At the extremes, some will see positive value; others will see negative value in a given change. The strength and magnitudes of the individual and aggregate values involved will vary from situation to situation. In other words, we have to not only be concerned with the unit values associated with the different interested group perspectives, but also the aggregate values involved in each instance. We also have to be concerned with changes over time, as discussed earlier

DIFFERENT USER VIEWS OF FOREST VALUES

Forests are not unique in terms of having conflicting values attached to them and their uses. Different persons attach different values to all resources, goods, and services.

No matter how many perceptions of value we identify, *what ultimately matters in terms of action is the value perceptions of those who actually will determine what happens to the forest.* Those decision makers are the ones we need to reach with the information derived from assessments of forest values, or benefits and costs. Who are these decision makers? Forests are owned, controlled and used by many different groups. The focus here is on public forests of various kinds - forests under the responsibility of communities, regional or state authorities, or national 1 governments. However, a word of caution is needed: Sometimes, the public decision maker is different from de facto decision maker, who also may be the client for public forest policy.

For example, in some remote forests, the actual decision makers may be the slash and burn farmers on the ground, if the government does not have an effective means to control forest clearing. Thus, to deal with problems of deforestation on public forest lands caused by forest margin or slash and burn farmers, one needs to understand the economic value perspective of this latter group. (We will get back to this point.)

MAIN INTERESTED GROUPS CONCERNED WITH FOREST VALUES

For the purposes of this discussion, we have identified four main categories of people who have differing interests in natural forest values. These are:

1. *Groups with commercial interests in specific parts or aspects of the forest.* These groups are interested in the market or barter values associated with uses of certain parts of the forest, e.g., timber industries and consumers of commercially sold timber.
2. *Local forest dwellers with their interest in livelihood/survival values.* These groups are interested in the forest as their living environment and as a source of sustenance and livelihood, e.g., indigenous tribal groups.
3. *Environmental advocacy groups and nonconsumptive users.* These groups are interested in the forest as an ecosystem or in saving particular species or groups of species. They also are interested in the educational, recreational, and spiritual values associated with forest preservation. The groups can be local, national, or international.
4. *Migrant farmers, ranchers, and others with an interest in the land under the forest.* This group may give a *negative* value to the trees and animals of the forests they want to clear, i.e., they would like to see them gone. To these groups, the forest is a nuisance: letting it stand

involves a cost; it harbors dangerous animals; it is the home for animals and insects that attack their adjacent agricultural crops; it hinders travel and road construction; it is in the way of progress and expansion of agriculture and ranching. From the point of view of these groups, the forest grown on the underlying land they want has a negative value at least equal to the cost of clearing it. Having said the above, we also should point out that in fact the forest has a positive value to the slash and burn farmer practicing shifting cultivation with forest fallows. This is so because the forest renews the nutrients in the soil for the farmer and possibly provides outputs during the fallow period. To these farmers, the forest near their agricultural plots also may have value as a source of fuel, food, fiber, and fodder. We come back to these types of value relationships later.

One might ask why we have not identified *government* or the *public sector* as a group that has a special interest in the value of the forest. The answer is that here we consider *the legitimate interests of government should be a mix of the varying interests of society,* i.e., the above groups and possibly others.

It also should be the role of government to advocate the interests of the voiceless interested groups of the future, i.e., future generations of the above groups. Indeed, it is with this in mind that governments should pursue not only economic efficiency objectives, but also those associated with sustainability and equity in distribution of benefits.

Of course, in many cases government officials have their own vested interests that they follow. In such cases, they as individuals may fit into various special interest groups.

PEOPLE MAY FIT INTO MORE THAN ONE GROUP

Confusion often arises because most individuals fit into more than one interested group. Thus, consumers of forest products, who have an interest in the monetary cost of the particular goods or services they are consuming, may also be ardent environmentalists, outspokenly advocating protection of forests against encroachment and unsustainable use. Generally, those conflicting interests apply to different areas of forest or different aspects of forest use. For example, a person may be a major consumer of forest products from the temperate forest and also an ardent defender of the preservation of the tropical forest and its biodiversity. The two value frameworks are consistent *from a valuation point of view.* It means that a person will be identified with one value perspective or another, depending on the specific forest area and situation being addressed.

As development takes place, people also move along the various value continua. Thus, as people move out of subsistence slash and burn farming, their value perspectives may change. They may eventually move out the group that values the forest primarily as a living environment to the group that values the forest for the commercial goods and services that it provides for theMarket. Similarly, local populations, as they get access to commercial medicines, may reduce the values they attach to the medicinal plants that they once collected. The dynamics of values introduce additional complications into the valuation equation, particularly in cases such as forestry, where long-term perspectives are needed.

Below we look at the value interests of each of the four major groups identified, keeping in mind the overlaps in terms of people fitting in various categories.

THE INTERESTS OF COMMERCIAL GROUPS

This is perhaps the easiest group to deal with in terms of economic value measures. Commercial interests are concerned with the market values of the goods and services derived from the forest. For instance, loggers are interested in the value of wood, while rubber tappers and gatherers of various commercial products are interested in the values associated with their products in specific forest situations. And, nature tourism companies are interested in the values they can derive from specific routes, areas, species, etc. In parallel with these producer groups, there are, of course, the consumers of the commercial outputs - consumers of lumber, paper, gums, oils, fruits, recreation trips, etc. derived from the forest. They also have a legitimate interest in values or the prices they pay for specific outputs (goods and services) derived from the forest.

Commercial producers in their role as such are interested only in market values - what they have to pay to get the products they want from the forest, what they have to pay to process and get those products ready for the market, and what they actually obtain when they sell the products in the market. Similarly, the consumers of the vast array of marketed products from the forest are interested in market prices - how much they have to pay in the market to obtain the goods and services they want.

LIVELIHOOD AND SURVIVAL VALUES OF FOREST DWELLERS

For people living in or next to a forest, its value is identified with both the products derived from the forest, and with the spiritual and cultural values attached to the forest environment. More specifically, the forest provides wood, fiber, and other materials for construction of homes, storage structures, and agricultural tools. The forest serves as habitat for a wide range of plants and animals that provide fuel, food, medicines, and saleable products that sometimes generate household income and employment. It also serves as the source of water. All these functions theoretically can be assigned monetary measures of value, using various shadow pricing techniques though monetary measures are the furthest thing from the minds of most forest dwellers. Also, the forest environment or ecosystem provides the religious and social context for life and ritual, which produce many values that we should not even attempt to measure in economic terms.

Typically, use and management of the components of the forest by local forest dwellers are dictated by an elaborate structure of constraints and obligations stemming from the values placed on forest vegetation because of spiritual and cultural associations. Forests have positive and negative values in this respect: as protectors and providers and as areas - to be feared or as deterrents to development.

One recent study of a situation in West Africa summarized the balance of interests and values involved as follows:

"It would seem that [for the local people] high forest is seen to have little value in and of itself. In practical terms, the bulk of subsistence-oriented forest products derives from secondary successions, not from high forest. But the greater value placed on 'bush,' compared to high forest, depends on more than practical considerations alone. In rural Mende eyes, social life begins and ends at the edge of a forest clearing. The energy released by the conversion of forest to farm and bush is a major source of power in society... the farmer about to fell trees to make a farm... will invoke the patient understanding of the ancestors and spirits of the land for the necessary damage he must inflict on the bush. The recovery of the bush from a period of cultivation... is a sign that ancestral blessing has not been withheld".

In practice, therefore, subsistence, income, environmental, and social and cultural impacts of the forest are intimately interrelated. People's decisions are dictated by their responses to the whole, rather than by assessments of the costs and benefits of each part separately. But their focus is invariably on present local needs, not on the wider values of the forest nor its more widely diffused benefits, nor future benefits.

Much of the value of the forest to forest dwellers lies in its importance in helping to maintain stability and control risk. Users therefore focus on products, such as fruits and leaves, which are available on an annual or continuous basis. They heavily discount the values of those products, such as timber or rattan, which are available only in the future or periodically . Lack of security of tenure or access tends to reinforce this focus on the short-term, secure economic values. If people have no assurance that they will have access to future harvests, they attach little if any value to them.

Access to markets will usually increase the value of a forest as a source of income for local people. However, many forest products are low value goods, and are sensitive to price and transport costs. Products such as fruits are perishable and so are marketable only locally. The seasonal nature of supply of many of these products easily results in supply/demand imbalances and a collapse in prices. Thus, there can be significant value fluctuations over time.

The ease of entry into many forest-based activities frequently leads to excess capacity and output. With improvements in rural infrastructure, the markets for many forest products are penetrated by low cost human-made or plantation grown alternatives. Though some product lines, such as woodworking and handicrafts, tend to have the potential to upgrade and become more competitive, most do not. Many forest-based activities are thus of low value. They are vulnerable to competition or deterioration in their raw material costs. They offer only a fragile and weak basis for livelihoods, and are likely to collapse or be abandoned in favor of livelihoods that offer greater income security and prospect for growth. The role of forest products in forest fringe communities can therefore change rapidly, with shifts toward or away from dependence on the forest often occurring over very short periods. Decision makers have to keep in mind that patterns of use at any one time may tell little about future values as perceived by local forest or fringe dwellers. The implication is that analysis has to be based on an understanding of the *patterns* of dynamic change in use of forest products.

VALUES OF ENVIRONMENTALISTS AND NATURE-BASED TOURISTS

Environmental groups have varied interests in forests. These interests can range from a concern with the impacts of deforestation on climate change and on reduction in biodiversity and loss of species, to local concerns to maintain the aesthetic values of a forested landscape or to save a particular area of native forest. For these groups, only those uses and attributes that can be sustained over time, without causing degradation of the forest, contribute to its value. It is also argued that the existence value of an environmentally intact forest is likely to differ from the aggregate of the value of the component goods and services that can be derived from it.

Many environmentalists consider that such values are not, and cannot be, satisfactorily reflected in economic or monetary terms. Indeed they argue that to attempt to place economic values on the forest results in partial or incomplete measures of forest value that are misleading, and can result in suboptimum decisions. Thus, many environmental groups resist attempts to put the forest in a conventional economic perspective, preferring other (more qualitative) approaches to assigning its value.

VALUE PERSPECTIVES OF THOSE WHO WANT THE LAND UNDER THE FOREST: SUBSISTENCE FARMERS, RANCHERS, ETC.

For many groups, the main value they see when they look at a forest is the productive potential of the land that lies under the trees. This value - in economic terms, and *from the perspective of the potential users of the land* - can be measured by the capital value of the land in the other intended uses, i.e., the present value of the annual or periodic net returns from using the land for those other purposes, minus the cost of clearing the forest and planting the new crop.

For such groups, the best thing that can happen is for the government to open up forest lands for settlement or for conversion to other uses. Often, governments become interested in pushing out the "frontiers of civilization." They provide subsidies to clear land for agricultural expansion, hydropower developments, road expansion, and so forth. These subsides become key factors in determining the economic value of the cleared land to the settler or other intended user. Naturally, such subsidies also can influence the value perspectives of various groups that want to use the forest as forest, e.g., loggers, rubber tappers, environmentalists, and recreationists.

Those who want the land under the forest oftentime prevail by influencing legislation that sets aside forest lands for settlement or other purposes. In cases where the decision to clear the land for settlement or other uses already has been made, the valuation task of the public forest manager or land manager is simpler: the manager does not have to worry about comparing values with and without the forest. If the decision has not been made, then the valuation task is to attach values to the potential losses from clearing, i.e., the opportunity costs involved.

ECONOMIC VALUES: USEFULNESS AND LIMITATIONS

Economic values do not exist in isolation. They merely provide an economic perspective of the value of goods and services associated with an activity or set of activities. They are attached to the inputs and outputs in production or transformation processes. Thus, a first, essential step is to identify the inputs and outputs that will be associated with a proposed change being looked at by the decision maker.

THE SAME GOOD OR SERVICE CAN HAVE POSITIVE OR NEGATIVE VALUE ASSOCIATED WITH IT

Goods and services can be associated with negative monetary values (costs) or positive values (benefits). It all depends on who is looking at them. Thus, to the worker, a wage is a benefit with positive economic value; it is an income. From the perspective of the forest company hiring the worker, the wage is a cost and takes on a negative value in the company's calculations.

At the same time, it should be kept in mind that valuation involves attaching positive values to goods and services. They become "costs" (and take on a negative sign) when we have to give them up. They take on a positive sign and become "benefits" when we obtain them. For example, even though we may use any number of proxy measures to estimate the cost of pollution, it fundamentally is equal to the *positive* value of the health benefits *we give up* due to the pollution. From society's point of view, the value of the labor will depend on the value of what it produces. When labor is hired away from one use and put into a new use, there is an "opportunity cost" involved. Opportunity cost is nothing more than a reflection of the value of the goods or services lost when a resource is diverted from one use to another.

The same physical good or service can have different economic and social values, depending on location and timing of the production of that good or service

The point that the same physical service (in this case the same reduction in erosion and soil loss, but in different locations) can be associated with quite different economic and social values. The basic point to remember is that there are no absolute economic values. They all depend on the particular conditions faced with regard to where and when the good or service is available, how much of the good or service is being produced, how much individuals want it, and how many people are willing to pay for it.

THE WITH AND WITHOUT CONCEPT

When a change in forest use or management is proposed, then the relevant costs and benefits to consider are the incremental ones associated with the change, i.e., the costs and benefits with and without the change.

POLICY PRICES REFLECT THE REALITY OF THE POLICY ENVIRONMENT

In theory, values assigned to a given good or service should reflect the best alternate use for resources (true opportunity cost), or the true willingness to pay for goods and services, excluding government interventions and including all externalities. In practice, this is not possible, nor always desirable.

The situation with regard to using policy prices for land. The situation is that a given area of land has been legally established by the legislature as a national forest, for use as forest. The question is whether the valuation of the opportunity cost of the land should consider options such as agriculture, or industrial park use, when in fact they would not be allowed under the existing law, which is expected to hold in the future.

We argue here that the opportunity cost associated with a proposed land use change should reflect only options that are permitted under policies that exist (and are expected to remain in effect during the life of the proposed change). The resulting values we call "policy prices," or prices/values constrained by the existing and expected policy environment. The cost of continuing the policy is another, separate and legitimate question.

Remember that the relevant policy environment is not only the one set by public law, but also through social and religious custom or law. A classic example is the sacred cows of India. They define certain realities of the country that should, appropriately, be reflected in any realistic economic valuation involving cattle.

CAPITAL VALUES AND FLOW VALUES

Under this heading there are several points that the decision maker ought to be aware of regarding forest values.

BIOLOGICAL RESOURCES HAVE BOTH FLOW AND STOCK (CAPITAL) VALUES

Forests have a standing stock of trees that can produce flows of timber, fruits, nuts, and other products. Both sets of values are relevant in considering proposed changes in forest use. The same is true of other forest plants and animals.

FLOW AND STOCK VALUE RELATIONSHIPS LIE AT THE HEART OF DEBATES ABOUT SUSTAINABILITY OF BIOLOGICAL RESOURCE SYSTEMS.

In fact, much of the argument for introduction of natural resources accounting, or taking changing stocks of natural resources into account in national accounts, relates to this point.

Policy prices in forestry project evaluations

Assume that an area of currently idle land technically could be used for two mutually exclusive purposes: agriculture or a forest plantation. The plantation alternative would yield $150 of benefits per year net of all costs except land cost. The agricultural alternative would generate a benefit of $200 per year net of all costs except land. There is, however, a policy restriction: the government has on various considerations decided that only forestry will be allowed in the area.

The analyst is asked to estimate the economic worth of the plantation alternative. To do this, he will need to estimate, among other things, the value of the land that will be used by the project. This value is equivalent to the net benefits given up by not being able to undertake the best alternative use for the land. Since the main*technically* feasible alternative is agriculture, with a net benefit of $200 annually, some would argue that this is the value of land which should be entered as the opportunity cost in the economic analysis of the afforestation project.

Others would say that, since a policy decision has ruled out the agricultural alternative, the relevant value of land for the afforestation project should be equal to the net benefits foregone by not undertaking the next best *forestry* alternative. If this next best forestry alternative generates a net benefit of $60 per year, again exclusive of land cost, which value should be entered in the analysis, $200 or $60?

Depending on which value is chosen, two radically different estimates of project worth might occur. As mentioned, the plantation would yield net benefits of $150, excluding consideration of land opportunity cost. If $200 is taken as the economic value of land, the economic worth of the plantation project would be equal to $150 - $200, or -$50, and the economic analyst would recommend against implementation on the grounds that costs outweigh benefits. On the other hand, if the policy restriction is taken into account, the net benefit generated by the afforestation project would be $150 - $60 = $90, and the project would have the chance to be approved since its worth is positive. Which approach is the correct one?

Using the traditional "with and without" principle, the analyst should consider only the estimated *actual* difference. The restrictive policy imposes real boundaries to feasible opportunities, as real as those imposed by technological constraints. Therefore, the value of the potential agricultural output should not enter the analysis of the plantation project. Failure to observe this principle would lead to the wrong decisions. In the example, if the policy restriction is considered as irrelevant, there would be no economic argument for approving the afforestation project. The project would not be implemented, but neither would the superior agricultural option, for the policy is in fact real. In consequence, society would receive neither the benefits of afforestation nor the benefits of the agricultural option.

The above should not imply that the worth of the unfeasible agricultural option is irrelevant. Quite the opposite. While this value should not be entered into analysis of the plantation project, it is very relevant in an analysis of the restrictive policy on land use. Since without this policy, $200 of net benefits would be generated, while with the policy the best alternative would yield only $150, the difference of $50 surely represents part of the societal cost of the restriction. This is relevant information.

Decision makers might or might not find this loss of $50 acceptable in pursuing noneconomic societal objectives associated with the land in question. The loss is of obvious importance in the analysis of policy implications, but it is not relevant to the evaluation of the afforestation project, given the policy.

Recently there has been a growing interest in developing such natural resources accounts associated with forests and other natural resources. To a great extent, this is due to an anomaly in national income accounts that leads to an overestimation of the value of income generated by natural resources by not deducting an amount for depreciation. Depreciation is an imputed cost that reflects both the declining productive capacity of a human-made asset - buildings, factories, equipment - and the investment that is necessary to sustain a certain level of productive capacity over time.

Unlike human-made capital assets, the value of production stemming from natural resources is calculated in national income accounts without deducting the cost associated with their depletion or degradation. Thus, when forests are cleared, no depreciation that would reflect their decreasing productive capacity is recorded. The resource itself is treated as free good, clearly a measurement failure. By including only the value of production without netting out the value of natural resources inputs, national income accounts overestimate income generated and provide wrong signals for decision making. Policies, which deplete forests or degrade the environment and decrease future productive capacity, appear to be desirable activities. To deal with this valuation problem, modified approaches have been designed. These approaches essentially try to redress the valuation discrepancy between human-made and natural capital by allowing a certain amount to be deducted from the value of production. This allows for the decrease in the productive capacity of natural resources associated with depletion and degradation.

FINANCIAL VALUES AND ECONOMIC VALUES

Financial values refer strictly to market priced goods and services. Financial values are always looked at from the perspective of a particular person or other unit. Thus, for that unit, financial costs represent outflows of money/resources, while financial returns are inflows of money to the unit.

TIME VALUE AND DISCOUNTING

Costs and returns, or benefits, occur over time and not all at the same time. For example, some costs may be borne today, with their corresponding benefits occurring sometime in the future. The basic question is how to compare present values with future values, since we know they are different. (A dollar in hand today is worth more than having to wait ten years to get that same dollar.) Economists use the widely accepted practices of discounting (bringing future values back to the present) and compounding (bringing present values forward to some future date). The basic concepts. The key to comparing values that occur at different times is to bring them back or forward to some *common* point in time so they can be compared.

"VALUE IN EXCHANGE" IS DIFFERENT FROM "VALUE IN USE"

It should be noted that in carrying out an analysis using any of the above means, it is important to distinguish between *value in use* (consumer value estimates) for some nonmarket goods and services and *value in exchange* (market prices) for market-traded goods and services. Thus, one should not compare, e.g., market priced values for timber with estimates of value in use for recreation. The two represent different concepts and often differ. Thus, for example, the market price paid (value in exchange) for an ecotourism trip to a Kenyan game park may be far below what a particular consumer actually is willing to pay (value in use) for the trip. The market price only reflects wtp at the margin. In sum, erroneous conclusions about relative values can be easily reached if the two are compared.

VALUING FOREST PROPERTIES

There are a number of valuation methods which can be employed to value a forest crop. The four main potential valuation methods include:

HISTORICAL COST VALUATION

This involves valuing the forest crop at cost (i.e. the total cost actually incurred to date in establishing and maintaining the forest crop) and increasing this value yearly to account for the growth increment in the crop. This method of valuation would generally only be applicable tovery young crops, and would generally be employed by an owner to update the value for accounting purposes on an annual basis. While there may be certain circumstances in young crops in which this valuation method might be used, it does not take into account the productivity of the crop, which ultimately will define its value. Also, sites of lower productivity may be more difficult and costly to develop and establish due to difficult site conditions, poor drainage, repeated fertiliser requirements, elevation, poor access and other factors. Because higher costs may be involved in establishing such areas they would be given higher values employing this valuation method than areas of higher productivity.

The most important factor that militates against employing this method of valuation in recent years is that grant aid will currently cover the entire costs involved in developing and establishing a plantation. Therefore, the actual cost incurred by a landowner in establishing the forestry investment is nil other than the land opportunity costs involved.

REALISATION/LIQUIDATION VALUE

The realisation value of a forest crop, as its name suggests, values a forest at the value it would realise if the crop is harvested at that particular point in time. It therefore only values the stage of a crop when timber is marketable, effectively from the time of first thinning onwards by assessing standing timber volume and valuing this using current market timber prices.

A problem with this valuation method is that a forest crop in the establishment and thicket stage up to the time of first thinning has no realisable value. This effectively neglects the potential value of the immature crop and therefore is not an appropriate method of valuation until there is a realisation value after first thinning stage. Also, as for the historical cost valuation method it does not take into account the productivity of the crop, which ultimately will define the longer term value of a forest.

NET PRESENT VALUE OR NET DISCOUNTED REVENUE VALUATION

The Net Present Value (NPV) or Net Discounted Revenue (NDR) value is unlike the two previous valuation methods in that it is based only on projected future incomes and expenditures and these are discounted to the present day at a particular discount rate decided by the valuer or buyer. Therefore, no account of either past income or expenditure is taken into consideration and the valuation is based effectively on the future potential of the crop.

This method should therefore more accurately reflect what an interested purchaser is likely to consider the value of a crop, as this valuation method will assess his future return on an investment.

The return which an investor is likely to seek from a forestry investment will be dependent on a number of factors, but the most significant influence will be the return he can achieve from competing investments and the comparative risks associated with these alternatives.

For general forestry valuation purposes the net discounted revenue valuation method is therefore the most appropriate basis of valuation to employ in most cases. This method of valuation is also recommended by the Society of Irish Foresters, which is the representative body for the forestry profession in Ireland, in their Policy Position Paper, "Investing in Forestry".

As the most important factor in determining the NDR valuation is the discount rate that is employed in the projected cashflow, careful consideration must be given to this rate. The internal rate of return (IRR) for a particular crop or investment is the discount rate at which the total of the discounted revenues equals the total of the discounted costs. This is effectively the real rate of return or the financial yield of the investment.

TRANSACTION BASED VALUATION

The transaction based approach involves the analysis of market transactions. It is the theoretically correct procedure to estimate the market value for a forest. The analysis essentially involves an interpolation or extrapolation of the values of past sales and applying the result to the forest of interest. Even if forest value is not inferred from past transactions, it may be possible to infer other relevant factors from sales e.g. implicit discount rate or timber price assumptions.

The availability of transaction information varies from country to country as does the volume of transactions. The volume of annually traded private forests varies from 0.1 to 0.15% in Austria and 0.17 to 0.23% in Finland. Transaction information is, as a general rule, more available in free market countries with a long forest tradition. Despite the availability of transaction information in Finland, the net present value is the preferred valuation method and that most widely used in the sales of forest properties.

6

Forest Project Management Planning

FOREST MANAGEMENT PLANNING

THE BASIC ELEMENTS OF PLANNING

Planning is an active process requiring careful thought about what could or should happen in the future and involves the coordination of all relevant activities for the purpose of achieving specified goals and objectives. Planning is an integral component of forest management; is about determining and expressing the goals and objectives which government, rural communities or companies have, and for deciding the targets and steps that should be taken in order to achieve those objectives.

Planning need not be a complicated process but it requires clear objectives which a government or other group aims to achieve. It requires imagination and a willingness to consider all points of view having relevance to a given situation.

The planning process should lead to the formation of a balanced outlook from which proposals for effective management can be written. An element of flexibility is desirable and necessary, however, in order to cope with unforeseen events which could affect the achievement of the objectives.

A range of information is used in planning to evaluate the benefits and drawbacks of alternative courses of action, which enables preferred options to be determined, coordinated with other activities, and expressed in writing. Information should be of good quality.

Information of questionable quality should either be discarded or, if used, it should be noted that it is of poor quality and one of the activities of the plan should be acquiring better quality information.

TWO TIME HORIZONS OF PLANNING

Forest management plans should have a minimum duration, or length, of 10 years. A shorter period than 10 years does not provide the medium-term stability that is needed to guide consistent implementation of sustainable forest management activities. A realistic maximum length is 20 years. The duration is also called the term, or period, of a plan. A management plan should include prescriptions that provide for:

- Review at the mid-point of the plan,
- Review in the final year of the plan,
- The preparation of a new plan upon expiry of the present plan.

Annual plans of operations are written for a one-year period and should be derived from a five-year (or longer) management plan. A Plan of Operations should express specific activities in tabular form for one year only and for a specific locality, such as a felling area. An example of the tabular structure of a plan of operations.

The relationships between elements of medium-term and annual forest management planning cycles. A tiered structure of long-, medium- and short-term management relationships. A number of commonly used terms in forest management planning and in the implementation of plans.

Table: The Tiered Forest Management Planning System

Management Level		**Time Frame**	**Key Elements of Forest Management**
Strategic Issues	*National*	> 10 years	Conservation driven forest policies
	Sub-national	> 10 years	Forest Sector Development Plans
Operational Issues	Forest Management Unit	10 years	**1. Management function - Planning** - Integrated forest resources inventory - Environmental impact assessment - Forest zoning by forest functions - Forest protection - Integration of customary land rights - Yield regulation
	Compartment	Annual	**2. Management Function - Implementation** - Low impact forest resources management - Yield allocation according to stand maturity **3. Management Function - Control** - Forest resources accounting - Periodic revision of management plans

LEGISLATION FOR MANAGEMENT PLANNING

A component of forest legislation that applies to a country or province should be that management plans are to be prepared for State forest land and for forest lands in non-State tenure the conservation of which is in the national or provincial interest or where subsidiaries or incentives are paid to promote forestry development.

The following guidelines indicate the primary requirements that should be included in forests legislation in respect of forest management planning:

- Subject to the rights existing in a forest when a management plan comes into operation, forests legislation should specify that a plan must regulate the management of forest land in conformity with the management objectives for a specified time period.. The maximum number of years for which a management plan can be in operation should be specified. It should not be less than five year nor more than 20 years. Scope for review of a plan during the planning period should be provided.

Forest Management Plan: A document that translates forest policies into a coordinated programme for a forest management unit and for regulating production, environmental and social activities for a set period of time through the use of prescriptions specifying targets, action and control arrangements.

Forest Management Unit: An area of forest for which an approved. Forest Management Plan is in operation, or any subdivision of it, such as a block (a specified locality) or a felling series.

Felling Series: Specific compartments of a Forest Management Unit that are being managed in a specific way for silvicultural reasons and also have an independently calculated harvest yield.

Plan of Operations: A tabular statement showing the order and extent of forest work to be carried out during one year and is based upon the prescriptions of a Forest Management Plan. The term is synonymous with Annual Work Plan.

Compartment: A permanent, geographically recognisable unit of forest land forming the basis of prescription and permanent record of all forest operations.

Sub-compartment: A sub-division of a compartment, sometimes temporary, where because of particular characteristics an area of forest has a special description and requires separate silvicultural treatment.

Prescription: A concisely written specification in a forest management plan that translates an objective, or a part of one, into an operational activity.

Mean Annual Increment (MAI): The total increment, usually volume, up to a specified age, divided by that age.

Current Annual Increment (CAI): The average increment, usually volume, for a management plan prescription, including where, when and how the yield should be extracted.

Yield Regulation: The determination of the yield and its expression in a management plan prescription, including where, when and how the yield should be extracted.

Working Circle: One or more parts of a working plan area, not necessarily adjoining, having the same objectives, silvicultural system and prescriptions.

Working Plan: A document that regulates wood production, silviculture and tending activities for a specific period of time through the application of prescriptions specifying targets, action and control arrangements. A Working Plan is not synonymous with a Forest Management Plan.

Source: Terminology of Forest Science. Technology, Practice and Products. Society of American Foresters. 1971.

- Each forest management plan should specify:
  - The maximum area from which forest produce may be harvested, or the maximum quantity of forest produce which may be harvested, or both, in a given time period,
  - The forest protection operations to be carried out,
  - The forest development operations to be carried out, including silviculture,
  - Other matters which are necessary or appropriate in order to implement management objectives effectively. This could include forest inventory, mapping, technical and social surveys, and public consultation.. A management plan to be applied to State or private forest land should be approved by the Ministry responsible for forestry or other specified authority.

BALANCE BETWEEN PRODUCTION, SOCIAL AND ENVIRONMENTAL OBJECTIVES

Forests provide a wide range of benefits at local and national levels. Log production is usually the main objective and revenue earned for governments and companies is the major driving force in tropical forest harvesting. Revenue earned from log harvesting will usually be the main funding source for long-term sustainable tropical forest management. Many communities depend heavily upon non-wood forest products for subsistence and as a basis for local trade, for example, canes, medicinal and food plants, gums, resins and wildlife. Tropical forests are an essential source of energy for many communities, directly through burning of wood for cooking and heating and indirectly to protect watersheds as source of water for hydroelectricity generation. They have an important role in protecting physical and biological environments at local and provincial levels. Tropical forests are dwelling places for many millions of people and are increasingly of value for recreation and tourism, notably "eco-tourism". They are important havens for wildlife and are the habitats of many endangered species of plants and animals. It is essential in tropical forest management planning to achieve a balance between the long-term between wood production, social and environmental management objectives.

THE PARTICIPATION OF ALL INTEREST GROUPS IN PLANNING

The initiative for the formulation of a forest management plan should be taken by the forest owner, such as the state, or by a concession holder on behalf of the owner. Local communities and others having historical rights or privileges in a forest are important stakeholders and must be involved in planning. The likelihood that sustainability will be achieved will be considerably enhanced if local people who live in and around tropical forests have a say in and participate in management planning and are able to share in the benefits of forest use to ensure that their basic needs are met. The steps that can be taken can include:

- Granting secure tenure to existing productive farmland within the forest
- Local participation in management decision-making.
- Guaranteed access to forest products.
- Provision of employment.
- Shared benefits in forest harvesting.

Accommodation of the respective interests of forest management companies and local community groups can be eased with the recognition that companies and indigenous communities are, in most cases, interested in different things - industrial logs by forest management companies on the one hand and small dimension wood and non-wood products by local communities on the other. A positive approach towards adapting the interests of both groups is to include rural communities as partners in forest management and to share the benefits of wood production with them.

YIELD PREDICTION

TYPES OF YIELD PREDICTION MODELS

A yield prediction model uses the quantitative relationships between measured growth variables to predict yields of forest types, and is a tool that helps to schedule and regulate harvests at sustainable levels. Two basic methods are available for their construction, diameter class (or stand table) projection and cohort modelling. Both depend upon the use of comprehensive growth data to construct and fit a yield prediction equation. Detailed development and application of both methods require specialized assistance that is beyond the scope of these *Guidelines* but descriptions of each are included to illustrate the basic steps involved in their construction.

THE BASIC STEPS INVOLVED IN THE CONSTRUCTION OF A YIELD PREDICTION MODEL

Diameter Class Growth Projection

The manual method of diameter class growth projection is the oldest method, first used in Myanmar in 1856, and used elsewhere for simulating the growth of tropical forests. A tree population/diameter class distribution is compiled using PSP summary data. DBH classes are in 5 or 10 cm intervals. Stratification of the tree population can be made on the basis of species groups. Average diameter growth and average tree mortality rates are determined from periodic measurements of PSP, for each diameter class. Growth is projected for a five-year period for each diameter class per hectare by applying growth and mortality rates.

Construction of a Growth and Wood Yield Prediction Model

The process of fitting a yield prediction model from forest data may be by fitting the field data to a pre-determined regression, for example, a linear regression, or manually by plotting the data on graph paper; equations can then be developed from the hand-drawn curves. The use of personal computers allows statistical procedures to be applied with greater precision and more quickly than manual methods.

Testing of a Yield Prediction Model for its Validity

A wood yield prediction model must be tested to determine its validity and precision. The precision of a yield model will depend on how well the PSP represent the forest, the number and period of the remeasurements, on covariances of the predictor variables and on coefficients used in the model.

Model testing is best done using a second set of forest data which was not used during the preparation of the yield model. The model is used to predict the behaviour of the forest from where the test data were collected and the results are compared with the actual observations. It is often necessary to repeat this stage several times.

Adjustments to the model are made as a result of anomalies, or irregularities, that show up at each stage of testing.

Application of the Yield Model to the Required End-Use

A yield model may be applied in one of three ways:

- To forecast timber out-turn through a simple table or graph or a set of both. These can be used by forest planners directly or tables can be entered into a computer for updating of inventory data.
- To test forest management options as a computer or calculator programme which produces a table or graph of growth and yield for a particular set of treatments.
- To provide information on timber outputs for wider aspects of forest planning

Readers will find references at the end of this chapter for detailed guidance on the development of yield prediction models.

EXAMPLES OF YIELD PREDICTION MODELLING TECHNOLOGY

A SIMPLE DIAMETER CLASS GROWTH PROJECTION MODEL

Data Assembly: Assemble the relevant tree population and size data collected from a CFI for a whole forest management unit, or a part of it (a felling series), for which a yield determination is proposed.

Stand Table Preparation: Using PSP summary data, compile a tree population/ diameter class distribution. DBH classes are typically in 5 cm intervals, e.g. 30-35 cm. Stratification of the tree population into smaller groupings can be made, based on species groups, e.g. "present commercial", "potentially commercial" and "presently non-commercial" species, and also on crown illumination classes.

Growth and Mortality Rates: Determine average diameter growth and average tree mortality rates from PSP data, for each diameter class.

Diameter Class Projection: Growth is projected for a five year period for each diameter class, on a per hectare basis, by applying growth and mortality rates. An adjustment is made to reflect the actual rather than the step-wise diameter class distribution of a stand because there are fewer trees in the upper part of a diameter class than in the lower part. In its simplest form, diameter class growth for each separate diameter class can be projected by applying the following formula:

$$N = S.I.\left(\frac{1}{q}\right)^{(1-I)}$$

where:

N = the number of trees growing from one diameter class to the next,

S = number of live trees in each diameter class,

I = average diameter increment for the class (cm),

q = an adjustment factor for each specific forest type and groups of diameter classes that is used to reflect the actual diameter class distribution.

The calculations can be carried out using standard spreadsheet software on a personal computer.

DIPSIM (Dipterocarp Forest Growth Simulation Model): an Empirical Individual-tree Growth Simulation Model

DIPSIM is an empirical individual-tree growth simulation model that has been developed in Sabah, Malaysia, as a management planning tool for natural Dipterocarp forests specifically for the purpose of:

- Predicting annual growth in terms of stocking, volume and basal area,
- Predicting changes in stand characteristics for periods of up to 60 years,
- Providing decision-support in yield regulation through the simulation of different harvesting prescriptions.

MAIN FEATURES OF THE DIPSIM MODELLING PROCESS

Diameter Growth

Developing a multiple regression that relates basal area increment of individual trees to tree basal area, site quality, stand basal area and overtopping basal area. Increment equations have been developed for groups of species having similar growth patterns; 20 growth groups in all. Diameter increment patterns are developed for each species group.

Mortality

Developing a model that reflects regular and catastrophic mortality and predicts the probability of mortality from tree size and stand competition.

Recruitment

The model predicts recruitment rates for species in seven timber groups into the lowest (10 cm) stem diameter class.

Harvesting

Three steps are included in the harvesting component;

- *Stocking assessment - the model compares the actual stocking of a stand against pre-defined post-harvest minimum stocking standards. In Sabah, a post-harvest minimum stocking of at least 8-10 trees/ha _ 60 cm dbh after 40 - 60 years.*
- *Tree selection and removal - predetermined minimum and maximum diameter cutting limits of 60 cm and 120 cm respectively are specified in the model.*
- *Harvesting damage - the user can specify in the model the percentage of trees expected to be destroyed in two size classes, 10-39 cm and_ 40 cm. The model randomly selects trees, removes them from the simulation database and places them into a mortality account database.*

Model Operation

The PC-based DIPSIM is programmed in relational database software and the model structure consists of three main modules, database preparation, simulation and output. The output module summarizes the simulation output in the following forms:

- *Stand and stock tables,*
- *Volume increment tables,*
- *Harvesting tables, comprising a harvest composition table and an annual harvest record table.*

Although practical and easy to understand, this and other diameter class projection methods do not effectively take changes in stand density or the consequences of spatial distribution (of diameter classes) of tropical forests into account. They are best used for preliminary yield analysis.

Cohort Modelling

The term "cohort model" refers to a group of trees of the same species group and size class which is the basic information unit used for cohort growth modelling.

- *Cafogrom Model:* A new and powerful tool for growth modelling research workers is the *Cafogrom* model, developed at the *Centro do Pesquisa Agropecuaria da Amazonia Oriental,* in Brazil. It is a cohort model that is directed towards the analysis of PSP data from mixed tropical forests to produce growth and yield models. Although the *Cafogrom* model is complex and does not provide, in itself, a standard set of computer programmes for the analysis of PSP data, the method is described in order that this new approach can become more widely known and to encourage local research on growth modelling.

DETERMINATION OF THE ALLOWABLE CUT

CLASSICAL METHODS FOR DETERMINATION OF THE ALLOWABLE CUT

Yield regulation, irrespective of the silvicultural system being applied, provides a basis for deriving a log harvest which is in balance with forest increment and for controlling the output to ensure that the cut is neither exceeded nor undercut. In many tropical forests where a knowledge of the uncut and regrowth forest resources is incomplete, where there is little or no information of forest increment and where forest management is being introduced for the first time, the allowable cut should be derived using one of the classical empirical procedures.

There is no alternative in these situations but to use an empirical approach. Four allowable cut determination procedures are explained to enable the reader to appreciate and understand the main features of each. In practice, the choice and use of each method depends upon the silvicultural system being applied, either polycyclic or monocyclic, in a specific forest situation. The methods are:

- A combination of area and the felling cycle.
- A combination of area, volume and the felling cycle.
- A combination of volume and forest increment.
- A consideration of volume only.

Each of these methods provides only a general guideline for deriving an allowable cut. Notwithstanding this qualification, a application of one of the methods having relevance to the technical characteristics of a forest management unit and the management objectives will be a positive contribution to sustainable forest management where at present no other basis for this exists. Selected technical reports listed at the end of the chapter explain each method and how they are applied in practice.

New computer-based methods of yield determination are currently being developed and have the potential for achieving much greater precision than do older methods. Their use depends upon having good quality information of tree diameter class distributions, tree volumes, growth, recruitment and tree mortality derived from CFI. The new procedures enable a user to calculate on a personal computer the increment of tree diameters and basal area over time, make allowances for tree recruitment and mortality, to simulate harvesting and logging damage and thus project forest growth and yield. Specialist technical assistance is required in order that these new methods are able to be applied in a specific forest situation.

Where the polycyclic silvicultural system is being applied in an uneven aged forest, the **Annual Cutting Area** (ACA) can be derived by dividing the area of the net productive forest into equal parts depending upon the length, in years, of the felling cycle. The most productive area is determined by zoning, by deducting the area of land which is "unproductive", from a wood production point of view, from the total area of a forest management unit. This method can also be applied in forest types being managed under monocyclic silviculture, such as in mangroves or bamboo. In equation form, the area control method is expressed as follows:

$$ACA = \frac{TA - UA}{n}$$

where:

ACA = the ACA; the maximum area of forest which may be cut each year,

TA = the total area of a forest management unit,

UA = the "unproductive" forest area,

n = the length of the felling cycle, in years.

The Annual Cutting Area method can only provide a general, though rapidly determined, indication of allowable cut. Because it is the simplest and least precise method it should not be applied without clear specification of species, tree diameter sizes and numbers of trees per ha which may be harvested.

A COMBINATION OF AREA, VOLUME AND THE FELLING CYCLE

In its simplest form, the Annual Allowable Cut (AAC) can be derived by combining the maximum felling area which may be cut each year with the volume of wood in the felling area that has been determined from a pre-harvest inventory. The nominated stem diameter is a variable figure and dependent mainly on the type of forest being managed. It can be as low as 30 cm in some forest types and more than 60 cm in others. This method is expressed as follows:

$$AAC = \frac{V.A}{n}$$

where:

V = the average volume per ha of commercial species above a specified stem diameter that is estimated from the first forest inventory.

A = the area of a whole forest, or of a felling series.

N = the length of the felling cycle, in years.

This approach is used in Dipterocarp dominant hill forest concessions in Indonesia where *n,* the felling cycle, is 35 years. It is a relatively simple and easily understood approach and allows yields to be determined easily. In practice, maximum and minimum values are determined and form the basis of the AAC for each concession. The method does not reflect the losses in volume which always occur during logging, caused by stem breakage, nor does it account for volume losses through stem decay. It also disregards increment of existing or potential timber trees. The AAC can be reduced by an "exploitation factor" and a "safety" factor (0.7 and 0.8 respectively in Indonesia) which provides some allowance for losses at harvesting and also for damage to a residual stand during logging.

A modification of this procedure is applied in the Dipterocarp forests in the Philippines. The procedure recognises the variability in size and distribution of large trees in different forest types and it considers an estimate of the volume which can be cut, derived from a yield table.

A COMBINATION OF FOREST VOLUME AND FOREST INCREMENT

In uneven-aged forests where selection cutting is proposed or is underway and where comprehensive forest inventory data and a confident knowledge of current annual increment are available, the *Gehrhardt Method* provides a basis for determination of the allowable cut. It is expressed as follows:

$$AAC = \frac{(If + In)}{2} + \frac{(Vf - Vn)}{AP}$$

where:

If = the Current Annual Increment for the forest,

In = the CAI for a theoretically normal forest,

Vf = the total volume for the forest determined by inventory,

Vn = the total forest volume for a theoretically normal forest,

AP = a planned adjustment period for the forest to reach normality.

A drawback in the use of the *Gehrhardt Method* is the difficulty of deriving a theoretically normal forest and the uncertainty of knowing whether it will be possible to plan cutting over a sufficiently long period to achieve a normal distribution of area classes.

An alternative approach which also depends upon having a reliable knowledge of increment but avoids the need to derive a theoretical normal forest structure, is the*Cotta Method.* It enables the cut to be determined for a forest being managed under an irregular shelterwood silvicultural system.

YIELD DETERMINATION BASED ON VOLUME ONLY

Where a forest management unit is being managed under a monocyclic silvicultural system and there is currently no knowledge of increment, the most simple method for yield determination is to divide twice the volume of the growing stock by the rotation or cutting cycle. Known as the *Von Mantel Method,* it does not consider increment, forest structure or variability in growth and volume at all and thus can only provide a very general indication of forest yield. It does however have the benefit of being simple, its use requires only a small amount of data and the yield determination tends to be conservative. In equation form the *Von Mantel Method* is expressed as follows:

$$AAC = \frac{2V}{R}$$

where,

R = the rotation (cutting cycle) for the major tree species comprising the growing stock.

V = the average volume of commercial species above a specified stem diameter that is estimated from the first forest inventory.

DETERMINATION OF THE AAC WHERE REGROWTH AND PREVIOUSLY HARVESTED FOREST OCCURS

For increasingly large areas of tropical forests the AAC needs to be determined where regrowth and previously harvested forest occur and where there are declining areas of primary forests. The empirical methods are less appropriate is these situations. A typical mixed forest resource structure where an alternative approach for determination of the AAC is required is as follows:

- Some primary forest, yet to be harvested;
- Some previously worked forest where a range of harvesting densities, from light to heavy, have been applied over the past 10 to 30 years, and regrowth has led to a new forest structure;
- Some land that has been cleared of forest through shifting cultivation or wildfires and where a pioneer forest has developed.

A helpful approach for determination of the AAC where a mixed forest structure occurs is as follows:

- Undertake forest zoning to determine the net productive area, being careful to exclude all forest land where social and environmental constraints will preclude any wood production at all.
- Update the forest resources statement for the net productive area of primary and secondary forests by undertaking new inventory.
- Calculate the AAC for regrowth forests that have been harvested previously, and for pioneer forests if applicable, plus the AAC for the remaining primary forest resources which can be cut over a period of “X” years.

- Define a "target growing stock" of commercially harvestable volume for the forest management unit. This is a value judgement based on ecological as well as commercial criteria.
- Using a growth simulation system, such as SIRENA or DIPSIM, derive a cutting cycle, in years, that will be required in order to reach the target growing stock. The cutting cycle will vary, depending upon species and their distribution, the damage pattern, the distribution of wood resources and site productivity. Several different harvesting prescriptions will need to be simulated in order to arrive at a practical and commercially realistic cutting cycle.
- Again using a growth simulation system, determine the adjustment period that will be required in order to achieve the target growing stock for the net productive area of forest.

YIELD REGULATION

GUIDELINES FOR YIELD REGULATION PLANNING

Yield regulation, or allocation, involves making decisions that lead to clear specifications of where and under what conditions a harvest may be cut using AAC and technical information about a forest. It is a critically important part of sustainable tropical forest management. Practical guidelines for yield regulation planning for each compartment that is included in an annual cutting plan are:

- Technical information;
  - The average volumes of different species,
  - diameter class distribution and the minimum diameter that may be cut,
  - Distribution of trees on the ground in relation to topography and practical road access,
  - site types and the characteristics of the silvicultural system, or systems, specified in a management plan that are being applied in the forest,
  - Technical information for unlogged, previously logged and secondary forests on each compartment should be considered separately because of differences in tree species, stem diameters and tree distribution that almost always occur. Yield allocation will inevitably be different for each of these classes of forest.
- Clearly define on maps and on the ground those areas of forest which are to be excluded, through zoning, from logging for environmental or social reasons. Harvest planning maps can either be manually drawn or GIS generated.
- It is desirable that yield allocation plans be prepared two and preferably three years in advance of logging to enable roadline logging

and road construction to take place, for roads to settle before use and, where necessary, for climber cutting to be completed.
- Wood harvested from roadlines should be allocated as a part of the annual allocation for the year; it should not be an additional allocation of yield.

YIELD CONTROL

On a year to year basis it is essential that frequent checks be made by a forest manager to ensure that the AAC and other details of cutting prescriptions are followed by logging crews. A programme of continuous log measurement, or scaling, provides an annual and a compartment-by-compartment basis for yield control. This is an essential practical aspect of sustainable tropical forest management and is a part of operational monitoring.

It is usually difficult to extract equal volumes of wood or other produce every year because of the variability within a forest and physical difficulties caused by wet weather and short term changes in market demand and prices. Some variation, perhaps as much as 15 per cent above and below a prescribed volume, in the annual rate of harvest can be expected and needs to be planned for. Three approaches for managing this situation are:

- *Subtract* an "overcut" from the prescribed harvest level for the following one (or two) years.
- *Add* all or part of an "undercut" to the prescribed harvest level for the following year.
- *Cancel* an "undercut" and add this volume to the total forest growing stock for the next five years and recalculate the AAC.

Long Term Control of Yield

Year-by-year indications of wood harvests and comparisons with the AAC does not enable the question of whether a forest is being managed sustainably to be properly answered. In order to monitor the yield over a longer term, of at least 15 years, the MAI for the whole of the forest management unit should be derived for this period and should be balanced against the total harvest for the same period.

Periodic and regular assessment of a forest is the most reliable method for determination of increment. Accurate mapping and CFI are able to provide reliable data on forest resources at the beginning and end of a planning period for which the MAI is to be derived.

The total volume of removals (including logging waste losses) are derived from accurate records of volumes cut each year, supplemented with an estimate of waste determined through logging waste studies. In equation form the relationship is:

$$\mathrm{MAI} = \frac{V(t+n) + Vp - Vt}{n}$$

where:

MAI = mean annual increment in m^3/year for a forest management unit during a planning period of not less than 15 years in length.

Vt & $V(t+n)$ = total standing forest volume in m^3 determined from CFI at the beginning (Vt) and at the end ($V(t+n)$) respectively of the planning period.

Vp = total wood volume in m^3 harvested during the planning period, including a logging waste estimate for the period.

n = length of the planning period, in years.

Sustained yield management of wood (or rattan, bamboo or other products) would, in technical terms, be considered to be achieved if the total harvest does not exceed the accumulated annual increment during a specified planning period. Conversely, sustainable harvesting would not be achieved if the total cut during a planning period does exceed the accumulated annual increment.

FOREST MANAGEMENT PLANNING

MANAGEMENT STRUCTURE AND FORMAT

To be effective a forest management plan should comprise basic information having direct relevance to the management of a forest, a long-term management goal, and specific prescriptions to achieve each of the objectives. The management plan structure should be flexible depending upon the characteristics of the forest for which long-term management is being planned. A logical, easily assembled and practical plan structure has four main parts.

A Model Forest Management Plan Format

The subject matter of a plan is likely to vary from one locality to another, depending upon the characteristics of the land and forest being considered as well as upon objectives, opportunities and risks. There is however a basic list of contents which should be considered where plans are to be assembled for tropical forests that are being managed for the production of wood. The model format which follows provides an effective framework for drafting a management plan for tropical forests.

GUIDELINES FOR FOREST MANAGEMENT PLANNING

Forest Management Plan Formulation

Guidelines for formulating and drafting a management plan are:

- A plan should be prepared in conformity with a country's forest policy, legislation and regulations.
- The planning process must overcome past managerial problems and should provide workable, positive and affordable solutions to these problems.

- Nomination by a government forestry office, a concession holding company or other agency having management responsibility that one person, or a group of people, will be responsible for plan preparation. It should be the primary task of that person, or planning group, and should not be undertaken in conjunction with other duties.
- Once a start is made on plan preparation every effort should be made to continue the process until it is completed.
- Summarise managerially significant resources information. Only information that is directly relevant to implementation of management objectives should be included. Be conservative when resources information is being assembled for the first time and where it is known that information is incomplete, or its quality is uncertain. In practice, conservative resources statements tend to be closer to future reality than do optimistic estimates.
- Assemble base maps, aerial photographs and satellite imagery and use these to compile forest maps needed to provide graphical support for management requirements. Subdivide the forest management unit into permanently defined compartments.
- The planning team must visit and acquire a good visual knowledge of all parts of a forest, villages and dependent industries.
- Summarise the managerial implications of specific features of basic information, for example, climate, topography and social issues. The summary should be a succinct statement of the decisive issues that are expected to influence the management of a forest. Assessments of the managerial implications of each specific feature of basic information become the link between the objectives and prescriptions in a plan.
- A plan should be no longer than is needed to present relevant information - the goal, preferably no more than five objectives and the supporting prescriptions that are related to those objectives.
- One or more people can contribute towards drafting different chapters of a plan but only one person should have responsibility for coordination and final assembly.
- Avoid identifying and specifying too many priorities for action. There should only be one priority on any one subject.
- Plans must be affordable and should be able to support the implementation of realistic budgets; it is unwise to prescribe action if it is unlikely that implementation can be funded.
- Plans must include provision for review at pre-determined intervals.
- Plans incorporate implementation of departmental technical instructions, guidelines and standards.
- Monitoring and reporting requirements should be expressed in the

form of prescriptions. A plan should not be approved without having monitoring and reporting requirements included.

- Frequent dialogue with all people having an interest in the formulation of a plan and in its implementation is to be encouraged.
- A plan should have a readable "user friendly" style and must be easily understood by all who will use it in practice.

Formulating Management Plan Prescriptions

The following guidelines for formulating management plan prescriptions are suggested:

- Prescriptions should be concisely written, specific to the issue being addressed and should be related to specific management objectives. They should not be vague or ambiguous.
- Prescriptions should not be too long or too technical. Lengthy or excessively technical prescriptions are likely to be misunderstood or simply ignored. Only include material that is directly relevant to support the implementation of forest management objectives.
- Prescriptions must be measurable, or capable of being monitored easily, so that progress can periodically be reported.
- Although a need for precisely written prescriptions should be recognised, it also needs to be acknowledged that there may be occasions where a manager should be allowed some discretion in the implementation of a prescription if local conditions or common sense indicate that a degree of flexibility is desirable. Losses of forest through fire, additions or losses of forest area, changes in the definition of forest resources or changes in community interests in a forest are cases of unforeseen events which may influence the progress of the management plan.

Management Plan Approval

The basic requirements for gaining approval of a forest management plan are as follows:

- When completed, an executive summary of a management plan should be assembled setting out the primary features of it, including the goal, objectives, the allowable cut and its location, operational features of the silvicultural system, community participation and forest protection arrangements.
- The principal features of the plan should be explained and senior staff in an oral presentation.
- The plan should be passed to the office of the approving officer with the support of a covering letter.
- Plans prepared for forests on private land should be approved by the government forestry authority to ensure that plan quality is

acceptable, to strengthen the basis of the national forest policy and to ensure that the rights of third parties are protected.

HARVEST PLANNING

Harvest planning provides a balanced and comprehensive foundation for sustainable harvesting practices to enable good technical control during harvesting to be reconciled with the need for reducing harvesting costs. Harvest plans are of two types, strategic and tactical, and both are an integral part of the forest management planning process. A map and a written plan are the basic components for both strategic and tactical harvest planning.

RECOMMENDED PRACTICES FOR STRATEGIC HARVEST PLANNING

A Strategic Harvest Plan explains why, where, when and what type of harvesting is proposed. Strategic harvest, planning cannot be undertaken without considering the issues which affect the management of the forest more widely. It is an integral part of a forest management plan, prepared by the planning team, and should never be a separate planning statement that is independent of it. Strategic harvest planning should rely upon a knowledge of:

- The area of forest that has been zoned for wood, bamboo or other production objectives; it should exclude all areas zoned as protected or protection forest and for settlement purposes, including buffer zones.
- The annual or periodic cut for woody produce.
- The silvicultural system, or systems, to be applied.

A strategic harvest plan map (or maps), at a scale of between 1:10,000 and 1:20,000, should show the following features which should also be identified in an approved forest management plan:

- Forest types, topography, existing and planned infrastructure.
- Forest land which is to be protected for watershed or biodiversity conservation or for community development reasons.
- Areas where harvesting is proposed, divided into annual felling areas that can be conveniently defined on the ground.
- Areas where major problems exist, such as rock outcrops, river crossings or swamps, that must be overcome when developing a transport system, or in carrying out forest operations.
- Areas of non-forest land uses.
- Locations of communities or indigenous populations that could be affected by harvesting or transport operations.

A written strategic harvest plan should briefly describe the items shown on the harvest plan map and include the following topics:

- The silvicultural system to be applied, and why.

- An explanation of how harvesting is expected to achieve silvicultural objectives, especially its effect on the next crop, and the extent to which this is expected to be achieved.
- A brief description of the types of harvesting equipment to be used in specific felling areas and why these are selected.. A tabular summary, derived from a general forest inventory, of the species, volumes and log size classes that are expected to be cut in each compartment.
- A schedule showing the year when each felling area is to be harvested.. A summary of special problem areas shown on the strategic harvest plan map, such as river crossings and difficult roading areas, with notes on how these might be overcome.. Information concerning the forest transportation system, such as road design requirements for different topographical conditions (valley bottoms, ridges, slopes), stream crossings and the design specifications for drainage structures.
- Annual labour requirements for harvesting and roading.. Arrangements for accommodation, health, safety and recreation of the workforce.
- The estimated cost of harvesting within each felling area and annual maintenance of the transportation system.

RECOMMENDED PRACTICES FOR TACTICAL HARVEST PLANNING

A Tactical Harvest Plan is a short-term plan, prepared by a team directly responsible for supervision of harvesting operations, that explains how and who will carry out the operations and when cutting will be undertaken in each annual cutting area. It should be linked through the Annual Plan of Operations with an approved forest management plan and should not be a separate planning statement. A Tactical Harvest Plan is formulated for the operational part of a year, for example, a dry season. It can apply to a single felling area or to a group of separate felling areas. The following basic steps are involved in tactical harvest planning:

- A pre-harvest inventory should be conducted to identify tree species, to estimate the size and volume of trees present and their position throughout a felling area. The pre-harvest inventory should extend over the whole area where harvesting is proposed. In the case of selection harvesting, trees to be cut should be identified, marked and numbered.
- A topographic survey, either on the ground or using remote sensing imagery, should be conducted during a pre-harvest forest inventory to provide information for mapping.
- Using field survey information, a detailed topographic map should be drawn at a scale of between 1:10,000 and 1:2,000 showing all

topographic features that will influence logging, and also the boundaries of the harvest area. Streamside protection strips, scientific, wildlife and cultural zones and any other special reservations specified in a management plan should be mapped. Contour mapping can be prepared either by manual drafting methods or through the use of GIS technology. It is the experience of many companies who are managing tropical forests that an investment in good quality mapping can lead to reduced harvesting, reading and other infrastructure costs.

- A felling area should be divided into administrative units, termed cutting units, that can be identified on the ground and used to control a harvesting operation. A cutting unit should be limited to a single extraction method because cable, tractor, draught animal and helicopter systems each have different characteristics.

Specific planning requirements are:

- Tactical harvest planning should be based on harvesting prescriptions set out in a forest management plan. The volume and/or number of trees per hectare to be extracted and the number of seed trees per hectare that are to remain should be specified.
- A cutting and log extraction plan should comprise a part of the harvest plan and should be undertaken using the topographical and tree position map. It can also be generated using vertical and oblique GIS imagery. The plan should be prepared jointly by forest planners and loggers and must be practical and realistic. The location of landings, skid trails (if ground skidding is to be used), cableways (if cable extraction systems are to be used), haul roads and feeder roads should be shown. Where possible, directional felling should be indicated.
- Harvesting equipment should be specified and a general operations schedule formulated, using actual or estimated production rates. Work studies may be necessary to determine appropriate production rates.
- A harvesting schedule should be prepared setting out the anticipated timing of harvesting in different felling areas. It should be flexible and able to be quickly modified, when necessary. For example, it should anticipate the onset of a rainy season, irregular wet season conditions, severe storms, roading problems, protection of specific endangered animals during breeding, fire hazard conditions (and wildfires) and periodic heavy seedfalls.
- Preparation of a harvesting schedule should, where appropriate, be prepared in consultation with local communities who might be affected by harvesting. The harvest of NWFPs and the dependency of local communities upon these for subsistence, employment and income generation should be considered. Examples are collection of rattan, fruit, resins and medicinal plants.

- Any legal requirements, such as right-of-way easements or specific local authority consents concerning roading, rivers, or aviation permits (for helicopter logging) should be obtained and listed.

IMPLEMENTATION OF FOREST MANAGEMENT OPERATIONS

IMPLEMENTATION OF FOREST MANAGEMENT PLANS

Neither the planning process, of itself, nor the approval of plans, will necessarily lead to the successful implementation of plans. Effective implementation depends upon a good level of understanding and acceptance by government officials, forest managers, forest workers, machinery operators, rural communities and others who will be involved in the task of implementation. No less importantly it also requires:

- A firm commitment to allocate funds, staff and other resources for the duration of a plan to enable prescriptions to be implemented.
- An appropriate organization structure and the appointment of people having appropriate knowledge and experience for specific, well-defined positions that are relevant to plan implementation.
- Training to ensure that people appointed to all positions are up-to-date with procedures, techniques and practices.
- A commitment to regularly monitor progress in plan implementation and to amend annual programmes when necessary.

IMPLEMENTATION OF HARVESTING OPERATIONS

Reading

Forest roads are an important aspect of tropical forest management because of their high cost and the adverse environmental impacts that can be caused in respect of soil erosion and sedimentation of watercourses. If unregulated, forest roads provide access to people, leading to forest damage through slash and bum agriculture. Roads should be designed and built by engineers who understand the need to minimise soil disturbance, maintain proper drainage and avoid stream crossings. Tropical forest roads are usually classified into two groups - haul roads and feeder roads.

- *Haul (or Arterial) Roads*/Haul roads form the transportation network over which the logged harvest is transported from landings to a mill or to an intermediate shipping point, such as a log pond or transhipment yard. Haul roads are permanent, should have an all-weather running surface and should be sufficiently wide to enable two vehicles to safely pass. They are also used for other management purposes, such as protection and silviculture.

- *Feeder (or Secondary) Roads:* Feeder roads are located in a cutting area and form the outer ends of the haul road network. They provide access for workers and machinery to the cutting area and reduce skidding and forwarding distances. Feeder roads are normally only temporary and are abandoned following logging.

The principles of forest road engineering that should be considered are:

- Roads should provide convenient low-cost access for the transport of logs and should also benefit forest communities.
- Access to roads built through forest land where the management objectives are watershed and biodiversity conservation, wildlife or scenery protection, or the conservation of cultural or religious values should be strictly regulated.
- The total road length, grades and curves should be minimised in order to reduce the erosion potential of roads, to reduce needless deforestation and to cut road construction and maintenance costs. Road density will depend on the forest type, topography, the cost of road construction and maintenance and the cost of log extraction. In general, because of the generally low volume of harvestable logs per hectare in selectively managed tropical forests, the optimum road density is lower than where clearcutting is practised.
- Feeder road density is related to skidding distance as follows:

$$D = \frac{a}{s}$$

where:
D = feeder road density in km/ha
a = a "road efficiency" factor, usually between 5 and 9;
4 - 5 for flat land,
5 - 7 for hilly land,
7 - 9 for steep terrain,
9 or more for very steep, rough terrain
s = the average skidding distance in metres

This relationship can be used for estimating average skidding distance when the road density is known, or for estimating road density when average skidding distance is known. Details of optimum feeder roading spacing, road density and skidding distance relationships. Although common sense needs to be shown in the use of the feeder road/skidding relationship it is a useful working guide.

- Road construction should be consistent with good design and maintenance practices, minimising road and landing areas while providing adequate roadside clearings to permit roads to dry quickly after heavy rains.
- Soil erosion associated with road construction and maintenance should be minimized, thereby reducing sedimentation in streams and damage

to stream ecosystems. Minimise cutting and filling and utilise natural drainage patterns in road design.

- Roads and landings should be kept away from streams and from streamside buffer (protection) strips. Where a stream crossing is needed the crossing structure should be designed on the basis of a site survey. Minimise stream disturbance during construction.
- When culverts are used for cross-drains or stream crossings, their size and spacing should be determined by local rainfall intensity and water runoff rates.
- Where practicable, roads should only be built during dry season conditions and should be allowed to stabilise through the next rainy season. Roads must be allowed to dry out thoroughly before being used by heavy machinery.
- Where possible, avoid areas of wet soils and high erosion risk; roads are expensive to build and to maintain in such areas.
- As a general guide, the average forest road width should be restricted to the minimum that will allow log transport to be carried out efficiently and safely. This will reduce forest loss and the potential for soil erosion. As a guide, the maximum clearing width should not be more than 10 metres for major roads nor more than 8 metres for minor roads.
- Road grades should be kept as low as possible, consistent with the need to provide adequate access to a forest. Maximum grades of eight to 12 per cent are suggested, except for short lengths of road where steeper grades are needed to provide access to higher ground. A ruling gradient of five to eight per cent is suggested for main and secondary roads. Formulae for conversion of slopes between slope per cent.
- Where practicable, avoid mixing horizontal and vertical curves during road line planning and construction.
- Good maintenance of road surfaces, roadside drains and culverts is needed to protect roads and to ensure that they can continue to be useable for post-harvest silviculture and for future log harvests.
- Feeder roads that are not expected to be used again until the next harvest cycle can be closed to prevent their use by local communities or others. Road closure can be achieved by ripping the surface and planting shrubs or grass.

TRAINING

All agencies involved with the management and harvesting of logs should make and implement arrangements for effective training of logging crews. The aim is to increase and maintain the professional skills, work performance, and work quality of workers, and to develop and maintain an awareness of social and environmental issues. In its simplest form, training can be "on-the-job" guidance on proper logging practices provided by supervisory personnel. It is also desirable that workers attend practical courses on safe harvesting practices. These should be repeated each year.

The following general training guidelines are suggested:

- All field personnel who are to be involved in log extraction that requires heavy machinery and suspended loads should be trained in the need for operational safety and working cooperatively as a team. Instruction should cover the need for an understanding of the role of each person in the team and their job and the need to practice good working methods.
- Field and aircraft personnel to be involved with helicopter log extraction should be trained in operational safety involving aircraft and suspended loads, radio communication between personnel and the need to practise good working methods.
- Training in fire prevention and control should be mandatory at all levels of organisation so that all personnel, including rural communities, know their role in the event of a wildfire. It should be in the form of short courses and practical training exercises. People who have not received some training should not be allowed to fight forest fires. Topics should include:
- The safety of people and equipment, including the use of fire safety clothing,
- The use of tractors, pumps, hoses and other equipment,. Methods of communication on a fireline,
- Simulated practical fire safety exercises to test that institutional arrangements, knowledge amongst personnel and equipment are able to cope with a forest fire emergency.

HARVESTING OPERATIONS

Pre-Felling Treatment

As road construction progresses ahead of cutting, it may be necessary to undertake pre-felling treatment within a felling area. Pre-felling treatment comprises cutting of the stems of large, climbing plants which have stems, branches and foliage in the forest canopy. The purpose is to cause climbers to die, allowing the stems to decay so they break during felling. Not to do so can lead to accidents during cutting and to tree damage because branches can be torn from residual trees. General pre-felling treatment guidelines are as follows:

- *Climber Cutting:* Climbers that bridge across the crowns of trees to be harvested or will influence the fall of a tree should be cut one to two years in advance of cutting. Depending upon the silvicultural system, climber cutting can be combined with cruising. It can be performed by a small crew of two or three who work systematically through forest where climbers have been noted during pre-harvest inventory. Climber stems are cut near the ground, using a bushknife, axe or powersaw.

- *Rattan:* Rattan stems can be cut and extracted on a commercial basis by the concession holder if this is appropriate. Alternatively, extraction can be offered or contracted to local communities.

Cutting

Cutting includes all activities undertaken to fell and prepare trees for extraction, including felling a standing tree, measurement to determine best log lengths, limb removal and cross-cutting to form logs.

The following principles, practices and standards should be applied in cutting:

- Forest land and trees that are not shown in a harvest plan, or marked otherwise as trees not to be felled, should not be cut, and the felling operator should be aware of such disposition.
- Operations should be safe for workers and others in the vicinity. Good worker supervision and good worker health are essential. Appropriate safety equipment must be worn. Chainsaws and other equipment must be properly maintained.
- Cutting should be carried out by personnel who have been trained in the correct use of chainsaws and safety equipment, such as protective clothing, and trained to interpret labels on trees that indicate which trees should and should not be felled.
- Chainsaws or crosscut saws should be used for felling and for crosscutting to form logs. Axes should not be used because of the wastage of wood that occurs. Directional felling should be practised to reduce damage to residual trees, saplings and seedlings, especially those that are expected to become future crop trees.
- Only trees that have been labelled and numbered, for harvesting, at the stump and at "dbh" height should be cut. Cutting crews should be trained to recognise labelled harvest trees and be properly supervised to ensure that only these trees are cut. Cruising labels should remain on stumps for post-harvest monitoring. Trees that are labelled as being seed trees must not be cut or damaged during felling operations. Checks should be made on a logging landing and during post-harvest checking to monitor whether reserved trees have been cut.
- The identity of all trees that have been measured and labelled for

harvesting (during cruising) should be maintained through to log formation. The following guidelines are suggested:

- A feller should carry a copy of cruising map showing the location and numbers of trees to be cut.. A cutter should remove each cruising label from the side of a fallen tree that has been cut and firmly attach it (using a flat-head nail) to the log butt.. The duplicate section of the label should be removed by the feller as a record of each tree that has been cut.
- The duplicate section of each label should be handed to the harvesting crew supervisor at the end of each day for use later in a harvest assessment of the cutting area. A record of the tree numbers cut each day should be maintained by the harvesting crew supervisor. This is a practical monitoring requirement to ensure that only trees labelled for cutting (the "compulsories"), are in fact cut.
- Practical guidelines for directional felling are:
- Cutting crews should be trained to carefully select the felling direction. On flat or slightly sloping land each tree to be cut should be felled either towards or away from skid trails or cableways, depending upon local experience, topography and the type of logging system being used. Directional felling simplifies log extraction and markedly reduces forest damage and overall logging costs.
- Trees should not be felled directly down steep slopes unless the downhill lean is so great that directional felling is unable to pull the tree in another direction. Felling across a slope or along a contour, will reduce the momentum of a falling tree and minimise breakage and damage to nearby trees.
- Where possible, trees should be felled in the direction of canopy gaps and alongside skid trails to reduce forest damage.
- It is desirable to direct the fall of a tree towards the crown of previously felled trees. This reduces both impact damage and damage to surrounding forest.
- Trees that are too difficult, too dangerous or that upon felling would cause too much damage to the remaining vegetation, should not be cut at all.
- The same applies for rare tree species or that are found few in numbers in the area to be harvested.
- The final assessment and decision on whether or not to fell a tree should always be made by the cutter.
- Tree felling should cause minimal damage to soils and watercourses. Trees should not be felled across streams where there is no streamside protection strip in order to minimise damage to the watercourse, to streambanks and to vegetation. National or local

regulations concerning streamside conservation should be observed.

- Operations should maximise the volume of wood that can be profitably utilized from each felled tree and maximise the value of logs that can be prepared for extraction. Cutting crews should be trained to follow proper log making procedures. The whole tree should be measured prior to crosscutting and log lengths determined according to market or mill requirements.
- Log formation involving the cutting of branches should take place within the forest in order that nutrients in foliage can be retained within the forest ecosystem. Branches should not be removed from a forest. This practice also reduces damage to the soil and to the remaining vegetation.
- Penalties should be imposed on felling crews for careless working practices that lead to cutting or damage of future crop trees or those reserved as seed trees. Penalty arrangements should be included in management contracts that are specific to the local situation. Frequent operational monitoring is necessary in order to detect cutting damage and to identify who caused it.

Extraction

The choice of extraction method and equipment selection will depend on topography, soils and climate, tree size, number and volume, the silvicultural system being applied as a basis for sustainable management of a forest and on the economics of the specific management and harvesting operation. The following guidelines for log extraction using different extraction systems should be adapted and applied to local forest situations:

- The safety of all personnel involved in log extraction is the foremost consideration in logging. Good training of logging crews is necessary to minimise accidents.
- Minimise damage to residual trees, to other vegetation and to soils and watercourses. Select the type of log extraction system that will minimise soil compaction and soil disturbance and also minimise runoff of water and soil erosion.
- Thoughtful and comprehensive harvest planning linked to a system of operational control to ensure that a plan is followed and adapted as required in response to changing conditions.
- Delivery to a landing or roadside of all logs prepared for extraction without loss of tree identity and without significant loss of volume or deterioration in quality.
- Achievement and maintenance of high productivity in the use of personnel and equipment.
- Maximise wood production during extraction. Two effective steps are:

- Extraction of "forest residues" as an additional income source, especially for forest dependent communities,
- Minimisation of logging waste through careful cutting, tree measurement and log formation.

Extraction must be continuously and closely supervised to ensure that safety and all technical aspects of a harvesting plan are being followed as proposed. In addition, animal skidding should be supervised to ensure that animals are not being abused.

Ground Skidding Extraction

Wheeled Skidders: Wheeled skidders are the primary means of log extraction in sustainably managed tropical forests. Skidders are preferred to crawler tractors for ground extraction of logs because their rubber tyres, ability to easily manoeuvre within a forest and to lift log butts off the ground can minimise soil and tree damage. Skidders are specifically designed for log extraction and are more suitable for harvesting than are crawler tractors. They should have a powered winch. "High-flotation" tyres or dual wheels mounted on wheeled skidders increase the effective tyre width where they are in contact with the ground, thus spreading the machine weight and its load over a larger surface area, reducing pressure on the soil and reducing soil compaction and disturbance.

Tracked Skidders: Tracked skidders are preferred to wheeled skidders and crawler tractors, especially for extraction of small to medium sized logs on forest soils that are easily compacted, because they cause minimal damage to residual trees and soils. Tracked skidders have the ability to move the load forward onto the machine for better weight distribution over the tracks. Low ground pressures lead to relatively little disturbance of soils and ground vegetation, which is an important feature for protection of seedlings and saplings and for soil conservation.

Crawler Tractors: Crawler tractors are often used for skidding as well as for road construction and maintenance. They have the advantage of being effective for log extraction from steep slopes if properly used, even if equipped with only a single drum winch. In spite of the damage that can be caused to soils, residual trees, poles, saplings and seedlings through insensitive use, crawler tractors are likely to continue to be important for log extraction in steep terrain and where rainfall is high. Effective training of operators and careful supervision is necessary.

Size and Power of Skidders: Skidders of the appropriate size and power configuration for a specific operation should be selected. The blade width should be between two and three metres. Machines should have a powered winch, with at least 50 metres of wire rope, and an arch that will lift log butts clear of the ground. These features help to minimise damage to residual trees, ground vegetation and soils.

Steep Slopes: Avoid steep slopes in ground skidding operations. As a general rule, the maximum slope should be about 30 per cent, except over short distances (less than 100 metres). Ground skidding on steep slopes greatly increases soil disturbance and erosion, reduces operating efficiency and leads to faster depreciation on skidders. Log butts should always be lifted above the ground during skidding. Steeper slopes should be logged by aerial or cable systems that cause much less physical environmental damage.

Skid Trails: A carefully designed and supervised system of designated skid trails should always be used for log extraction. The following guidelines are recommended:

- Skid trail routes and density should be indicated in the harvesting plan and flag-marked within a forest. The aim is to extract logs causing the least possible damage to residual vegetation. Marking skid trail routes can assist the felling crew to align trees along skid trails. This practice reduces felling damage and extraction costs.
- Skid trails should be as straight as possible to minimise soil and vegetation damage. Sharp comers should be avoided in order to protect trees and smaller plants growing nearby.
- Skid trail formation using a blade should be kept to a minimum. Manual cutting of skid trails is much to be preferred.
- Skidders should always remain on a skid trail. Rope should be manually pulled from a skidder to each log that is to be extracted to avoid the need for skidders to leave a skid trail. This practice minimises soil disturbance, soil compaction, and damage to residual trees, poles, saplings and seedlings. Skidder ropes should be at least 50 m long.
- Skid trails and skidders should not be allowed within streamside protection strips defined in a management plan or in national or local regulations. Skid trails and skidders should not cross gullies or streams unless it is absolutely unavoidable. If crossing a stream cannot be avoided, the crossing should be on solid rock or on an installed culvert. *Uphill Skidding:* Uphill skidding is to be preferred to downhill skidding because it tends to cause less damage to soils and vegetation and also leads to more dispersed runoff of surface water. Logs being skidded uphill are more easily controlled, although uphill pulling does require more power and is more expensive. The choice of either uphill or downhill skidding in a harvesting plan needs to be evaluated and specified in a tactical harvesting plan in respect of the prevailing local forest conditions.

CABLE EXTRACTION

Cable Log Extraction in Hill and Swamp Forests: Cable log extraction is only justified in sustainably managed tropical forests that are growing on long steep slopes or hilly terrain where log harvesting is technically and economically justified and watershed conservation is not impaired. It is also appropriate for log extraction in swamp forests. Cable extraction can be operated in conjunction with tractors for harvesting in previously logged forests where there is low and variable stocking. It does however have the advantage that it is less expensive than helicopter logging.

Skyline Cable System: Only the skyline cable log harvesting system should be permitted for selection harvesting in sustainably managed tropical forests because it is much less damaging to the forest structure than is the high-lead cable system. The high-lead system should not be allowed.

LOG EXTRACTION USING DRAUGHT ANIMALS

Animal Skidding of Logs: Draught animals - specifically water buffaloes and elephants - are effective for extraction of small to medium sized logs on both flat and slightly hilly land. Animal skidding causes relatively low compaction and disturbance to soils and minimal damage to residual trees and smaller plants.

Planning

- Extraction distances should be short, not more than 200 metres and preferably down slope.
- Depending upon the type of animal being used, a maximum slope of 20 to 30 per cent for downhill skidding and 10 to 15 per cent for uphill skidding are suggested.
- Depending upon climatic conditions, terrain and log size, draught animals may not be able to work every day and may require relatively short days, no more than four hours. A reserve of animals (20 to 30 per cent) is desirable in order to maintain log production continuity.
- *Ground Preparation:* Skidding paths should be laid out and undergrowth vegetation cut to provide easy access for animals. Undergrowth should be manually cut close to the ground and thrown clear of the path. Stumps and old logs that could be an obstacle or a danger to animals should be cut low or removed. Stones should be rolled aside.

Case Study 7: Summary of Results of Skyline Logging Studies in Malaysia

A. Results of a Soil Disturbance Study After Harvesting with A Skyline Yarder

Soil Disturbance Class	Area (%)
No disturbance	97.6
Litter layer disturbed	1.1
Top layer exposed	0.7
Subsoil exposed	0.4
Subsoil heavily disturbed	0.2 100%

B. Skyline Yarding Costs for Three Operational Skyline Systems

(based on an average harvestable volume of 40 m^3/ha on a set-up of 10 ha)

System price (RM)	544,000	806,000	628,000
Work days/year	250	250	250
MOH/year	900	850	900
Production/MOH (m^3)	8.0	8.0	7.6
Labour cost (RM/hr)	9.6	11.4	11.4
Litre diesel/MOH	5	10	5
Interest (12% per year)	36.1	56.9	44.3
Insurance (1% of price)	6.0	9.5	7.4
Repairs	56.8	108.2	74.0
Fuel & Oil	3.9	7.8	3.9
Labour cost	128.0	187.0	176.0
Total Costs/MOH	331.4	524.2	428.6
Total Costs/m^3	41.4	65.5	56.4

Note: MOH == Machine Operating Hours

Working Practices

- Sledges and skidding pans can increase the productivity of animal skidding through reducing ground friction with logs and should be used if this is practicable.
- Cutting should be coordinated with skidding, both operations proceeding together towards a log landing. This working practice enables animals to walk on clear skid paths, helps to avoid accidents and increases logging productivity.
- Animals must be well cared for, fed, watered and rested regularly.
- When a skidding operation has been completed, cross-drains should be cut across skidding paths to divert surface ground water into the adjacent forest thereby reducing soil erosion.

Helicopter Extraction

Rationale: Helicopter log extraction is justified in sustainably managed tropical forests for four reasons:

- Where forests are growing on hilly land, close to stream buffer zones or on swampy land where the use of ground-based logging systems and roading could lead to unacceptable damage to soils, watercourses or to forest structure.
- Where it leads to the most economic extraction of logs to landings, given the high production rate of aerial extraction, the high value of wood, the low roading density, construction and maintenance costs, the absence of skidding trails and minimal real costs for overcoming environmental damage caused by ground-based environmental damage caused by ground-based log
- Where logs are inaccessible to ground-based extraction, such as across a gorge or above a long steep slope.

- Where it is wished to limit entry of "slash and bum" farmers to a forest where the social pressure to use land for unsustainable agriculture is both a forest protection and management risk.

Planning: Helicopter log extraction needs to be thoroughly planned and should involve teamwork by foresters, harvesting and helicopter management personnel. A harvesting plan should incorporate some flexibility to enable adjustments to be made in the event of rapidly changing working conditions. Planning should be carefully integrated with ground-based logging where there are economic, environmental or management benefits linking the use of both systems.

The guidelines for log identification and labelling are suggested:

- The identity of trees that have been cruised and labelled for harvesting should be maintained through to log formation and delivery, at least to the landing.
- Log loaders should ensure that cruising labels are firmly attached to the butt of the first log and that secondary labels are painted onto the large end of upper logs cut from the same tree. Skidder or tractor drivers should remove each cruising label that has been attached to the log butt by a cutter and carry these during log extraction to a landing. Each label should be handed to log scaling personnel on the landing. In the case of helicopter logging the identity of logs should be advised to log scaling personnel by the loader using two-way communication radio as each load is extracted to a landing.

LANDING OPERATIONS

The following practices should be applied in the design, construction and efficient operation of landings for log trimming, sorting and loading:

- *Safety:* The safety of all personnel is the foremost consideration in the conduct of landing operations and the safety and protection of all personnel and equipment working on a landing or nearby should be safeguarded. Effective training of logging crews is necessary to minimise accidents.
- *Location and Number of Landings:* Where possible, landings should be located on slightly sloping ground. A gradient of about 2 per cent is often followed. Landings should be sited away from streams to minimise soil runoff. The number of landings should be kept to a minimum to reduce the loss of productive area and to minimise costs.
- *Size of Landings:* Landings should be as small as possible, bearing in mind the need for storage and sorting of logs, vehicle turning and loading.
- Where large logs are being handled and a knuckle-boom loader is being used for loading, landings can be as small as 20 m × 25 m (500 m^2).

- Helicopters and cable logging systems require larger landings. A typical landing area for these systems is of the order of 40 m × 30 m ($1,200m^2$).
- Where landings are not needed, logs can be decked temporarily on roadsides and loaded onto trucks from there. This reduces the loss of forest, soil runoff and costs of landing operations. The use of knuckle boom loaders or self-loading trucks enables logs to be loaded directly from roads.
- ***Quality Log Handling:*** All logs should be delivered to a landing and transferred to the transport system without loss of log identity and without significant loss of volume or deterioration of quality.
- ***Site Protection from Spillage of Fuel and Lubricants:*** Care should be taken to prevent spillage of fuel and lubricants during refuelling and servicing of machinery. The refuelling area must be placed away from streams and earth ridges should be constructed to contain any spillage.
- ***Site Restoration:*** When landings are no longer needed they should be cleared of debris, including oil cans and machinery parts, compacted soil should be deep ripped and they should be planted using nursery-raised seedlings. Tree species selected should comprise those that are ecologically dominant in the locality **and** are expected to be commercially important as part of the next main crop.

LOG MEASUREMENT (SCALING)

All logs should be measured, or scaled, at landings in order that log volumes can be calculated. The measurement of log production in relation to a production target prescribed in a forest management plan is based upon consistently accurate log length and diameter measurements for deriving log volumes which is a critical indicator of sustainable management of a forest.

There are a variety of measurement methods used to estimate log volume. The choice should be made on the basis of value and log size, the scale of harvesting, the required accuracy, or as a negotiated part of a sale or management agreement. Whatever scaling system is used it must be fair to the buyer and to the seller of wood. The following practices and standards are suggested for scaling operations in tropical forests involving large logs:

- ***Responsibility:*** The forest owner as the seller of forest produce should be responsible for measuring log production. This approach is preferred to others because the owner is able to maintain firm control over the scaling procedure. In practice, the owner may not always have the personnel and supporting facilities to enable continuous scaling to be undertaken. Where this occurs, as it does on many large forest concessions, the responsibility for scaling should be delegated, as a condition of license or concession contract, to the concession holder, subject, however, to check-scaling by the forest owner.

- ***Scaling Practices:*** The following guidelines can be adapted to prevailing local conditions for scaling of logs:
  - Log identity should be painted onto both ends of every log and it should correspond with the cruising label tree number and the species code. Log identity, recorded as a code number, should be tallied against the tree number, taken from the cruising label. The species code should also be tallied.
  - Log length is assumed to be equal to the axis of the log and is measured using a logger's tape in metres and tenths of a metre along the surface. The tape must be kept parallel to the axis. The total log length should be measured and no allowance made for trim. Any trim taken off log ends should be paid for by the buyer, not the seller. This feature should be made clear in the sale and purchase agreement.
  - Log diameter used for log volume derivation is mid-length diameter, measured over-bark, using a diameter tape or callipers at a point midway from the log ends. Any debris on the log, such as mud or loose bark, should be removed from the point of diameter measurement and the tape should be kept at right angles to the axis of the log. Log diameters from circumferences, measured using a tape, should be recorded in centimetres and tenths. A bark allowance, or twice the average bark thickness, should be subtracted. Bark allowances should be determined by separate studies for each species, or groups of species. The resulting under-bark diameter is usually rounded to the nearest even diameter class.

Table: Application of a Bark Thickness Allowance

	Example 1	**Example 2**
Species	*A*	*B*
id-length diam. (over bark)	93.6 cm	81.8 cm
educt bark allowance	3.0 cm	4.0 cm
	90.6 cm	77.8 cm
ally to nearest even cm	90 cm	78 cm

- Log measurements should be tallied against the log number.
- Log volumes should be calculated using a volume table based on cylinder volumes computed using *Huber's Formula,* defined as follows:

$$V = d^2 1.\frac{\pi}{40\,r}$$

In practical terms the formula can be simplified by replacing p /40 with *0.0785398;* Huber's formula then becomes:

$$V = d^2 \, l \, 0.0785398$$

where:

V = log volume,

d = is the mid-length log diameter without bark,

l = log length

The log medium length cross-sectional diameter is also measured as the average of the small and large end diameters, under bark. This is the practice in parts of Africa.

Where exact log volumes are required, a log volume table based upon sectional measurement of logs can be used. It enables log volumes to be estimated from measurements of log length and the average diameter of the small end of logs. A volume table is calculated from a representative population of logs spanning the range log lengths and diameters of one species or of species groups that are being produced from a specific locality. Log volumes used to construct a volume table are calculated using *Smalian's formula.* It is applied to each section of log from under-bark measurements at the butt, 1.5 m, 3 m, 6 m, and so on from the butt until the small-end of the log is reached. *Smalian's formula* is defined as follows:

$V = (d^2 + D^2) \, l_s \, 0.03927$

where,

d^2 = small end diameter (under bark)

D^2 = large end diameter (under bark)

l_s = log with length 1_s

p /80 = 0.03927

V = log volume

Check Scaling: An essential feature of scaling practice is check scaling of the work of the scaling team. It should preferably be conducted by a two-person team led by a planning forester, or a qualified person who is directly supervised by a forester. Check scaling should be conducted regularly, but at randomly selected times. It should be a routine aspect of monitoring of log measurement practice.

Where a forest management unit is being managed by a concession holding company, or by an NGO on behalf of customary owners, the check scaling team should comprise company or NGO supervisory staff. Government forestry officials should conduct separate checks on scaling quality where the forest land is in State ownership. Check scaling should involve monitoring of the following three aspects of the scaling procedure:

- Log labelling and numbering practices, ensuring that log identity is clearly painted onto both ends of every log.
- That log identity is tallied against the corresponding tree number, taken from the cruising label.
- Measurements of log length and diameter and allowances for rot.

The extent of check scaling will depend upon the confidence limits imposed by a forestry authority or set by the management of a concession company or cooperative. As a working guide there should not be more than a+/- 1% difference in calculated volumes between the scaling report and check scaling of the same batch of logs. Check scaling data should be processed in the same way as the main scaling data to ensure that valid comparisons can be made. The reasons for consistent differences between check scaling and scaling should be examined and discussed with the scaling team leader with a view to eliminating the differences.

TRANSPORT OPERATIONS

Although log transport does not influence the management of tropical forests it can have an adverse impact on the forest environment and on the business operations of a company. It is for this reason that guidelines on log transport operations are provided. The aim should be to deliver logs safely to a point of destination without significant loss of volume and without adverse impacts on the forest environment. The following practices and standards should be applied in log transport operations in tropical forests:

Safety: Good training of drivers in log loading, including "tie-ing down" of loads, daily care and maintenance of vehicles and careful driving is necessary to minimise accidents.

- Trucks should never be overloaded and the load must be evenly distributed.
- Loads must be secured by binders that are of sufficient capacity to prevent logs from falling off the truck if a load should move during transport.
- Roads being used by logging trucks should be posted with warning signs, especially where trucks enter main roads.

Road Maintenance

- Roads being used for heavy log transport should be properly maintained in order to minimise erosion of the road surface and edges and for the safety of all road users. The need for adequate grovelling and grading should be planned and undertaken as a matter of practical road management where roads are being regularly used by logging trucks.
- Roads should not be used, especially by loaded trucks, after heavy rain where there is a risk of serious road surface damage. Although local conditions can vary widely it is often advisable to allow a road surface to dry out for several hours before being used again for log transport. A waiting period to enable a road to dry will often reduce road damage markedly. Earth roads should not be used at all during periods of heavy rainfall.

Refuelling: The same rules apply as for refuelling logging equipment.

HARVESTING ASSESSMENT

A harvesting assessment is a systematic check made in the field during or following harvesting to determine the degree to which the operation is or has followed a harvesting plan and has complied with its objectives. It is an essential aspect of monitoring of the operational performance of a forest manager. A harvesting assessment provides information about the quality of operations, including the volumes cut and the condition of a forest following harvesting. It may be carried out while an operation is in progress (*in-progress assessment*), or after it is completed (*post-harvest assessment*). The following guidelines should be applied in forest harvesting assessments:

- *Qualified Personnel:* Assessments should be carried out by qualified planning and supervisory staff in the presence of operational personnel who are directly responsible for harvesting activities.
- *Objectives:* The extent to which operational performance has complied with the objectives of a tactical harvest plan should be assessed by examining key aspects of the plan.
- *"In-progress" Assessment:* An "In-progress Assessment" should monitor aspects of harvesting performance that need to be checked frequently. It should be a continuous or semi-continuous activity. Specific topics that should be checked are:
  - That location and standards of roads, landings and skid trails compare with those specified in a tactical harvest plan. The use of GPS equipment can assist with checking road location.
  - That the harvest comprises only trees that have been cruised and labelled for cutting and that residual trees remain and are undamaged. Check that trees that were marked "not to be cut" but have not been felled, damaged or destroyed. If no, determine whether disciplinary action and imposition of penalties on those responsible is required. Check if trees that should have been cut have been left.
  - That protected areas, such as streamside buffer strips and places of cultural importance, remain undisturbed.
  - That directional felling, cross-cutting and log-making requirements are being complied with.
  - That all logs have been extracted and transported from landings. Ensure that no logs have been left behind.
  - That equipment and working practices conform with local safety requirements.
  - That soil disturbance is being kept to a minimum.
  - That fuel, oil and other possible contaminants are effectively contained and any spills have been properly disposed of.

   - Whether roads have been closed, where specified.
   - The effectiveness of directional felling for avoiding damage to residual trees.

Consideration should be given to applying penalties to harvesting crews where poor working practices are consistently observed.

- *"Post-harvest" Assessment:* A *post-harvest assessment* should monitor aspects of harvesting performance following an operation. It need not be carried out immediately but after sufficient time has passed for the environmental impacts caused by harvesting to become clear. This might be from six months to one year after harvesting has been completed. Specific topics to be checked are:
   - The survival status of damaged trees, especially labelled "mother" trees.
   - A comparison of the location and standards of roads, landings and skid trails with specifications in the harvest plan.
   - The extent and long-term effects of soil disturbance caused by log extraction, and determination of remedial action if any. What remedial action is required?
   - Whether protected areas, such as streamside buffer strips, have remained undisturbed,
   - Whether landings have been cleared of logging and mechanical debris and, where necessary, have been drained to prevent ponding of water. Check also whether landings need to be ripped for establishment of nursery raised tree seedlings.
   - Assess whether oil and other contaminants have been properly disposed of and what remedial action is required.
- *Reporting:* The results of harvest assessments should be reported to the relevant authorities and to logging crews who carried out the work. Where it is appropriate a report should make recommendations for remedial action, for financial payments to personnel for work meeting specified performance criteria and penalties for poor performance. Questions of specific performance criteria, rewards and penalties should be determined by the management agency in relation to prevailing local conditions.

IMPLEMENTATION OF POST HARVEST OPERATIONS

FOREST PROTECTION

Sustainable forest management can not be achieved in the absence of a firm commitment and action to effectively protect a forest management unit. Policies and legislation establishing a permanent forest estate, providing secure forest tenure, permanent definition and maintenance of forest boundaries, an operational capability to protect forests from fire and cooperation with forest communities, all contribute towards achieving effective forest protection. The following guidelines should be adapted to local forest conditions.

Forest Guards

Forest guards have an essential role for patrolling forest boundaries, roads and tracks and the interior of forest compartments to observe and monitor whether unauthorised operations may be taking place.

- Guards should work closely with harvesting, inventory and silviculture crews who also operate in a forest management unit.
- Guards should be trained for their duties, including in public relations and in fire control. Where it is practicable, they should have earlier security experience. Distinctive uniforms are essential in order that guards are easily identified when patrolling in a forest.

Fire Prevention and Control

An effective capability should be organized and maintained in a condition of operational readiness in order that a rapid and effective response to forest fire emergencies can always be made.

Fire Plan: When wildfire is perceived as a possible problem a fire plan for the prevention and control of fires should be prepared for a forest management unit, or specific parts of it, as a requirement of a forest management plan. Following approval, the fire suppression plan should be annexed to and form a part of the general management plan. Action to be taken by staff and workers if an accidental fire occurs should be clearly outlined in a fire plan, including the use of available equipment, the necessary manning strength in anticipation of a fire outbreak and the efficient clean-up and patrol of a fire area to prevent recurrence. Each fire plan should specify the following:

- The lines of command, control and communication amongst all personnel. A senior fire control officer (a fire boss), responsible to a chief forester for a forest management unit should be appointed. The fire boss could be a permanent officer having fire control responsibilities as a part of the job that also involves wood production.
- Definition of the area to be protected on a topographical map at a 1:50,000 scale. Several copies of a fire control map should be available to operational staff to assist with communication. It should show:
- Road and track access routes for vehicles, and aircraft landing points.
- Location of existing water points and proposals for construction of new water points.
  - Vegetation fire hazard class map, identifying "levels of risk" for each broad vegetation zone.
  - An equipment resources statement and specifications for procurement of new fire control equipment.

– A programme of public relations, education and advertising directed at strengthening public awareness of the need for protection of forests from wildfire.

Communications: Radio and telephone arrangements should be provided to enable a fire control organisation to work efficiently to help prevent fire and to assist in suppressing fires quickly. Telephone and portable radio systems are also valuable for general communication for other forest management operations.

Fire Danger Rating System: A fire danger rating system should be developed that is suited to the physical conditions of a province or to a forest management unit. Fire danger ratings show defined levels of fire danger, such as low, moderate or high, and are useful for explaining forest fire problems to local communities, to other sections of the general public and for putting forest staff on alert.. *Records:* A register and supporting maps should be established and maintained by a forest manager, recording the location, dates, reasons, areas and vegetation types lost or damaged by wildfires.

THE PARTICIPATION OF FOREST COMMUNITIES IN FOREST PROTECTION

Where forest communities have a traditional dependence upon tropical forests which are being managed for wood production, their participation in the overall management process is important for achieving effective forest protection. Dialogue between representatives of local communities and forest managers is essential in reaching an understanding of the respective interests, and concerns, of each side and from which the foundations of forest protection can be developed. The following guidelines can be adapted to the prevailing local conditions for protection of a forest management unit:

Sensitivity: Consultations with forest communities need to be positive, constructive and conducted with sensitivity and care using traditional as well as official discussion processes.

Informality: Consultations should be informal, conducted in the local languages, and be as easily understood as possible. It will be through informal and frequent discussion that the aspirations of local people may best be determined and understood thereby providing a firm basis for effective forest protection arrangements.

Buffer Zones: Through community consultation, promote an understanding and acceptance of the use of buffer zones as a management and protection tool in localities where forest communities interact with wood production operations.

- Buffer zones should be developed within the context of specific forest management plans. The aim is to encourage investment in agriculture, agroforestry and other perennial crop systems and to discourage utilization of forests for which firm protection is needed.

- The definition of buffer zones is a part of a wider strategy for classifying forest land where multiple use and protection of forests is contemplated. A medium to long term time horizon is necessary.
- Buffer zone development might be enhanced through the transfer of long-term land use and conditional management rights over buffer zones.

Road Closure After Harvesting: Feeder roads that are not expected to be used again until the next harvest can be closed to prevent their use by local communities. Road closure practices can include ripping the surface and planting short rotation tree crops, shrubs or tall grass.

Helicopter Logging: The reduced impacts on soils and forest vegetation that can be achieved through helicopter logging can have a protective effect on forests in relation to community relationships, as follows:

- Low road densities associated with helicopter log extraction reduces opportunities for squatters to encroach on forests and practise "slash and bum" agriculture,
- Low impact harvesting causes little damage to medicinal, food and other plants that are of traditional value to forest communities.

POST-HARVEST SILVICULTURE OPERATIONS

General Guidelines

Silvicultural operations should be implemented in accordance with specific prescriptions set out in an approved management plan for a forest. The type and purpose of tending operations to be applied in each compartment, or sub-compartment, should be determined by diagnostic sampling. Tending decisions may also be based upon the conclusions of studies that have been made to gain a better understanding of forest ecology problems which are considered to be barriers to the effective practice of silviculture.

Responsibility for the implementation of silvicultural tending should be with the director of forest operations in the forestry agency, concession or a cooperative.

Operations being implemented should be part of a silvicultural system that has been designed to contribute towards the achievement of the management objectives of a forest. Silvicultural treatments should be applied within one or two years of harvesting, before regrowth makes movement difficult. Specific post-harvest silviculture operations can include:

- Enrichment planting using nursery-raised seedlings or forest transplants.
- Release weeding, or forest cleaning, of undergrowth to reduce competition to existing seedlings, or to seedlings that might become established from seedfall.

- Liberation cutting of dense stands of trees and poles of commercial and non-commercial species.

Guidelines for Enrichment Planting and Release Weeding

The objective **of enrichment planting** and **release weeding** is to establish an acceptable stocking density of commercial tree species in a severely degraded and heavily logged forest.

Planning

- General enrichment planting standards should be expressed in the forest management plan.
- Specific proposals should be set out in the annual operational plan, based on diagnostic sampling. Compartments, timing of planting, and species to be planted should be specified.

Species to be Planted

- Species should be selected from a list set out in the forest management plan. Importance should be placed on species comprising the forest type where enrichment is proposed and those having commercial potential for wood production.

Forest Practices

- Planting lines or spots should follow contour.
- Planting lines should be at least 1.5 m wide.
- Secondary vegetation larger than 6 cm diameter within a planting line or spot should be girdled. Vegetation outside the planting line or spot which will affect the planting site should be girdled.
- Generally, the best time for planting is near the beginning of the rainy season.
- The success of establishment should be evaluated in the forest regularly by field inspection of planted trees.
- Weeding should be carried out to keep transplanted trees free of competing plant growth. The need for weeding should be determined by field inspection.

Guidelines for Silvicultural Tending

The objective of silvicultural tending is to create or maintain favourable conditions for the growth of **potential crop** trees by removing competing vegetation.

This is called*liberation.* A PCT is a species having wood of commercial value that is selected from the residual stand after logging and is tended to form the next crop of harvestable trees.

Selection Criteria for a Potential Crop Tree

- A PCT should be a listed timber species for the locality, known to grow to loggable size (over 50 cm dbh). From an economical point of view, listed species should be defined by the forestry authority and should be shown in two lists, *preferred species* and *acceptable species. Protected species* should be listed separately and should include rare or endangered species and fruit trees.
- It should be at least 5 cm dbh. A cluster of small trees may be equivalent to one PCT, providing the cluster has three or more individuals between 2 m in height and 5 cm dbh. There should be more than five individuals if less than 2 m in height.
- A PCT should have a vigorous, well-developed crown.
- It should have a straight, clear stem with no visible defects or injuries and should be a stable tree without a pronounced slant.
- A tree standing on the edge of a steep slope, a road cutting or within 20 m of a watercourse should not be selected.
- It should not be under the shade of another selected PCT.

Selecting between Two Potential Crop Trees

- When a choice between two trees has to be made select the tallest tree having the larger diameter.
- If both PCTs are of the same size select the *preferred* species over the *acceptable* species. If both are either *preferred* or *acceptable* species, select the tree having the longer bole. If both are equal in all respects, select the tree with the most uniform spacing.
- Select the PCT which is least likely to be damaged by the falling of a poison-girdled tree.

Liberating a Potential Crop Tree

- Except for protected species, all trees competing directly with a selected PCT for overhead light should be removed. Trees whose crowns are well below those of a PCT need not be cut.
- Individuals of preferred or acceptable species which are defective may be removed. Individuals of pioneer species may be removed if it is considered that they will compete with a PCT. Trees whose stem or branches may be or are rubbing a PCT should be removed.

It is not the purpose of these *Guidelines* to provide more specific guidance on the technical aspects of silviculture that can be applied in the management of tropical forests.

7

Indian Forest Law and Policy

After Independence, however, and according to the newly enacted Indian Constitution, forests were placed under the so-called 'state list' according to which state legislatures have a primary right to make laws. In 1976, the Indian Forest Act was added to the concurrent list of the Constitution of India, giving the Central Government and states shared responsibility and control over forest matters. Thereby the Government of India does have the power to legislate on forestry issues but only after consulting the states. The responsibility for administering the forests lies primarily with the state government. The relative position of the Government of India depends on several factors, such as its contribution to the state budget and state polities. The balance of power between central and state governments has remained a key issue in forest management ever since. After 1947, in a post-independent India, commercial exploitation and degradation of India's forests increased dramatically. Indeed, the 1952 National Forest Policy set out guidelines which were, for the most part, directed towards the supply of cheap timber and non-timber forest products for state-sponsored industrialization and modernization. In 1980, with the passage of the Forest Conservation Act, the central government reasserted some of its control over forest-based resources. The Act restricts the state government's power to de-reserve a forest, and it restricts the use of forestland for non-forestry purposes without the prior approval of the central government. Unilateral decisions from the centre have prevailed from then onwards. Only six centres were set up to monitor forests and conservation (as per the Act), which is obviously insufficient for effective regional implementation in a country the size of India. Thus the Forest Conservation Act of 1980 has been problematic for a number of reasons, and has achieved little improvement in the 'conservation' of India's forests.

The National Forest Policy of 1988 envisaged people's involvement in the development and protection of forests *for the first time*. It stipulated that the requirements of people living in and near forests for fuel wood, fodder and small timber should be treated as the top priority, and forest communities should be motivated to identify themselves with the development and protection of forests from which they derive benefits. A primary task of all agencies responsible for forest management, including the forest development corporations, should be to engage tribal peoples closely in the protection, regeneration and development of forests, as well as to provide gainful employment to people living in and around the forests. However the 1988 National Forest Policy has never been translated into law. It remains essentially a broad statement of government intent and does little in the way of specifying any legal rights or duties owed to forest communities-especially the tribal/indigenous peoples.

FOREST POLICY

1894. Although the foundations of regular forest management were laid in the sixties of the nineteenth century, it was not until 1894 that the Government of India adopted the forest policy that constitutes the Magna Carta for the forests of India. Since then the vital role of the forests in relation to agriculture, industry, transportation and defence, has received increasing recognition. Their protective functions have also come to be better understood.

The old forest policy was designed largely for the former British provinces. Its provision for the relinquishment of forest land "without hesitation" for the extension of agriculture-subject to certain conditions honoured chiefly in the breach-led to undesirable consequences.

In the original policy no mention was made of sustained yields, working plans, forest education, or forest research; nor was any cognizance taken of wildlife, an important and attractive feature of India's forests.

THE NEW POLICY

The recent constitutional changes have directed attention to the shaping of an over-all policy for the country. The government has revised the forest policy in relation to the progress that has been made in the physical, economic and political fields. The New Policy of 1952 provides, among other things, for the classification of forests into:

- Protection Forests, the preservation of which is directed by purely physical and climatic considerations;
- National Forests, to be maintained and managed to meet the needs of defence, industry and transportation;
- Village Forests, to be maintained for their role in the agricultural economy of the country, such as provision of firewood and of small timber for agricultural implements and dwellings;
- Treelands, or areas covered with tree growth of some sort, which, though outside the scope of regular forest management, are essential to the amelioration of the physical environment. These classes are by no means mutually exclusive, since each forest usually fulfills functions subsidiary to those specifically assigned to it.

The notion, once widely entertained, that forests as such have no inherent right to land, but may be permitted on sufferance on residual land not required for other purposes, is being effectively dispelled. In the New Policy, the protective and productive role of the forests finds recognition in a directive to the effect that a proportion of the whole land area to be determined by each state should be permanently maintained under forest. Each group of villages is to have a complement of forest, constituting a fuel, fodder and timber reserve.

Under the New Policy, moreover, attention is given to such matters as:

- Balanced land use; putting each type of land to such use that it will produce most and deteriorate least;
- State control of private forests;
- Preservation of wildlife;
- Control of grasing;
- Control of shifting cultivation;
- Provision against fluctuating budgets.

Special provision is also made for the training of forest personnel, for forest legislation and for research. The principle of sustained yield and the need of setting up an organisation for dealing with working plans have both been especially stressed.

POLICIES IN INDIA ON PRODUCTION FORESTRY

NATIONAL AGRICULTURAL POLICY

National Commission on Agriculture (NCA) recommended a change over from the conservation-oriented forestry to more dynamic programme of production forestry. According to the Commission, production of industrial wood would have to be the main reason for the existence of forests and should be project-oriented and economically feasible.

The NCA recommended against leasing forestlands to industry and instead wanted government to allocate them forest raw material through enhancing commercial forestry. For the purpose of commercial forestry, it further recommended that out of 64 million hectare (Mha) of forest lands available in India at that time 48 Mha should be brought under production forestry and remaining 16 Mha for biological diversity.

NATIONAL FOREST POLICY (NFP)

NFP, 1952 acknowledged the need for sustained supply of timber and other forest produce to meet the developmental need of various industries. The policymakers had two major objectives in mind while framing NFP 1952. First to ensure that forests were preserved and managed on a sustainable basis, and second to use them for meeting national interest as a source of timber. Since both these objectives somewhat opposed each other, NFP came up with a concept of '*treelands*'. It identified the scope for involving state governments as well as various other institutions, such as, Defence, Rail-ways, Public Works Departments, Universities and Colleges, Boards, Municipalities and other local authorities, associations and institutions in the process by converting the land at their disposal into treelands. To ensure that the needs of forest-based industries are met without putting undue pressure on forests the need to substitute tree-species of commercial importance in place of inferior tree–species was advocated. The policy also mentioned involving both the industries and individuals in a bigger manner and emphasised on considering commercial and industrial interests for establishing closer contacts and bonding between Forest Research Institutes and industries utilising timber and forest products.

Forest Conservation Act, 1980

The Act put a ban on the de-reservation of forests or use of forestland for non-forest purpose. The Act of 1980, consequently, brought the subject of forests from state list to concurrent list enabling the parliament of India to look into the matter of forests. After the Act, no state government could use forestland for non-forest purposes without prior endorsement by the central government. This put up a check not only on the conversion of forests but also brought to halt the fragmentation of the remaining forests. This ensured that a local party could not take the decision of diverting the forests for taking up any political mileage. The centre acted as an independent agency, to which the state governments and their decisions were answerable.

National Forest Policy, 1988

The NFP, 1988 looked upon forests not as a source of raw material for commercial purposes, but primarily for conserving soil, water and biodiversity besides meeting subsistence requirements of the local people. The policy clearly mentioned that the economic utilities coming from the forests would be secondary to this prime aim.

The NFP 1988 shifted the official focus from fuelwood and timber to the management of forests primarily for their services. It made it imperative to ensure that the forests are not only conserved but also their cover and productivity is increased so as to meet the demand of goods and services coming from forests. The policy, while addressing the production forestry programme, expressed its concern in plugging the increasing demand-supply gap of fuelwood and meeting the national needs. But it explicitly mentioned that no such activity should result in any sort of clear felling of already existing natural forests. It expressed the desire that such programmes should help the country meet with its objective of achieving one-third forest cover. The policy put a thrust on meeting two important concerns of utilising the wastelands and increasing tree cover by promoting major forestry programmes. To reduce the pressure on forests, it also aimed at promoting substitution of wood besides encouraging better and efficient utilisation of forest produce. Since land plays an important role in taking up plantations, it advocated that a slight modification in land laws should be taken up so that the process becomes smooth for the investors.

At the same time, it maintained that any sort of leasing should be in coherence with the existing land ceiling act. The policy discouraged the earlier trend of meeting raw material requirements of forest-based industry by operating on natural forests. It directed these industries to meet their requirements by establishing a direct relationship with individuals who had the capacity to do so. The industry was encouraged to chip in by contributing its resources and expertise at various levels during the total project duration. The policy also gives more importance to native species over the exotic species. It discourages the use of exotic species without prior scientific trials to establish that there are no adverse effect on the environment.

National Forestry Action Programme, India (NFAP), 1999

The NFAP aimed to prepare an action plan for next 20 years, in conformity with NFP 1988. It is a comprehensive strategic plan to address the issue underlying the major problems of the forestry sector and to reverse the process of degradation for sustainable development of forests. The consumption of fuel-wood in India was reported to be about five times higher than what could be sustainably removed from forests. Further, a large tract of forestland was claimed (nearly 4.3 Mha) for undertaking industrialisation and developing infrastructure necessary for meeting the development goals of the nation. The NFAP aimed at meeting the requirements of forest based industries without compromising the conservation and protection of natural forests.

The basic purpose of NFAP was to establish direct linkage between the NFP and the National Five-Year Plans (FYP). In the past, a comprehensive and constant programme structure for forestry was found missing. Every plan had its own programme structure. So it was difficult to find linkages and establish trends. Although plans had specified objectives and programmes, the main activity under most of them was tree planting. NFAP recognised the capability of plantations to help conserve the natural forests by providing an alternative source for forest products. The Programme was also optimistic regarding the capability of plantations to earn foreign exchange, besides meeting the domestic requirements of the country. The Programme admitted that despite the policy addressing direct relationship between industry and farmers, the government did not adequately support private initiatives. It raised concern on the inability of the government to provide these initiatives with relevant research, extension, technological packages, input delivery, and market information or credit facilities. It felt and remarked that it was imperative to encourage small operators, keep them interested in sustainable forestry development and understand their needs adequately.

NFAP suggested looking at these plantations as a means of raw material for industries or for meeting energy requirements. It intended to conserve and rehabilitate 31 Mha of degraded forests (less than 40 per cent crown density) in addition to bringing 29 Mha of non-forest land under plantations. It advocated the use of different strategies for both these targets. The problem of degraded forests was to be tackled by involving local communities, especially the areas near villages through Joint Forest Management (JFM). For non-forest land, market-oriented massive tree plantation drive involving multiple agencies was proposed. The NFAP came up with a strategic approach to meet its objectives. The approach had five interrelated 'strategic areas' which formed the very basis of the Programme. These approaches were:

- Protect existing forest resources
- Improve forest productivity
- Reduce total demand
- Strengthen policy and institutional framework
- Expand forest area

The state governments while preparing the State Forestry Action Programmes (SFAPs) incorporated all planned activities as part of these activities.The NFAP recommended that for the sustainability of forests, the productivity of forest plantations was to be increased at least 3 to 5 cubic meter per ha per year (m^3/ha/yr) by promoting regeneration and enrichment of plantations. Plantations to be carried out on all categories of wastelands were also suggested. Keeping in mind the fuelwood requirements of the country, emphasis was paid on taking up plantations of fuelwood species on non-forest wasteland. Strengthening the institutions for people's participation in protection and development of degraded and fringe forests was emphasised.

Regarding the financing part of the programme, the sources of funds were grouped under four broad categories, namely, domestic public financing, domestic private financing, external public financing, and external private financing.

NATIONAL ENVIRONMENT POLICY

National Environment Policy (NEP), 2004

NEP emphasised the need to develop a strategy to meet the goal of raising the forest cover of the nation to 33 per cent by 2012. It promoted the involvement of non-forestry sector as well. For increasing the forest and tree cover of the nation, multiple stakeholder partnerships have been recognised where each stakeholder would have his role clearly defined. For achieving the aforesaid target of 33 per cent forest cover, the NEP 2004 suggested that the afforestation activities should be taken up on degraded land, wastelands as well as private land holdings. Key elements of the strategy would include: (i) implementation of multi-stakeholder partnerships involving the Forest

Department, local communities, and investors, with clearly defined obligations and entitlements for each partner, following good governance principles, to derive environmental, livelihood, and financial benefits; and (ii) rationalisation of restrictions on cultivation of forest species outside notified forests, to enable farmers to undertake social and farm forestry where their returns are more favourable than cropping. The policy called for development of a strategy to achieve the targets set for the eleventh five-year plan.

The problem of climate change and its underlying causes in global warming and increased usage of GHGs has been addressed in the Policy. It identifies deforestation in the country as one of the reasons for climate change expresses concern that India and other developing nations would be affected the most by climate change. The current level of emission in India is substantially lower than that of the developed nations; however, India's economic growth could result in an increase in GHG emission. However, government policies favouring renewable energy and afforestation projects as well as the growth of less energy intensive service sectors would result in a decrease in the level of emissions.

PLANNING COMMISSION REPORTS

Report on Leasing of Degraded Forest Lands, 1999

The Report was of the view that the degraded forestland should not be leased out to private entrepreneurs. In accordance with NFP 1988, it recommended that industries needing forest raw material should establish contact with farmers. The government would lease land to Forest Development Corporation (FDC) who, in turn, would enter into proper MoU with the user agency without leasing the land to them, as per the GOI guidelines of 1994. This MOU would give the user agency the right to undertake afforestation and take a fixed percentage of forest produce at the time of harvesting.

The Report recommended leasing barren land far away from habitations, available in plots of 1000 ha or more, and of no use to the villagers. These are desert or ravine or saline lands, which require huge investment before they can be made productive.

The Report gives reference of Investment Promotion Scheme of Ministry of Rural Development, Government of India wherein such enterprises would be entitled to 25 per cent subsidy on their capital investment. This means that the land needed for production purposes could be mobilised for meeting the demand of industry provided the industry is ready to put in huge investment besides following the guidelines. The report estimated that 33 Mha of degraded non-forest lands and 27 Mha of degraded forests (a total of 60 Mha) would be available for tree growing.

The Report also addresses the issue of difference between barren and degraded lands. Uncultivated public land was classified under these two categories. Barren land were defined as having forest/tree cover less than 10 per cent whereas degraded land were classified as having forest/tree cover between 10 to 40 per cent.

Greening India for Livelihood Security and Sustainable Development, 2001

Greening India Programme proposes to cover 43 Mha degraded land (15 Mha of degraded forestland, 10 Mha of degraded irrigated land, and 18 Mha of degraded rainfed land). It recognises that there exist numerous problems that make the implementation of agroforestry programmes difficult:

- Cumbersome legislation with respect to tree felling, wood transportation and processing.
- Lack of market information and infrastructure
- Dearth of appropriate agroforestry models
- Absence of economic security and incentives for tree growers
- Lack of extension training and demonstration
- Non-availability of quality planting material
- Unfavourable Import and Export policy

The Report highlighted the lessons learnt from the farm forestry programme:

- Tree planting should not be undertaken in uncultivable lands, but in cultivated-field and homesteads.
- All wastelands, non-forest areas and degraded forestlands should be brought under silvi-pastoral system with suitable species for fuel and fodder production. This can be addressed through JFM.
- Coastal land through afforestation, ravines and sand dune area for land reclamation, area under mining leases, water-logged areas can be targeted for converting into forested land.

Five-Year Plans

Forestry has also been covered from the first five-year plan, though it remains neglected most of the time in the planning process. Of the total fund allocated to various sectors, funds for forestry in India hovered around 1 per cent only. The expenditure on forestry sector has increased substantially since sixth five-year plan in accordance with the increase in afforestation activities undertaken to meet the desired targets. The sixth five-year plan coincided with the FCA 1980. So the increase in spending on forestry sector can be attributed to a shift in governmental policies. In the fifth plan, the spending was a meagre ₹.107.28 crore, which increased to ₹.15964.06 crore at the end of ninth five-year plan. The area afforested under the same time period has increased from 12.21 hectares to 80.50 hectares. The comparison shows that the spending has increased at a much higher rate than the afforested area. The area afforested under seventh, eight and ninth year plan has been almost same, but the spending has almost tripled in same time period. This shows that growing trees alone will not make these afforestation activities successful. Proper care and maintenance of the area afforested needs higher allocation of money. In fact, money spent in ninth five-year plan was close to 90 per cent of what had been spent till date in the country on these activities. This sends positive signals regarding finance to the project proponents and implementers about the success of afforestation.

Tenth Five-Year Plan (2002-2007)

The current five-year plan targets to increase the forest/tree cover to 25 per cent. It agrees that no strategy would be successful unless and until the basic needs are met. Recognising the role played by JFM in regeneration of degraded forests, the plan recommends taking further steps in identifying its strengths and weaknesses, so that the area under implementation can be increased. Raising concern on high imports of round timber and other forest produce, it expresses a desire for reversing this trend. This could be achieved by utilising community land, degraded forests or private farmlands of the country.

Implementing the same would mean removal of government subsidies, regulation of tariff on imports and other such policy modifications, which will make the plantation activities more desirable among farmers and village communities. Promotion of technology, credit support, developing marketing infrastructure and providing extension and training to interested farmers has also been recommended. Policy recommendations for tackling the problems related to constraint of felling, transportation and selling of forest produce which act as disincentive for growing trees are also suggested. This asks for creating a favourable policy environment, which promotes positive interaction among various stakeholders.

Keeping up with the challenges facing the society, plan proposes to utilise the wastelands and degraded lands for taking up CDM projects. This would help in utilising the wastelands besides generating additional incentives for taking up plantations. Emphasis has been put on growing species such as *Jatropha curcas* and *Pongamia pinnata*, which also grow naturally and can be utilised for generating bio-diesel, although success of these schemes are yet to be fully realised.. These plantations are cost-effective and easily replicable. To take up the afforestation activities more seriously all programmes have been merged under a single scheme called 'National Afforestation Programme (NAP)'. It is being operated through Forest Development Agencies (FDAs). Similarly, another programme named National Action Programme to Combat Desertification under UN Convention to Combat Desertification (UNCCD) has been taken up by MoEF. A 20 years' comprehensive NAP to combat desertification in the country was prepared with the following objectives:

- Community based approach to development,
- Activities to improve the quality of life of the local communities,

- Raising awareness,
- Drought management preparedness and mitigation,
- R&D initiatives and interventions which are locally suited,
- Strengthening self-–governance leading to empowerment of local communities.

For the Tenth Five-Year Plan, it has been proposed to initiate activities that include, among others, assessment and mapping of land degradation, drought monitoring and early warning system groups, drought preparedness contingency plans, and on-farm research activities for development of indigenous technology, etc.

The growing demand of raw material from our natural resources is threatening them. Envisaging the threat to the natural resources due to growing demand of raw material,is, the plan Plan proposes to take up plantation, which would reduce pressure on the natural forests and reverse the negative impact of deforestation while meeting the increasing demand. The Plan proposes to encourage agro-forestry by promoting technology, extension, and training, credit support, marketing infrastructure, etc., and providing a policy environment, which assures the farmers of a remunerative price. It also proposes to removes the constraints of felling, transport and marketing of forest produce from private holdings in different States and to formulate a common guideline for this purpose.

The current mean annual increment (MAI) of forest plantations varies from about 2 m^3/ha/year for valuable timber species to about 5-8 m^3/ha/year for eucalyptus and other fast growing species. Generally, MAI is around 10 m^3/ha/year in good quality plantations in various countries. This poor performance of forest plantation remains a great concern in the area of policy decisions. The Plan suggests measures including appropriate site selection, site-species matching, planting of elite clones, proper maintenance and protection, timely tending, thinning, irrigation, application of manures and pesticides, etc. for improving the productivity of plantations. For improving the utilisation of plantation, the plan identifies Indian Plywood Industries Research and Training Institute (IPIRTI) to be actively involved. IPIRTI can also help develop programmes that will not only fulfill the demand, but also provide with more wood substitutes.

POLICIES GOVERNING FOREIGN TRADE IN FORESTRY PRODUCE

Timber price in India has been increasing at the rate of 15 per cent per year, making import of timber more attractive, and Tthe current import policy allows duty free import of timber and pulp. In order to help wood-based industries meet their requirements, the government removed the trade barriers and liberalised the import of timber on Open General License (OGL). For industries, it was a welcome step and had an additional benefit of growth of industries in the coastal belt. This policy change led to increased import of timber. However, the produce from the imported timber is sold mainly in domestic market and there is practically no export of products against import. Export is less than one tenth of import. India's foreign exchange reserve as well as interest of tree growers has been put under an unwanted pressure. It created a sense of insecurity among tree growers of the country who now had to be satisfied with a smaller share of the market, as global players offered attractive deals to capture a bigger share of the growing market. Despite tough competition from the forestry sector and importing agencies, farmers are still supplying 50 per cent of wood supplies from their holdings. The importance and potential of agroforestry and several other such models has not been realised.

The acceptance of timber from plantations as raw material in wood based industries has opened new avenues for these farmers. However, to give a boost to tree growing activity as a means for import substitution, certain policy initiatives were felt necessary and were recommended.

- To impose heavy import duty on such wood products, which are/can be produced within the country to meet domestic needs.
- Enhance R&D efforts to manufacture quality products from plantation grown wood and other renewable fibres for import substitution.
- Export of wood and natural fibre based products promoted through incentives and simplification of procedure.
- Evolution and implementation of minimum mandatory material and product standards.
- Mechanism for collection and dissemination of information regarding import, export, prices and trade of timber needs to be developed.

The import of various wood-based commodities has been quite high than the exports both in terms of quantity and money involved. Though the exports have increased a bit compared to import in year 1999-00 over 1998-99, huge gap still remains. Besides, the farmers would find it difficult to make a financial comeback to take up this activity again if their initial investment does not return enough profit. Moreover, import of wood reduces the option of generating additional employment opportunities in the country, which would be easily taken up by the low-income class. A general reason cited for this import has been to reduce pressure on forests. Production forestry, farm forestry, agroforestry, if utilised to their hilt can do away with this import, which as of now puts a burden of ₹. 8,000 crores annually. Moreover, this would also help achieve the goal of one-third forest cover. Now the industries are also interested in taking up these activities by building relationship with farmers. The north-western part of the country took these efforts on a large scale, and massive plantations of eucalyptus and poplar were raised. However, a lack of organised market along with government policies, which make the process of harvesting trees and their transportation cumbersome, did not allow this effort to get the optimum revenues.

Wood import under Open General License (OGL) made the proposition of importing wood raw material more attractive. Generally, this imported wood comes from natural forests outside the country. In many cases, the harvesting procedure is unsustainable. In a way, these steps save Indian forests at the cost of forests in other wood-exporting countries. In today's scenario of climate change, a phenomenon occurring at one place can have complex implications at far off distances as well. So the problem gets transferred instead of getting solved. So the solution lies in raising more trees within the country. This will provide incentive for local farmers and a disincentive for those countries indulging in these unsustainable activities by taking benefit of imperfect market conditions.

Financing Schemes

Institutional funding is very important in areas where a farmer-industry relationship is to be established. In order to promote the afforestation activities, the central government has been spending money through the five-year plans. Schemes such as Investment Promotional Scheme have been instrumental in initiating and promoting production forestry throughout the nation, though not as successfully as they were initially conceived.

The experience in the last two decades show that institutional funding has been minimal in forestry programmes. These are some important reasons:

- Dearth of technical and economic data on different farm forestry models. This limits the ability of banks to evaluate bank ability of various farm forestry projects.
- Producers and banks often find the associated risk unacceptable. There are no insurance system to guard against the loss to producers and banks arising from various natural calamities.
- The lending banks do not have adequate capability to assist in formulation and appraisal of projects for farm forestry.

Investment Promotional Scheme

The Scheme was launched in the year 1994-95 in order to stimulate involvement of the corporate sector/financial institutions, etc. to pool in resources for development of non-forest wastelands.

The principal objectives of the scheme were:

- To facilitate/attract/channelise/mobilise resources from financial institutions, banks, corporate bodies including user industries and other entrepreneurs for development of wastelands in non-forest areas belonging to Central and State Governments, panchayats, village communities, private farmers, etc.

- To promote group of farmers belonging to different categories, namely, large, small, marginal and SCs/STs for bringing wastelands under productive use.
- To facilitate production and flow of additional biomass including farm-forestry products used as raw material inputs for different types of industries.
- To facilitate employment generation through land development and other allied land based and related activities including plantations.

The Scheme was restructured to make it broad-based and circulated to all the states and other concerned in August 1998. Under this Scheme, Central Promotional Subsidy was limited to ₹. 25 lakhs or 25 per cent of the project cost for on-farm development activities, whichever was less, subject to condition that the promoter's contribution in the project shall not be less than 25 per cent of the project cost. The projects promoted by the Scheduled Commercial Banks (SCBs), Regional Rural Banks, Land Development Banks and Cooperative Banks were eligible for promotional grant/subsidy under the Scheme. Under the Scheme, 41 projects covering an area of 1435 ha with a total cost of ₹.16.88 crores (firmed up by the bank) and subsidy of ₹. 1.09 crores have been sanctioned up to March, 2004. Because of slow progress, the Scheme was discontinued in 2003-04.

Tax Deductions

Tax deduction is an important financial incentive for production forestry. The Government of India announced tax deduction to companies for carrying out projects of softwood plantation on degraded non-forest land.

NATIONAL FOREST POLICY OF JOINT FOREST MANAGEMENT

One outcome of the National Forest Policy was the launching of Joint Forest Management (JFM) initiatives by all the States and Union Territories. However, there have been no accompanying changes in the legal framework for JFM, and in almost all states it has been implemented through administrative orders, which do not take the existing infrastructure into consideration. Forests continue to be looked upon as the property of the Government and the delegation of management responsibilities to local communities is merely an administrative arrangement, falling short of any real devolution of power to local communities. As an illustration. Prakash Kashwan has looked into JFM from various points of view and highlights some other problems. One of the most important findings is that JFM has been allowed only in degraded forest, but in order to bring more communities under the ambit of such programme, communities have had to actively pursue degradation of natural forest. Furthermore, JFM requires the demarcation of boundaries between villages, often for the first time, but poor implementation has resulted in many boundary conflicts. Joint Forest Management (JFM) in the state of Jharkand.

- JFM in the state of Jharkand is based on the premise that people are to blame for the destruction of the forest. The objective, therefore, is gradually to diminish people's dependence on forests.
- The Resolution to introduce JFM has been made unilaterally by the Forest Department. There is no scope for consultation with the people, no effort at consensus building, and no mechanism for dissemination of information.
- The resources required for villagers' needs are to be extracted from the protected forest according to the micro/annual-working plan. There is no mention of the existing rights of the villagers to use the produce from these forests. This is a gross violation of customary rights.
- A 33 per cent share in net profits was promised. Now the promise is to share 90 per cent of net profits with the forest dwellers. The profits however, are from commercial productions, which are not based on local needs, thus indicating the focus on commercialization of forest. The JFM Resolution in Jharkhand is simply an extension of the undivided Bihar Forest Policy (Jharkhand used to be part of Bihar before it became a separate state), which adopted Joint Forest Management in 1990. Jharkhand Forest Department adopted the JFM Resolution on 27th September 2001
- The Forest Department claims to have formed 2034 Village Forest Management and Conservation Committees and Eco-Development Committees managing an area of 5,589 sq. km. in a remarkably short time span. However, local people emphatically rejected JFM. Apparently, the figure is manipulated and incorrect.

Eviction of communities as Forest Encroachers

Indigenous peoples feel that measures that were put in place in the name of protecting the forest have only deprived them of their resources. The JFM initiatives have failed from the point of view of indigenous peoples, and there has also been widespread eviction of communities from forests. The forest department uses any means available to alienate the forest communities from the forest, reduce their dependence on the forest in the name of forest protection and conservation, and invite private partners and multinational companies to negotiate directly with village committees to access forests for carbon trading, Clean Development Mechanisms and trade in eco-services.

The direction of forest management is thus very far from anything that takes traditional forest related knowledge into account or that recognises the rights of indigenous peoples to maintain their traditional forest practices; rather, it aims to separate them from the forests, and sets up an externally imposed process of commodification and marketing of forest goods.

Indigenous Peoples' Rights and Forest Management

The Government of India is not a signatory to the ILO Convention 169 and as such does not recognize indigenous peoples. It does recognise "Scheduled Tribes", but not all indigenous groups are scheduled. Some of the indigenous groups are recognized by the Government of India as Scheduled Tribes and enjoy a degree of special status. Some of the areas where the Scheduled Tribes live have been demarcated as Scheduled areas and under the Indian Constitution Sixth Scheduled provisions, Autonomous District Councils have been set up for local administration of the Scheduled Tribes. In theory there are some measures to protect the interests of Scheduled Tribes. The Constitution empowers the President of India and state governors to withhold any law considered detrimental to tribal/indigenous peoples' interests in Scheduled Areas. Items V and VI of the Indian Constitution give special privileges to the Scheduled Tribes and the Panchayats Act (Extension to the Scheduled Areas), 1996 (PESA) is also designed to offer some protection. However, in practice most of the laws restrict the rights of and control of forest communities. Specifically, the Indian Forest Act (IFA), Forest Conservation Act (FCA) and Wildlife Protection Act (WLPA) continue to be used to hound forest dwellers.

JFM and CFM are present in most Indian states, but are simply plantation programmes related to timber and other economic products, which have nothing in essence to do with forests. They should include Village Forest Committees directly representing the community living in or using the forest. These programmes are operational to varying degrees in different places with varying degrees of participation of indigenous peoples depending upon the local situation. The involvement of indigenous peoples is focused on providing them with a share in the economic benefits and *de facto* also acts to wean them away from their dependence on forests. In other words, integral to these programmes is a subtle (in some cases blatant) redefinition of indigenous peoples' relationship to the forests. The degree of incorporation of TFRK is varied, if there is any at all; the expertise is provided by the forest department, sometimes in partnership with NGOs.

Indigenous peoples' rights to the forests are progressively minimized. In some cases, indigenous peoples do receive some economic benefits (though in others non-indigenous peoples dominate the Village Protection Committees), and in the context of the takeover of resources necessary for basic survival and consequent deprivation, these economic benefits at times are seen as a steady source of survival income. This in certain cases has superficially reduced tensions and conflicts between the forest department and the indigenous peoples as a sense of co-existence is manufactured. However, this also means that the forest department is able to stifle protests and resistance. In many places, where the indigenous peoples' political consciousness is well developed, they keep away from or oppose these programmes leading to conflicts, as has happened in parts of Madhya Pradesh. India's report to UNFF3 (2002) describes measures taken to make use of indigenous capacity and local knowledge in participatory forest management. Clearly, the picture painted by this report is not matched by the situation on the ground.

RIGHTS OVER FOREST RESOURCES

The tribal people are facing serious problems with regard to utilisation and rights over forest resources. Due to the increasing pressure on forests by various interest groups, there is a corresponding pressure on the tribals to reduce their dependency on forests. This is creating serious situations of conflict, as tribal life is symbiotic with land and forests and their livelihood and culture are based on their relationship with the natural wealth around them. The tribals are being harassed for using forestlands and being evicted in many places. Such reports have come from places like Khammam, Visakhapatnam, Vizianagaram, Adilabad, Srisailam and other places. In Khammam in one particular village, the forest and police departments allegedly branded the tribals on their shoulders as an indication that they were destroying the forests. There are ambiguities in forest-revenue land demarcation. In some places like Nellore district, a lot of land on Velugonda hills is indicated as 'poramboku' in revenue records and as RF as per the forest department. These lands do not have any forest growth. The FD is taking up palm oil plantation in these RF lands (which is not a forest species). However, landless tribals are booked in criminal cases or prohibited from using these lands for agricultural cultivation. These lands should be given to tribals with pattas for cultivation.

In some areas like in Visakhapatnam district, the lack of clear forest boundaries is making tribals vulnerable to the exploitation of both the forest and revenue departments. A joint survey and demarcation of boundaries by both departments should be immediately taken up to arrest these conflicts. Such Joint surveys need to involve the villagers at various levels. The Forest-Revenue Boundary dispute is a perpetual problem in Adilabad and Warangal districts, leading to booking of cases by the Forest department and tension in these tribal villages. In Visakhapatnam Agency and Nallamala areas, there is the unique problem of Enclosure Villages. There were many tribal villages that were not enumerated in the forest surveys. Due to such sheer negligence, the villages were not given revenue status and to this day, they do not have pattas for their lands. They face constant harassment from local forest officials, as they do not possess land records. Recognizing these enclosure villages and issuing pattas to tribals should immediately resolve this problem. In Buttapur

(Adilabad district) and in Nellore Dt. (Yanadis), the tribals were given lands decades ago under the social forestry scheme and are cultivating there. But due to lack of pattas, they are being harassed by the police and forest departments and also do not have access to bank loans as they cannot prove their ownership. These tribals have to be given pattas as promised.

Attacks on tribals, their properties and livestock by wildlife are not compensated by the Forest Department. Several cases are pending where tribals have been either killed or disabled and yet have not received any monetary compensation as due to them under the Wildlife Act. The tribals should not be prohibited from entering the forests to collect NTFP for their domestic requirements, like firewood, medicinal herbs, food, or agricultural and housing material.

The tribals should not be defined as 'encroachers', as is being projected by the forest department and also as indicated in the Circular of IG Forests, MoEF dated 3rd May 2002. In districts like Visakhapatnam, East Godavari and Vizianagaram, where there is high prevalence of podu cultivation, the tribals are facing threats of eviction from the forest department. There was a notification issued by the government of A.P in 1987 ordering that pre-1980 settlements will not be evicted until further orders. This should be implemented. The JFM programme now renamed as the Community Forest Management programme of the A.P Forest Department has caused grievous violations with regard to tribal rights. One major violation is the displacement of tribals from their podu lands by reclaiming them back into the forests through the JFM programme. The official reports of the forest department and the World Bank (which has funded the project) reveal that 37,000 hectares of forestland has been reclaimed back from the people§. The APFD further states its intention of displacing tribals in G.O. where it calls for voluntary surrender of lands by involving NGOs to motivate people under the CFM programme. The APFD has come up with a proposal for rehabilitation of tribals displaced from their podu lands through a monetary and schematic approach. This should be condemned as it bypasses the issue of eviction and rights of people over their podu lands. Their act of reclaiming lands under JFM programme and the APFD's forestry project under World Bank assistance has to be scrutinized closely by the Commission.

Samata and a few other NGOs raised this issue by writing to the World Bank on its violations of its own Operational Directives 4.2 and 4.3 in its financial support to the APFD. This has led to the Bank's insistence on an R&R policy to be proposed and implemented by the APFD in its CFM programme In Srisailam area, the Rajiv Gandhi Tiger Sanctuary has led to eviction of tribals from their original homes. They have not been properly settled so far. The concept of EDC (Eco Development Committees) that was introduced is working to the detriment of the tribals, as the objective of this programme was to reduce the forest dependency of the tribals. The tribals are given income-generating programmes and alternate sources of firewood by the forest department. This is an artificial mechanism that is not sustainable in the long term.

In the Srisailam Tiger Sanctuary area, the Chenchus, who are traditional hunter-gatherers, go into the forest everyday for all their needs. They are being harassed by the forest department for trespassing into the sanctuary. The groups who came from the chenchu area felt that the Chenchus should atleast be given identity cards to prevent harassment from forest department and the police department who mistake them for naxalites. Another serious problem with regard to Sanctuaries is the settlement of people's rights. The Settlement Officer is the Conservator of Forests whereas the forest department is one of the interested parties in the land acquisition for the sanctuary and hence it is not appropriate to make the forest officer the settlement officer**. It should be the revenue department (District Collector) who should be authorised to settle the people's rights. G.O.No.112 which calls for involvement of private industries like ITC, Reliance and others for taking up commercial plantations through the VSS should be withdrawn immediately, as this is a backdoor method of allowing private industries to enter forest and tribal lands. Such tripartite agreements between the government, the industries and the tribals can never provide a level playing ground for the tribal people and make them more vulnerable to the exploitation of private industries.

The historical injustices to the tribal people in this region and that of the tribals in southern Orissa due to construction of several 'development' projects and industries like Nalco, HAL, Sileru, Machkund and others which have displaced tribals in large numbers without any rehabilitation, and has forced them to migrate in search of livelihood. They are now being treated as encroachers and criminals in forestlands. This definition should be condemned and Commission should recommend proper mechanisms for resolution of conflicts. The Commission should strongly recommend the orders passed by the Ministry of Environment and Forests in 1990, on the recommendations of the Commissioner of Scheduled Castes and Scheduled Tribes, to ensure that such conflicts are resolved. Infact, the first two orders alone show a way forward to settle disputes concerning forestlands. All the groups consulted strongly felt that the pressure on forests and the destruction of forests is taking place more due to increase in industries and private commercial activities like Mining, paper-mills, timber smuggling and the growing non-tribal population settling down in Agency areas, than due to the podu cultivation practised by tribals. Eco-Tourism is also causing destruction of forests. For example, the A.P Tourism Department built huge infrastructure close to Farhanbad, near Mannanur (Srisailam) for Tourism purposes in the middle of the protected area and in Araku, Borra and Anantagiri (Visakhapatnam). While tribals are prohibited from entering these forests for their survival needs, it is totally unjust to allow tourism, which is causing a lot of degradation. Hence, the constitutional provisions of the Fifth Schedule, the Samatha Judgement and the PESA Act should be strictly implemented following the right spirit with regard to industries and non-tribal settlers, which includes the Tourism Department.

The Tourism Department also conducts tours through tribal villages, especially in Chenchu settlements, and exhibits them like museum pieces. The groups felt that this degrading exercise further underscored the lack of empathy among the various government departments towards the tribals. Because of a shift in the policy of the government, profits to G.C.C. are more important than benefits to tribals. Although there are 32 items in the procurement list of GCC Ltd, it procures a limited number of commodities and at very low prices compared to the market rates. The tribals face several constraints in collection of NTFP and marketing these items because of the monopoly rights enjoyed by GCC Ltd. They do not have the right to sell their produce to private traders even when their rates are higher. Hence, a long-standing demand has been for removal of the monopoly restriction of GCC Ltd. and instead a minimum support price should be provided by GCC to protect the tribals from exploitation of traders. The monopoly of forest department over Beedi leaf collection and sale should be removed. The tribals or VSS should be given 100 per cent rights over income from beedi leaf and also the right of sale, with the forest department providing the support price.

THE NATIONAL FOREST POLICY

The forest policy of the United States may be said to have had its origin in 1799 in the enactment of a law which authorised the purchase of timber suitable for the use of the navy, or of land upon which such timber was growing. It is true that laws were in force under the early governments of Massachusetts, New Jersey and other colonies, providing for the care and protection of forest interests in various ways, but these laws were distinctly survivals of tendencies acquired in Europe and for the most part of little use.

It was not until the apparent approach of a dangerous shortage in certain timber supplies that the first real step in forest policy was taken by the United States. Successive laws passed from 1817 to 1831 strove to give larger effect to the original enactment, but without permanent influence towards the preservation of the live oak, which was the object in view. A long period of inaction followed these early measures. *The unshaded areas are treeless, except along the Streams* 1831 the solicitor of the treasury assumed a partial responsibility for the care and protection of the public timber lands and in 18 55 this duty was transferred to the commissioner of the general land office in the Department of the Interior.

The effect of these changes upon forest protection was unimportant. When, however, at the close of the Civil War railway building in the United States took on an unparalleled activity, the destruction of forests by fire and the axe increased in a corresponding ratio and public sentiment began to take alarm. Action by several of the states slightly preceded that of the Federal government, but in 1876 Congress, acting under the inspiration of a memorial from the American Association for the Advancement of Science, authorised the appointment of an officer under the commissioner of agriculture, to collect and distribute information upon forest matters.

As the railways advanced into the treeless interior, public interest in tree-planting became keen. In 1873 Congress passed and later amended and repealed the timber culture acts, which granted homesteads on the treeless public lands to settlers who planted one-fourth of their entries with trees. Though these measures were not successful in themselves they directed attention towards forestry. The act which repealed them in 1891 contained a clause which lies at the foundation of the present forest policy of the United States.

By it the president was authorised to set aside " any part of the public lands wholly or in part covered with timber or undergrowth, whether of commercial value or not, as public reservations and the President shall, by public proclamation, declare the establishment of such reservations and the limits thereof." Some eighteen million :acres had been proclaimed as reservations at the time when, in 1896, the National Academy of Sciences was asked by the secretary of the interior to make an investigation and report upon " the inauguration of a rational forest policy for the forest lands of the United States." Upon the recommendation of a commission named by the Academy, President Cleveland established more than twenty-one million acres of new reserves on the 22nd of February 1897. His action was widely misunderstood and attacked, but it awakened a public interest in forest questions without which the rapid progress of forestry in the United States since that time could never have been made.

Within a few months after the proclamation of the Cleveland reserves the present national forest policy took definite shape. Under this policy the national government holds and manages, in the common interest of all users of the forests or its products, such portions of the public lands as have been set aside by presidential proclamation in accordance with the act of 1891.

These lands are held against private acquisition under the Homestead Act, the Timber and Stone Act and other laws under which the United States disposes of its unappropriated public domain, but not against private acquisition under the Mineral Land Laws. They are selected from lands believed to be more valuable for forest purposes than for agriculture and are managed with the purpose of securing from them the best and largest possible returns, present and future, whether in the form of water for irrigation or power, of timber, of forage for stock, or of any other beneficial product. The aggregate area of the reserves, or national forests, has been steadily increased until they now include nearly all the timber lands left of the public domain.

The general lines of this policy were in part laid down by the commission already mentioned, in its report submitted to the secretary of the interior, May 1, 1897 and by the act of June 4, 1897, which was largely shaped by the work of the commission. Until this act was passed the national forests had been in theory closed against any form of use; nor had the possibility of securing forest preservation by wise use received much thought from those who had favoured their creation. Such a state of affairs could not continue.

Before long public opinion would have forced the opening to use of the resources thus :arbitrarily locked up and in the absence of any administrative system providing for conservative use, the national forests would inevitably have been abolished and the whole policy of government forest holdings would have ceased.

The act of June 4, 1897 was therefore of the first importance. This act conferred upon the secretary of the interior general powers for the proper management of the national forests through the general land office of his department. It provided for the designation and sale of dead, mature and large timber; authorised the secretary to permit free use of timber in small quantities by settlers, miners and residents; empowered him to "make such rules and regulations and establish such service as will insure the objects of such reservations, namely, to regulate their occupancy and use and to preserve the forests thereon from destruction "; and made violation of the act or of such rules and regulations a misdemeanour.

The statute limited the power to establish forest reservations to the purpose of improving and protecting the forest, securing favourable conditions of water flows and furnishing a continuous supply of timber for the use and necessities of citizens of the United States.

Lands found, upon due examination, to be more valuable for other purposes than for forest uses might be eliminated from any reservation and all mineral lands within the reservations were left open to private appropriation under the mineral laws.

The rights of settlers and claimants were safeguarded and civil and criminal jurisdiction, except so far as the punishment of offences against the United States in the reservations was concerned, was reserved to the States.

While the administration of the national forests was entrusted to the general land office, the same act assigned the surveying and mapping of them to the United States Geological Survey, which has published descriptions and maps of some of the more important.

No attempt was made in the general land office to develop a technical forest service. There were, indeed, at the time of passage of the act, less than ten trained foresters in the United States, no means of training more and very little conception of what forestry actually meant. The purpose of the administration was therefore mainly protection against trespass and fire, particularly the latter.

Regulations were made giving effect to the provisions of the act of June 4, set forth above, but in the absence of technical knowledge as to what might safely be done, the tendency was rather to restrict than to extend the use of the forest. Meanwhile, however, there was rapidly developing in another branch of the government service an organisation qualified for actual forest management.

One year after the passage of the act of June 4, 1897, the division of forestry in the Department of Agriculture ceased to be merely a bureau of information and became an active agency for introducing the actual practice of forestry among private owners and for conducting the investigations upon which a sound American forest practice could be based. The work awakened great interest among forest owners and exerted a powerful educational influence upon the country at large.

The division extended its work and became the Bureau of Forestry. It drew into its employment for a time nearly all the men who were preparing themselves in increasing numbers (at first abroad, then in the newly-founded schools in the United States) for the profession of forestry and was soon recognised as qualified to speak authoritatively on technical questions connected with the administration of the national forests. This led to a request from the secretary of the interior for the advice of the bureau on such questions. Working plans were accordingly undertaken for a number of the forests.

The general land office, however, was not ready to attempt active forest management. Though some timber was sold and the grasing of stock regulated to some extent, the main object of the land office administration continued to be protection against fire. Many of the regulations which it made could not be enforced.

The disadvantages of dispersal of the Federal government forest work among three separate agencies grew more and more apparent, until, on the 1st of February 1905, control of the 63,000,000 acres of forest reserves which up to that time had been set aside was transferred from the general land office to the Bureau of Forestry. In recognition of its new duties the designation of the bureau became the Forest Service.

Other provisions of the act which affected the transfer were that forest supervisors and rangers should be selected, so far as possible, from qualified citizens of the state or territory in which each forest was situated and that all money received from the sale of any products or the use of any land or resources of the national forests should be covered into the treasury and constitute a special fund for their protection, administration, improvement and extension.

Five days later a statute gave forest officers the power to arrest trespassers; and on the 3rd of March the lieu land selection law was repealed. This law had opened the way for grave abuses through the exchange of worthless land by private owners within the forests for an equal area of valuable timber lands outside.

The law has been modified since by the change of the old name " Forest Reserves " to " National Forests."

The act of June iz, 1906, opened to homestead entry lands within national forests found by examination to be chiefly valuable for agriculture. The administration and improvement of the national forests are now provided for directly by congressional appropriation. The power to create national forests conferred on the president by the act of March 1891 has been repealed for the states of Washington, Oregon, Idaho, Montana, Wyoming and Colorado, but for no others.

8

Forestry Conservation Management Practices

Forestry Conservation Management Practices (CMPs) are specific, science-based guidelines for conservation of rare species during forest harvesting. CMPs are somewhat analogous to Forestry Best Management Practices (BMPs), except whereas BMPs focus mainly on protection of water resources, CMPs specialize in protection of rare wildlife. The primary objective of CMPs is to guide harvesting activities such that rare species listed under the Massachusetts Endangered Species Act (MESA) are not impacted in a way that jeopardizes long-term viability of local populations. CMPs first identify and describe potential impacts of forest harvesting to state-listed species, whether impacts may be direct (*e.g.*, physical injury or death of individual animals) or indirect (*e.g.*, alteration of habitat in a way that reduces overall reproductive success of a local population).

Then, CMPs provide specific guidelines to avoid or minimize impacts that would be considered negative or potentially detrimental to a local population; the guidelines are based on scientific knowledge of the habitat requirements, reproductive strategy, dispersal ability, survivorship, and other ecological factors that influence population dynamics of the species. CMPs are based on the principle that protection and enhancement of the long-term viability of local populations is prerequisite to statewide recovery of imperiled wildlife.

Simultaneous with the objective of protecting local populations of state-listed species, CMPs aim to maintain adequate opportunity for sustainable management of timber products in Massachusetts. To this end, CMPs tend to focus forest harvesting restrictions on the critical areas within known habitat of state-listed species, thereby allowing timber management to proceed with fewer restrictions over as large an area as possible. This strategy is based, in part, on recognition that forest harvesting typically results in temporary habitat change or sometimes even habitat improvement rather than permanent habitat loss.

Thus, the CMP strategy is designed to help maximize the protection of state-listed species and the ability of Massachusetts landowners to manage their forests for timber and other wood products.

MANAGEMENT OF FORESTLAND IN MASSACHUSETTS

Management of forestland in Massachusetts involves multiple stakeholders with multiple objectives, so communication among stakeholders and development of management standards are essential to guiding compatible and sustainable uses of the land. State-owned forestland in Massachusetts received Forest Stewardship Council certification in May 2004, and this certification requires that there be coordination of forest management among the three state forest management agencies (Division of Water Supply Protection [DWSP], Bureau of Forestry [BOF], and Division of Fisheries and Wildlife [DFW]).

In addition, there is a need for state forestland managers to work closely with the Natural Heritage and Endangered Species Programme (NHESP) to develop and implement a formal and consistent process for determining appropriate mitigation of potentially adverse impacts of forest harvesting to state-listed species on both state and privately-owned forestlands. In light of these goals, CMPs are needed to ensure adequate protection of state-listed species during forest-harvesting operations. Without CMPs, a landowner and/or forester must develop a Forest Cutting Plan without having prior knowledge of possible harvest restrictions required by the NHESP to mitigate potential impacts of forest harvesting to state-listed species. Under these circumstances, activities proposed in the Forest Cutting Plan must often be modified after the plan is reviewed by the NHESP, which tends to result in delay of the harvest, changes in the amount and distribution of timber to be harvested, or changes in the number, type, or location of stream and wetland crossings. However, CMPs shall make potential harvest restrictions available to the landowner and forester before a Forest Cutting Plan is developed. This gives the landowner and forester an opportunity to develop a plan that is more likely to be approved by the NHESP without need for modification, thereby saving the landowner time and money. With proper planning and attention to detail, use of CMPs shall maximize the efficiency of the cutting-plan filing and review process and enable landowners to better understand how forestry and conservation of rare wildlife can be integrated as compatible uses of Massachusetts forestland.

Benefits of CMPs

CMPs benefit both state-listed species and forest management by (1) being based on scientific knowledge of the ecological factors influencing population dynamics of state-listed species, thereby enabling focused protection of key habitats and other resources, (2) improving the predictability and consistency of review of Forest Cutting Plans by the NHESP, and (3) providing detailed guidance to landowners and foresters for developing Forest Cutting Plans that have high probability of being approved by the NHESP without modification. An additional benefit, which is a byproduct of the first listed above, is that time-of-year harvesting restrictions mandated by CMPs tend to apply to smaller areas than those to which restrictions applied in the past. In this sense, intensive conservation measures are concentrated, which should be more effective in achieving conservation objectives than a strategy by which lighter measures are applied over a broader area. Furthermore, this strategy affords the landowner greater liberty in managing a larger proportion of a given tract of forest.

Process for Developing CMPs

The NHESP is the primary partner responsible for development of CMPs. However, staff of the Natural Resources and Environmental Conservation (NREC) Extension Programme at the University of Massachusetts Amherst and foresters of the DWSP, BOF, and DFW collaborate with the NHESP in this effort. This group of scientists and land managers meets regularly to work together on every aspect of the CMP development process.

The first step in developing CMPs is to determine which state-listed species should be addressed. This decision is based largely upon the frequency with which forest harvests are planned in habitat of each state-listed species, whereupon species that most frequently coincide with harvests are considered top candidates for development of CMPs. A second factor is the degree to which protection of each state-listed species is expected to impact the logistics of forest harvesting, whereupon species that are likely to require highly protective measures are considered top candidates.

A third factor, which often is related to the second, is the sensitivity of a state-listed species or its habitat to forest harvesting, whereupon species that are highly sensitive are considered top candidates. When multiple species have similar ecological requirements and conservation strategies, groups of species may be lumped into a single CMP document (*e.g.*, Blue-spotted Salamander, Jefferson Salamander, and Marbled Salamander are lumped together in a "Mole Salamander" CMP document).

When there is agreement between the NHESP and its collaborators about which state-listed species to address in a CMP document, the NHESP conducts a thorough search of scientific literature pertaining to the ecology of the species of interest. The information is then consolidated into a species account that includes a physical description of the species and a discussion of its range, distribution, habitat requirements, seasonal movements, reproductive strategy, survivorship, and other concepts associated with its life history. Additionally, the account includes a discussion of known and potential threats to population viability, including those posed by forest harvesting.

The NHESP and its collaborators then develop the actual management practices that scientific evidence suggests is necessary for successful conservation of the species. These management practices are specific to forestry-related activities and, like Forestry BMPs, are split into two categories:

required management practices and recommended management practices. Required management practices (denoted with "R" in the CMP document) are those which should be considered mandatory during most harvests, barring special circumstances. Recommended management practices (denoted with "G" in the CMP document) are optional guidelines that are expected to provide additional benefits to the species of interest.

FOREST CONSERVATION AND THE RURAL POOR

FORESTS–POVERTY NEXUS

Forest conservation efforts have achieved significant successes worldwide in the last 30 years. These include increasing the variety and number of protected forests; enhancing the visibility of forest issues, both nationally and internationally; promoting new national and international policies and partnerships in support of forest conservation; and working with communities, consumers, and producers to foster sustainable forest management and logging practices. One of the areas where review and additions seems warranted is that of the forests–poverty nexus. First and foremost, worldwide concerns about poverty alleviation and the need for new strategies to address poverty are putting the onus on the conservation movement to show that forest conservation helps rather than hinders poverty alleviation. If we do not step in with convincing proposals to support this contention, we may witness further attacks on forests in the name of poverty reduction.

Second, there is growing frustration among conservation and social development practitioners with policies that have not lived up to their claims of being able to deliver both poverty alleviation and forest conservation. These include many market-oriented reforms, agricultural intensification programmes, and integrated conservation and development projects. Third, we must reopen discussion on this issue because the current state of affairs, in which a rich urban world demands that the poor rural world embrace what is essentially the environmental agenda of the former, is not sustainable. The situation will continue to be unsustainable until the needs and concerns of the poor rural world are brought on board, and until its role as steward of the world environment is duly acknowledged and rewarded.

New Answers to Pressing Questions

The conservation movement has for several decades viewed the forests–poverty nexus with a vicious circle conceptual framework, within which population growth, limited environmental carrying capacity, natural hazards, and market failures combine to perpetuate poverty-cum-environmental degradation traps. This diagnosis led to the implementation of local integrated conservation and development projects (ICDPs), which were viewed as a win-win strategy that could deliver both environmental conservation and poverty alleviation. WWF embraced the ICDP approach in the mid-1980s, and a decade later was devoting more than half of its budget to this approach. Outcomes, however, as assessed both inside and outside WWF, were mixed. Although there were many success stories, with credit given to the commitment and efforts of participants, there is a sense of frustration with the limitations of the ICDP approach.

Some ICDPs fail because they are unable to insulate themselves from national or international changes, from the building of new roads and infrastructure to market and economic changes, that may threaten years of local-level conservation efforts. Others fail because they do not deliver sufficient profits to make them an attractive option among the local population (for example, they may be more complex, less productive, and provide fewer market outlets than originally touted). In part as a reaction to the shortcomings of ICDPs, several conservation organisations have now moved to larger, ecoregion-based conservation strategies—an approach that increases the need to address conservation and rural poverty issues.

One alternative to the vicious circle theory is the pro-market approach. Sometimes complementing and sometimes competing with the vicious circle theory, this approach blames insufficient markets and a lack of property rights for deforestation and rural poverty, and has been used to justify the drive by international development banks and development agencies for land titling, for the scrapping of price controls and subsidies, and for the opening up of rural production to international competition, on the assumption that expanded markets and private ownership would foster rural development and protect natural resources.

In some cases, such as in China, these initiatives have paid back in terms of rural poverty alleviation; in others, such as in Africa, they have not. Nowhere have they fostered forest conservation.

These failures suggest that the conceptual approaches used in the past were deficient, or at least incomplete, and in the last decade new answers and strategies have been proposed to address four basic questions:

- What are the immediate, intermediate, and root causes of deforestation?
- Are the rural poor a threat to forests?
- Are forests an important source of current or potential income for the rural poor?
- How might the conservation movement better mainstream forests–poverty issues into its policy and activities?

The following sections address these questions in turn, summarising current thinking and perspectives. To close, I offer a number of specific suggestions that I believe can strengthen the conservation community's response to the challenges posed by poverty to the world's declining forests.

Drives Deforestation

Research into the immediate causes of deforestation has grown significantly in the last decade, and although some disagreements linger, the overall picture is clear. After reviewing more than 150 economic models of tropical deforestation, Kaimowitz and Angelsen (1998) report: "A broad consensus exists that expansion of cropped area and pastures constitutes a major source of deforestation.... Pasture expansion is especially important in Latin America." "There is no similar consensus with regard to logging, although it seems to be a direct source of deforestation in some contexts.... Southeast Asia has been identified as one region where logging contributes to deforestation." "Evidence regarding both fuel wood and open pit mining is weak, although it points to them being occasional sources of deforestation, particularly for fuel wood in Africa."

Several studies investigating the intermediate causes of deforestation find that higher agricultural prices (particularly for annual crops), higher timber prices, increased opportunities for land titling through deforestation, more rural credit, more roads, lower rural wages, and a shortage of off-farm employment opportunities foster the expansion of cropped areas, pastures, and logging—all of which are immediate causes of deforestation. Intermediate causes are usually linked to broader processes. Also known as root causes or ultimate drivers, these are the national and international processes that trigger the chain of events that eventually put in motion or accelerate deforestation. While such root causes are similar the world over, the direction and magnitude of the deforestation processes they drive are usually country- and site-specific. Consider, for example, these findings regarding the impact of countrywide economic crises and ensuing adjustment programmes:

- Bolivia's economic crises of the 1980s and the ensuing structural adjustment policies saw poverty rising at the national level, but produced no trace of poverty-induced deforestation. While deforestation did increase significantly, it was as a result of the expansion of soybean and logging for export.
- In Cameroon, the economic crises of the mid-1980s and the subsequent adjustment programmes caused widespread deforestation in the country's southern regions. This was due to an increase in rural population and a move from export-oriented plantation crops such as cocoa and coffee, whose prices were falling, towards food crops. This change required more land, both because food crops are more extensive and because some farmers kept their plantation plots, instead clearing new land for the food crops.
- On the island of Java in the Indonesian archipelago, the financial crisis of the late 1990s and subsequent adjustment programmes fostered significant forest clearance by small farmers, who reacted to the crisis

by increasing their holdings of rubber and other tree crops, mostly as a source of future income security. (Sunderlin *et al.*, 2001b and 2001c)

More generally, Geist and Lambin (2001), in a review of 152 deforestation case studies, conclude that: "Tropical deforestation is driven by... economic factors, institutional and national policies, and remote influences.... Our findings reveal that too much emphasis has been given to population growth and shifting cultivation as primary and direct causative variables at the decade time scale."

These interactions between immediate, intermediate, and root causes have important consequences for forest conservation strategy. According to Sunderlin *et al.* (2001a): "The implication of these findings is that a wide gamut of polices not heretofore considered relevant—for example, exchange rate, trade, urban employment, and infrastructure policies—must be taken into account and modified if the goal of reducing inappropriate deforestation is to be taken seriously."

RURAL POOR A THREAT TO FORESTS

While there are many cases of poor farmers cutting natural forests, the role of poverty as a major immediate, intermediate, or root cause of world deforestation is contested. Quoting from the Kaimowitz and Angelsen (1998) review: "Some authors argue that poorer families deforest more because they have shorter time horizons... while others say they deforest less because they lack the necessary capital to put additional land into production.... The popular and professional literature often refers to a link between poverty and environmental degradation, yet poverty is rarely integrated into economic models in general, and deforestation models in particular.... Existing models provide rather weak and conflicting evidence on these issues."

Part of the difficulty of reaching a definitive conclusion lies in the variety of circumstances in which the rural poor or other indigenous groups may be involved in deforestation.

For example, are we looking at the interaction between remote forests and a sparse local indigenous population? Are we looking at an area of small farmers in the fringe of the forests, or at a contingent of would-be colonists pouring into the rural frontier, spontaneously or as part of a colonisation programme?

Are we looking at large forests, or at patches of forest amid farms? The question of whether poor farmers deforest more or less than the better-off ones furthermore depends on where the poverty line is drawn and on the level of aggregation. For tropical countries, neither aggregate models nor local-level studies have found an inverse relation between income and deforestation rates (*i.e.*, that deforestation declines as income increases), nor have they found a

Kuznetz curve relation (*i.e.*, deforestation growing as income increases, up to a point where the relation would reverse and deforestation would decline with further income increases).

There is also a time dimension. For example, in Africa it is the poor that are responsible for most forest cutting, but a lot of cut forest is allowed to grow back. By contrast, in the Philippines logging companies were first responsible for deforestation in the 1960s and 1970s; small farmers have since followed suit, preventing forest regrowth. In many cases, the rural poor are an immediate cause of deforestation processes that are driven by other intermediate and root causes; some of the worst episodes of deforestation, for example, can be attributed to sudden countrywide or regionwide shocks, such as economic crises, natural hazards, and major price and market changes. Geist and Lambin (2001) find that episodes of social disorder, crisis conditions, population displacement, and abrupt policy shifts are frequently associated with deforestation bursts in Africa and, to a much lesser extent, Asia and Latin America.

Rural poverty should therefore not be seen, *per se*, as a factor driving world deforestation. While it is true that in Africa, for example, most of the farmers that deforest are poor, it is far from clear that African farmers deforest because they are poor. Recent research in Africa and elsewhere shows that market and policy changes are far more important drivers of deforestation.

Potential Income for the Rural Poor

It is important to consider also the relationship between the rural poor and the forest from the opposite perspective: What can the forest do for the poor? Most observers agree that forests are important sources of livelihood for the rural poor—particularly ethnic minorities, forest dwellers, and rural women. However, estimations vary widely regarding how many people and to what degree they rely on forests: “The livelihoods of over 200 million forest dwellers and poor settlers depend directly on food, fibre, fodder, fuel and other resources taken from the forest or produced on recently cleared forest soils.” (Barraclough and Ghimera, 1988) “Forest resources directly contribute to the livelihood of 90 per cent of the 1.2 billion people in the developing world that live in extreme poverty.”

Forest services are particularly important for the poorest of the rural poor, and this fact alone provides a powerful reason to protect forests and the stream of services that they provide to poor rural dwellers. While acknowledging that forests are of immediate importance to the rural poor, some analysts do not believe that forests have the ability to lift the rural poor out of poverty. They point to the fact that, as rural household income increases, the proportion coming from forest services decreases sharply and conclude like Wunder: “A general conclusion is that, in most settings, natural forests tend to have little comparative advantage for the large-scale alleviation of poverty, especially compared to their great land use competitor, agriculture."

This statement describes the situation extant in some countries, but it fails to assess the full range of sustainable forestry benefits, and how a larger portion of these benefits could accrue to the rural poor. The benefits of sustainable forest management include the following:

- On-farm and local benefits from harvesting and selling marketable products (timber and non-timber), plus other forest services. These benefits directly accrue to the rural households and communities that embark in sustainable forestry activities.
- Regional and national benefits from forest environmental services provided to the region or country at large; for example, erosion protection, water regulation, biodiversity conservation, tourism, and carbon sequestration. Little of these benefits accrues to the rural households and communities that engage in sustainable forestry activities, for example through increased land productivity or new market and employment opportunities in the conservation sector. By and large regional and national benefits are captured by downstream populations, particularly urban populations.
- Global benefits from forest environmental services; for example, biodiversity conservation, carbon sequestration, tourism, and scientific research opportunities. Again, little of these benefits accrues to the rural households and communities engaged in sustainable forestry activities, for example, through employment opportunities provided by international ecotourism, or through support from international non-governmental organisations (NGOs). By and large, global benefits are captured by the international community.

For understandable reasons, most local conservation programmes focus on helping rural communities increase on-farm and local benefits, through the introduction of land conservation or high-yield, multipurpose sustainable forest management, for example.

Successes are rare, however, due in part to the low density of occurrence of most non-timber forest products and to management, processing, and market complications.

To address these shortcomings, some practitioners are focusing on improving ecoagricultural techniques, and others on reforming market structures and national forest policies that discriminate against the rural poor (Scherr, White, and Kaimowitz, 2001). Even if these proposals are successful, increased on-farm and local benefits may nonetheless be insufficient to make forest conservation attractive. Actually, unsustainable forest logging of natural forests may be the most profitable option when only market-based benefits are considered.

This picture changes if the regional, national, and global benefits of sustainable forest management are included. Lampietty and Dixon (1995) estimate that in rich countries these types of benefits—and particularly the regional and national benefits—are three times greater than on-farm and local benefits.

This explains in part the strong appeal of forest conservation among developed countries. In poorer countries, and particularly in tropical countries, the picture is different: while the regional, national, and global benefits of forest management in developing countries are roughly equivalent to on-farm and local benefits, they are mostly made up of global benefits—*i.e.*, the ones accruing to the international community. If we are to increase the appeal of forest conservation among the rural poor and if we are to preserve the world's forests, it may be necessary to make significant income transfers from the rich urban population to the poor rural population to pay for the environmental stewardship services that the latter are asked to perform.

The provision of such transfers has its precedents. At the country level, for instance, there are many examples of payments that are made for watershed management services. At the international level, this type of transfer is an integral part of the European Union's Common Agricultural Policy, in the form of payments made to European farmers to care for Europe's countryside and environmental resources. It also provides the rationale for the Global Environment Facility (GEF) and for a large part of the activities of northern hemisphere NGOs in the south.

The overall message of this chapter is simple: The conservation movement must address forest–poverty issues as part of its forest conservation policy. Failure to do so would be to permit increased pressures on world forests that most probably would benefit neither the poor nor the forests. The ensuing question then is how to do it. Based on the preceding discussion, I would like to offer the following recommendations.

At the overall policy and programmatic level:

- At a global policy level, the conservation movement should acknowledge explicitly that most forests around the world are not empty. This acknowledgement should include recognition that, particularly in developing countries, natural forests are an important component of rural livelihoods. National and international forest policies and the conservation movement should address both the sustainable management of natural forests and rural poverty alleviation; one should never be addressed at the other's expense.
- The above guidelines for global policy should be translated into specific targets linking forest conservation goals and rural poverty alleviation goals at the forest or ecoregion level. For example, the long-range WWF/World Conservation Union (IUCN) forest vision

proposes that by 2050, 30 per cent of the world forest should be community-managed. We should extend this to the establishment of specific percentages representing the rural poor's share of these community-managed forests.

- Given that many forest services do not carry a market price, the realisation of sustainable rural environments and livelihoods will require that the urban world pay the rural world for its environmental stewardship services. The conservation movement should make this principle a key component of its forest policy

At the project level, including policy research and advocacy:

- Support should be given to ICDPs that increase the on-farm and local benefits of sustainable forestry and agriculture that accrue to the rural poor.
- Local conservation activists and advocates should focus more closely on national policy and market issues, because the rural poor are clearly at a disadvantage when competing with politically and economically stronger stakeholders. It is imperative that these policy issues be addressed, because to be effective an ecoregion conservation strategy demands a broad policy approach. The concrete programmes and interventions at the local level should be coupled with enabling policies at the national level.
- In addition to on-the-ground projects, we should develop a policy research and advocacy agenda related to the proposals above. That agenda would allow us to better understand and address local or country-specific situations, including country-specific forest–poverty dynamics, institutional and economic changes affecting forests, and ecoregion-specific forest management alternatives. Specifically, what is needed is to strengthen the conservation movement's capabilities both for analysis and advocacy, and its ability to learn from, and partner with, other stakeholders in the conservation and poverty alleviation arena.
- Last but not least, we recommend that the conservation movement undertake a policy research and advocacy initiative to advance the proposal of paying the rural poor for regional, national, and global forest conservation services. Similar proposals have been made in the past, but what is different here is our focus on the rural poor. This focus would change the underpinning payment ethic (who pays and who is paid) and may increase institutional complexity (a large number of potential recipients). Local and international NGOs are nonetheless well-positioned to tackle both issues. What is needed here is a concerted effort to bring the pieces together in a coherent framework, and to move the proposal to the policy advocacy arena.

ENVIRONMENTAL CHANGE AND BIODIVERSITY CONSERVATION

In the Convention on Biological Diversity signed by many member states at the Earth Summit held in Rio de Janeiro (Brazil) in 1992, explains biodiversity as follows: "Biological diversity" means the variability among living organisms from all sources including terrestrial, marine and other aquatic ecosystems and the ecological complexes of which they are part; this includes diversity within species, between species and of ecosystems.

TYPES OF BIODIVERSITY

Biodiversity is a generic term that can be related to many environments and species, for example, forests, freshwater, marine and temperate environments, the soil, crop plants, domestic animals, wild species and micro-organisms. Basically it can be classified according to three types of diversity:

- Ecosystems and landscapes (habitat diversity)
- Animal, plant, bacterial species (species diversity)
- All genes (genetic diversity)

Of particular importance are the taxonomically isolated species, as they have little similarity to other species and therefore are unique with respect to their genetic structure. These species are often endemic meaning limited to one specific area.

Their extinction would mean a greater loss for global biodiversity rather than just the extinction of a species.

Distribution of Biodiversity

In Europe, biodiversity is very unevenly distributed with the least variety of ecosystems and lowest diversity occurring in Northern Europe. Centres of high biodiversity are to be found in the Mediterranean (Italy, Spain, Greece, France) and on the fringes of Europe (Bulgaria, Ukraine, Georgia, Armenia, Turkey), with over 5,000 endemic plant species that occur only in these countries. The Mediterranean is Europe's richest sea in terms of biodiversity.

The Importance of Biodiversity

Biodiversity is often used to draw attention to issues related to the environment. It can be closely related to

- The health of ecosystems: For example, the loss of just one species can have different effects ranging from the disappearance of the species to complete collapse of the ecosystem itself. This is due to every species having a certain role within an ecosystem and being interlinked with other species.
- The health of mankind: Experiencing nature is of great importance to humans and teaches us different values. It is good to take a walk

in the forest, to smell flowers and breath fresh air. More specifically, natural food and medicine can be linked to biodiversity.

Biodiversity in the Black Sea

The Black Sea region used to be one of the most important areas for fisheries and for food and income for local people. Sturgeons (Acipenser sp.), mullets (Mugil sp.), and mackerel (Scomber sp.) as well as other species have been extensively exploited in this area. However, human activities related to agriculture, shipping and tourism now exert strong pressure on the environment, especially in the northern part of the Black Sea, and are taking their toll on biodiversity and damaging fish stocks.

Threats to Biodiversity

Large amounts of fertilizers were carried to the sea from agricultural areas along the large rivers, such as Don, Dnepr, and Dnjestr. Oil leaked into the sea from ports on the eastern shores and directly from tankers crossing the Mediterranean.

Wastewater from cities and heavily visited coastal tourist towns was discharged without any purification.

Consequences for the Ecosystem

All of this leads to pollution and eutrophication meaning the enhanced blooming of planktonic algae due to increased nutrient loads. Planktonic algal blooms lower the water transparency letting only a little amount of light through the water where makrophytes usually grow. This is how the natural belt of bottom vegetation along the Black Sea coast has been destroyed. For example, the vertical distribution range of Cystoseira spp. decreased from 0-10m to 0-2,5m.

The consequences were drastic because the habitat is of major importance as a nursery for spawn and hatchlings of many marine species. This led to a drop in reproduction rates and hence fish stocks.

Biodiversity of the Coastal Zone

Coastal areas are exceptionally productive environments, rich in natural resources, biological diversity and with a high potential for commercial activity. The importance of biodiversity in the coastal zone can be demonstrated by 8 out of the 40 EU listed priority habitats of wild fauna and flora falling into the coastal habitat. Approximately a third of the EU's wetlands are located on the coast as well as more than 30 per cent of the Special Protected Areas designated under the Directive for the conservation of wild birds. The reproduction and nursery grounds of most fish and shellfish species of economic value also comes from this area, which accounts for almost half of the jobs in the fisheries sector.

Pressure on Coastal Biodiversity

Coastal areas are increasingly vulnerable to stresses from both human activities and the forces of nature. The complexity of human activities, natural systems and ownership in the coastal zone, requires an integrated management scheme to allocate coastal resources efficiently and minimize environmental degradation. Choices have to be made between competing uses and limits of resource exploitation if escalating conflicts and resource degradation are to be avoided.

The attitudes of community and industry to the use of biological resources should change from the 'maximum yield' approach to one of 'ecologically sustainable', which recognizes the need for conservation of biological diversity and maintenance of ecological integrity. Integration of management regimes within and between different sectors to meet environmental, economic and social objectives must be realized in order to achieve sustainable development.

Integrated Approach

Integrated policies will also provide the opportunity for all the people to accept responsibility for their actions and the impact they may have on biological diversity. The development of integrated policies for managing the coastal resources is necessary:

- To coordinate activities within and between all levels of government;
- To ensure that full social and environmental consequences (and costs) of development activities are considered;
- To ensure that the public interest is properly taken into account.

ASSIGNING ECONOMIC VALUE TO BIODIVERSITY

Biodiversity refers to the diversity of life in all its forms and all its level of organisation, not just plant, animal and microorganism species. At its most elemental level, biodiversity, encompasses the varied assemblages of organic molecules that comprise the genetic basis of life. On the other end of the spectrum there are biomes-the vast stretches of tundra, desert, forest, ocean, etc. In between come-population, race, sub-species, community, ecosystem.

Why is Biodiversity Important?

For many people the very questioning of the worth of biodiversity is illicit. They would argue that humankind has a moral obligation to conserve biodiversity, an obligation that comes with the fact that humans have the capability to destroy much of that biodiversity. Others find a religious support for such a view there is some stewardship responsibility on behalf of some deity. One problem with these moral views is that they often conflict with other moral views about, say, the right to earn a living, the right to have access to basic needs such as food, cloth and shelter, and so on. If conserving biodiversity conflicts with those rights, then some 'meta-ethical' principle is required for deciding which moral view should prevail. One aspect of the process of changing popular perceptions about biodiversity resources is to show that the sustainable use of biodiversity has positive economic value and that this economic value will often be higher than the alternative resource uses which threatens biodiversity.

Valuing Biological Diversity Conservation

The issue at hand concerns the measurement of natural capital, great difficulties arise in assigning values to natural capital precisely because the market in which it is traded are limited. In the past few decades a number of techniques have been developed to place monetary value to the benefits of conserving an area for biodiversity. Some rely on market prices of related goods and services both to value benefits and to estimate costs, while other rely on survey based approaches to infer values.

Hedonic Pricing Method

Property values are affected by a number of variables including environmental quality. After excluding other variables, including environmental quality, the residual price difference can then be ascribed, at least theoretically, to differences in environmental quality, *e.g.*, the increased value of property located next to natural areas. According to a report by Nelson (1982) traffic noise, measured in Leq (equivalent continuous sound level), a one unit change produces property price depreciation of 0.5-1.0 per cent.

Ravel-cost Method

This approach looks at the pattern of recreation use of a natural parks and uses this information to derive a demand curve to estimate the total amount of consumer's surplus. For example, travel behaviour reveals that Costa Rican visitors are willing to pay USD 35 per household to visit a tropical rainforest site in Costa Rica. Foreign visitation is likely to be worth far more than domestic, as foreign visitors have higher travel costs.

Contingent Valuation Method

The Contingent Valuation Method (CVM) bypasses the need to refer to market prices by asking individuals explicitly to place values upon environmental assets.

This is also referred to as an expressed preference method. An interesting advantage of the CVM approach is that it can, in theory, be used to evaluate resources, that people have never visited personally *e.g.* the Antarctica which people are " Willing to Pay" to preserve but would not in general ever want to visit.

Consumptive Benefit Method

There are a number of products which can be harvested on sustainable basis and marketed. For example, a probable number of higher plant species, which are widely used as basis for pharmaceutical drugs, is some 500,000.

According to Pearce and Moran (1994) economic value of these plants can be approached by looking at:

(i) The actual market value of the plants when traded,

(ii) The market value of the drugs of which they are the source materials,

(iii) The value of the drugs in terms of their life-saving properties, and using a value of a 'statistical life',

(iv) The lost pharmaceutical value from disappearing species.

As there is absence of 'global markets' in the benefits of biodiversity, the developing countries face major problems of appropriating the global benefits of sustainable use of biodiversity. As long as these global values cannot be captured by host countries, biodiversity will be a risky investment in many contexts.

THE VALUE OF BIODIVERSITY-THREATENED HABITATS

Biodiversity is not just some benign backdrop for hiking holidays, but the very substance and foundation of our survival, whether we realize it or not. We are entirely dependent upon the plants, animals, fungi, and micro-organisms that share the world with us. Individually, they alone feed us, and without them we would starve. Yet we frequently act to undermine these very species essential to our welfare. In addition to food, they provide many of the drugs and other medicinal and industrial products on which the quality of our lives increasingly depends.

They offer the promise of sustainable economy-productivity that the Earth can support on a continuing basis, so our children and, in turn, their children will survive and be able to live peaceful lives of abundant splendour.. We live in an age driven by the apparently insatiable desire of industrialized nations to go on getting richer, and of free-market economics driven by equally insatiable multi-national corporate organizations, competing to exploit the remaining resources of the planet. Though we are now beginning to consider atmospheric changes such as the ozone hole and global warming as significant international problems, we have yet to demonstrate we can hold good to effective action. However at the same time the threats to biodiversity, which are much more long-lasting are not being taken seriously politically. The fact is that up to a quarter of the species on Earth may be lost in the course of the next three decades-within the lives of the majority of us alive today, and a majority of biodiversity is likely to have perished by the middle of next century.

"Each year, we are cutting and burning 1.5 to 2 per cent of the world's remaining tropical rainforests; losing an estimated 24,000 million tonnes of topsoil; and adding some 93 million people to a world that is already far too full, judging from the extent of human misery, and starvation, let alone from the depletion of every conceivable resource." (Peter Raven "Porritt 71"). Since Rio, the rate of felling of the Amazon has increased some 30 per cent, finally exacerbated by drying from accentuated El Nino, a possible consequence of global warming.

Every, point on the Earth's surface, from the frozen wastes of Antarctica to the most remote stretches of the oceans, receives a steady shower of man-made chemicals. We are clearly "managing" the entire planet now, for better or for worse, whether we acknowledge this responsibility or not. In this sense, there is no longer any region that can be said to be truly "natural". The future impact of genetic engineering technologies is likely to be vast and has barely even been considered in the midst of runaway technological initiative.

Stewardship of Planet Earth

"Will we act as responsible stewards of the many organisms that share the Earth with us? We have certainly not given much evidence so far of our commitment; having given names to only 1.4 million of them, we don't know whether the total number may be 10 or 100 million. We understand even less-often nothing at all-about their individual properties, or the ways in which they interact with one another. Moving beyond our growth-orientated mentality which assumes that every, productive system on the planet can be expanded indefinitely to meet our needs, regardless of its biological basis, is an essential ingredient of stewardship.

Every nation must work to develop its own base of information on biodiversity, and strive to understand, to use, and to save it, both for its own purposes and for future generations. For rich nations, this means understanding that we cannot continue to ravage our strictly limited home planet as if its productivity and stability were simply inexhaustible. For poorer nations, the challenge will be even greater, and will not be met without reversing the tragic flow of many millions of dollars from poor, starving countries to the rich industrialized North. Environmental stewardship and social justice go hand in hand".

Multifarious Insects

There are more insects in the world than any other group of organisms. Until recently, virtually all the natural medicines we have developed have come from plants and fungi, but there is no reason why a sector which produces both cochineel and potent stinging toxins cannot have diverse biochemicals, especially to resist predators and to give protection against diverse plant toxins. "Currently only about 20 per cent of all insect species have been identified, let alone chemically characterized.

Bioprospecting in the insect species has only begun and is barely explored, yet the diverse insect species could be rapidly reduced in number with the destruction of habitats" (Peter Raven "Porritt 71"). There are currently some efforts under way to develop cooperative relationships with the governments of some developing countries in which wide assays of insect species are carried out.

A Case: Cone Snails

Just as arrow poison frogs are famed for their toxins, so are cone snails. Typical cone snails contain between 200 (chemical analysis) and 2000 (genetic analysis) types of polypeptide toxin of between 10 and 30 amino acid units. By contrast, snake toxins frequently contain 80 peptides and spider toxins up to 1000 units. Magic sponge Sea creatures could be a goldmine for powerful drugs

Left: Detail of the shell pattern of Olivia porphyria and wave-like cellular automaton with long-range and local autocatalytic interactions. The cone snail toxins represent both acetylcholine blockers similar to cobra venom toxin and ion blockers, which instead of the stopping flow of sodium ions like puffer fish, block one of the seven types of calcium channel. They also contain glutamate NMDA receptor blockers. No two species have the same toxins and many change their output over time. Their extremely varied shells, which mimic know cellular automata have fetched more than a Vermeer painting.

Scientific American Feb. 96 reported their use in a new pain-killing drug SNX-111 which proved effective in 5 out of 7 cases of intractable pain which had become tolerant to opiates. It thus represents the first of an entirely new class of compounds to treat severe pain. A second case of medicinal toxins: The Platypus New Scientist Jan 3 98. The poison from the spurs of the duck-billed platypus could point to ways of designing new types of painkiller, physiologists say. They believe that a toxin in the poison acts directly on our pain receptors. The male of this strange Australian species has spurs on its hind legs that contain at least four different toxins. They are thought to help the animals defend their breeding territory. "It's an unusual venom that's not designed to kill or paralyse its victims," says Rosemary Martin of the Australian National University in Canberra. Humans that are pricked by the platypus experience intense pain that can sometimes last for several weeks, she adds. "it seems designed as a deterrent to induce pain." Martin and her colleagues, led by Greg de Plater, have now pinned down how at least one component of the poison of the platypus's spurs behaves. The researchers tested the effects of a protein in the toxin on the neurons of laboratory mice. It turned out that the protein binds to a channel in the membranes of the neurons which allows positive ions to enter and leave the cells.

Snake oil and Cancer The protein contortrostatin named after the copperhead has been found to have a dual anti-cancer action stopping cells spreading and reducing blood-vessel formation. The African saw-scaled viper also produces a heart drug Aggrastatis.

Case Study: The Wollemia Pines

In a remote stretch of national park in Australia, was accidentally discovered this stand of an exceedingly ancient pine Wollemia nobilis known only from fossil records dating back to 250 million years. The trees stand in a formation of Wollemi sandstone dating itself from around 250 million years ago. Wollemia was common in Pangea from 200 million years and existed worldwide until 65 million years ago and continued in Gondwanaland up until 30 million years ago. This single stand later proved to be genetically monoclonal suggesting it has survived by vegetative sprouting from the forest floor. A second stand has been found a kilometre away. Otherwise this is the only specimen of this ancient and widespread species still on Earth.

Endemic Diversity: Hot Spots and Fragile Niches

Almost every corner of the earth supports some form of life but while in some areas there are only a limited number of species, others, particularly certain tropical forest areas appear to have living diversity in superabundance. "Ecuador has many more plant species than the whole of Europe, which is more than 30 times as big. Madagascar has five times as many kinds of trees as the whole of temperate North America. The United States contains fewer woody species of plant than a single volcano, Mount Makiliang in the Philippines-and the entire 20 million square kilometres of the North American continent contain fewer bird species than a 2,000-square kilometre national park in Costa Rica".

A species is called endemic to a region if it is found only in the specific locality and nowhere else in the world. Some areas have many endemic species. Indonesia has one sixth of the world's bird species, and nearly a quarter of them are endemic. Half of Papua New Guinea's birds, half of the Philippines' mammals, and about 80 per cent of Madagascar's plants are unique to them. Many islands have unique endemic species because of their evolutionary isolation, which are often exceedingly vulnerable because they have small populations easily wiped out by a single disaster.

"Tropical rainforests contain the greatest diversity of species; the US National Academy of Sciences reports that a typical patch, just 10 kilometres square, contains as many as 1,500 species of flowering plant, up to 750 species of tree, 400 different types of bird, 150 butterfly species, 100 kinds of reptile, and 60 species of amphibian. Insects are so abundant that no-one has yet been able to count them, but the Academy estimates that there may be as many as 42,000 in a single hectare".

The Amazonian rainforest helps to make South America the richest continent for wildlife and for biodiversity generally. It covers an eighth of the world's land surface, but harbours around a third of the world's birds diversity of species. Some local hotspots can contain comparable diversity to whole temperate habitats.

Coral reefs are the rainforests of the oceans; the Great Barrier Reef, for example, contains more than 3,000 animal species. "The rainforests' nearest rivals on land are areas with a Mediterranean climate-such as coastal California, the southern part of Western Australia, and the Mediterranean basin itself. These lack the rainforests' diversity of large animals, but have a huge number of endemic plant species".

The Impact on Diversity of a Changing World

Climate and geography play a part in determining why some areas have so many more species than others. Areas with high temperatures and rainfall and little seasonal variation-like tropical rainforests and coral reefs-can support many more species than cold, dry places with distinctly different seasons. History also plays a role in determining why some habitats have more species. When areas became isolated from each other, as a result of continental drift, mountain formation, ocean in welling or drying out of large rainforests into smaller islands, their animal and plant life evolves in different ways.

The longer an area is isolated, the more distinct and different its inhabitants are likely to become. The best examples are islands and super-islands, such as Madagascar and Australia, with highly distinct fauna and flora, but a similar explanation has been proposed for the high diversity of the Amazon involving insular dry periods during ice ages and re-integration of these island forest sanctuaries during warmer wetter epochs.

The theory of continental drift suggests that all the major land areas were once joined in a single "supercontinent", Pangea. Between 200 and 80 million years ago this broke up, first into two land masses, Laurasia and Gondwanaland-and then eventually into the modern continents. Australia and Antarctica broke off relatively early, while Madagascar probably did not separate entirely until about 60 million years ago. New Zealand has been isolated so long it contains no land mammals. As these land masses separated they carried plants and animals with them. Some of the ancient forests of Gondwanaland are still detectable scattered as ancient beech forest stands.

As evolutionary paths begin to diverge, different species form, filling the available ecological niches. For example, Madagascar and Gondwanaland probably had very similar kinds of primitive primates when they separated. "However, over vast periods of time, Madagascar's primates (sheltered from the fierce competition that species still faced on the mainland) developed into lemurs, lower primates found nowhere else. Gondwanaland's primates, subjected to greater pressures, evolved into higher forms-including modern monkeys, apes and, ultimately, man. Madagascar has more than 6,000 unique flowering plants and half the world's species of chameleons are endemic to the island."

Similarly in New Zealand many of the niches usually filled by mammals have been adopted by flightless birds. Australia's unique array of species evolved similarly in isolation from the rest of the world. Antarctica probably set out on a similar path, but became a snow-bound pristine wasteland with a few specialized species.

CONSERVATION AND MANAGEMENT OF BIOMASS RESOURCES MANAGEMENT

Conservation and management of biomass resources and environment are embedded in an array of knowledge and local practices. Most development projects tend to ignore the ingenuity of rural people in responding to the local problems based on their local knowledge. Initiatives intended to grow trees through Social Forestry projects have not taken cognisance of the existing local practises. For example in the Himalayan region, common practices of obtaining biomass resources from forests are through pollarding, pruning or selective cutting and not by felling of tress. Similarly studies from Nepal have shown that, communities adjacent to forests mostly use dry wood as fuelwood and grasses for fodder that normally does not involve cutting of trees. For many local communities across South Asia, forests are not only of consumptive value, but also revered as places of great socio-cultural and religious significance. The other factors that regulate resource extraction from forests include (a) traditional rights (b) religious practices (c) and non-use of certain tree species in the region. For example, people have a strong belief that felling of certain tree species such as 'neem' (*Azadirachta indica*) and 'pipal' (*Ficus religiosa*) brings evil to the members of the household.

Thus local systems of knowledge and management are sometimes rooted deeply in their religion and belief systems, which help in conserving the resources. But, state management was often based on flawed premises or a lack of understanding of the people-nature dependency. Gradually local communities have lost access and control of the resources, resulting in conflicts with the state and other stakeholders.

In many parts of south Asia, local people maintained strict rules to manage natural forests in their vicinity even until the 60s. The examples given below are illustrative of the diversity of informal or traditional institutional arrangements at the local level:

(i) A grazing fee was levied on herders in some pasturelands. In some regions, grazing was banned in pond catchments to prevent siltation of ponds.

(ii) Cutting of grass and fodder leaves from the certain tree species, 'Sal' (*Shorea robusta*) in the *Terai* region in the Himalayas, or 'Palas' (*Butea monosprema.*) in central and western India was regulated on forestlands.

(iii) Collection of dry wood did not require individual permits from the informal councils at the village level, whereas special permits were required for felling trees on the hill slopes and catchments. In case of some species that are less in abundance such as Shisham (*Dalbergia sisoo*) and Bamboo (*Dendrocalamus* spp.) there was a ban on felling. These species had market value for their timber.

The village community performed collective work to enhance and maintain the tree cover, by fencing, planting, trenching in forests, fire lines maintenance and desilting of ponds. Each household had an obligation to contribute a share to such efforts, failing this its rights to resources were curtailed. These duties are no longer followed as the local rights to resources are curtailed with state control.

The indirect non-consumptive values were represented in day-to-day life in the form of rules and conventions regulating use of resources. The informal institutions tend to reduce the environmental uncertainty faced by resource users especially in arid and semi-arid regions and also contribute to the conservation of natural resources. In some cases, the local institutions are better informed than the state departments about local ecological, economical and social conditions and about problems and constraints, which may be important from the management point of view. According to some studies, traditional management systems of CPRs have contributed to the protection of natural resources from being over used and have played a vital role in the management and conservation of natural resources.

TENURE RIGHTS AND BIOMASS RESOURCES

Prior to 1950s, local landlords controlled and had the authority to grant rights in forests in India, Sri Lanka and Nepal. In different areas, the tenure systems varied, for example the *Birta* system in mid hills of Nepal and the *Zamindari* system in northern part of India. The colonial regime in India and Sri Lanka significantly influenced the land tenure system. Under colonial management systems which continued in some areas even during the postcolonial period, the local landlords had the responsibility to manage forests and granted rights to the local households.

These include access rights, use rights and entitlement rights, which determine the access and end use of resources from the forests. Timber extraction in general was regulated, but there was free access to non-timber forest products. These resources were treated by local communities in many parts of south Asia as a "free good" which were easily available. But these rights and duties ceased with the land reforms during 50s and subsequent development policies initiated by respective governments. In Nepal, forests were nationalized as a part of a wider move to break feudal structures. In India, it was the Land Revenue Act in the respective states, which was implemented to nationalize forests. Nationalization of forests did more harm to landless and rural poor whose access to common pool resources was restricted as part of these resources were declared protected. In addition, communal sources of fuel wood, fodder and non-timber products have been reduced as a result of the forestry projects under the management and control of state functionaries. Due to nationalization of forest, the lack of local tenure and rights meant there was no incentive for local users, especially the poor and landless to exercise restraint. The rights to access and use of forest resources was further restricted with social forestry interventions enclosing forestlands.

For example, in the middle hill region of Nepal, the poorer sections of the people have less access to forest products for subsistence use and income today, than they had before the implementation of social forestry projects. This is also the case in India and Sri Lanka, where common lands, which were accessible to the landless prior to the social forestry intervention, are no longer freely available. In such a situation, the cultural overlay of rights creates paradoxically huge 'scarcity' differentials between households in villages, especially for the landless and poor.

This tends to inhibit effective development and active participation by marginalized groups. Currently, the average poor household receives only one third to one fifth of the wood from forests than collected before the social forestry intervention. The rights to use resources from forestlands, which were formerly guaranteed by customary law, were banned after the land reforms and land acts came into existence in 1950s.

The choice of species or location of social forestry plantations was often made by people who had practically little local knowledge. The fact that there are local variations, even in small countries like Sri Lanka and Nepal, wherein women traditionally prefer certain tree species for fodder or fuel wood is important for any afforestation project to consider. The practice of use restrictions and the issue of land tenure, when viewed in the context of cultural and property rights based on gender inequalities and power relations within the households, presents a complex scenario.

The tenure rights to land and resources in many South Asian regions are held by men, giving them legal rights over the resources, although women perform the frequent work of collecting biomass resources for household needs, cooking etc. Attached daily to the forest, women thus have a better knowledge on forest management and conservation, but are the most neglected group in social forestry projects.

There is no equity between men and women in land tenure specified officially in the land laws of the respective countries. Neither are women's rights in resource use are ensured in practice. Local traditions seems strongly influence on the women rights in land tenure, as it is the male child who inherits land. As a consequence, women's involvement in forestry projects is less, at the most they are being used as labourers in planting or watering the plants.

ADAPTATION AND MITIGATION PRACTICES IN FOREST MANAGEMENT

Adaptation practices could be incorporated synergistically in most mitigation projects in the forest sector. However, in some cases, mitigation strategies could also have adverse implications for watersheds in arid and semi-arid regions and biodiversity. To achieve an optimum link between adaptation and mitigation activities, it is necessary to clearly define who does the activity, where and what are the activities for each case. Several principles can be defined: prioritizing mitigation activities that help to reduce pressure on natural resources, including vulnerability to climate change as a risk to be analysed in mitigation activities; and prioritizing mitigation activities that enhance local adaptive capacity, and promoting sustainable livelihoods of local populations.

In many places, forests have disappeared due to conversion to lands for the cultivation of high value crops. In other places, fall in prices of crops or beef have led to abandoned agricultural lands, on which forests regenerate. Increased prices of agricultural crops lead to increased production and increased need for packaging material, which in turn stimulated the establishment of plantations of fast growing tree species. An increase in the value of forest products and services may make it more attractive for forest owners and users to manage the forest than to convert them into marginally producing agricultural or livestock lands. An increased demand for international enterprises to behave in an environmentally responsible manner makes them incorporate forests and trees into their agricultural production plans. All these examples show that markets, whether for agricultural products, forest products or ecosystem services, have a complex and close relation to the way forests are used or conserved and thus can influence the mitigation and adaptive capacities of these forests. With the recent discussions on climate change, three types of relations between markets and forests have become crucial; markets for forest carbon, markets that require social and environmental responsibility of a wide range of companies and markets that influence the relative value of forest use in relation to other land uses.

MARKETS FOR FOREST CARBON

Since the KP has been in force, several carbon emissions trading schemes have been established. By far the biggest is the EU ETS, which currently trades more than 80 per cent of all carbon credits with prices significantly higher than in the voluntary carbon markets. Within the scheme, large GHG emitters have been assigned a maximum amount of GHG that they may emit during an established period of time. Those that emit less than this 'cap' can trade the difference with those that emit more, earn emission reduction units through the Joint Implementation programme of the KP flexibility mechanism, or buy Certified Emission Reductions (CERs) through the CDM, also part of the Kyoto flexibility mechanisms. The EU ETS does not recognize sinks, effectively eliminating forest carbon credits from the scheme. Forest carbon credits can be traded in the voluntary carbon market and its proportion in that market has increased considerably after REDD+ was recognized by the UNFCCC as a regitimate form of emission reduction. Overall, however, the value of carbon traded in the voluntary market has declined, possibly because the expected international agreements did not get through, nor did climate change legislation in the United States.

The World Bank (2011) indicates that future demand and supply of carbon are expected to be in balance and it is not very attractive to set up new carbon initiatives, unless GHG emission reduction commitments in developed countries are strengthened. It is, however, difficult to predict the demand, since it depends also on other (macro) economic factors, such as fossil fuel prices, type of economic development and growth. There is another way of trading carbon, through direct transactions between buyers and suppliers. Some examples exist where communities or community associations in developing countries entered into agreements with companies in developed countries. Such companies are often prepared to pay more than market prices for carbon credits because they also look for additional benefits, usually contributing to their social and environmental responsibility.

Social Responsibility Requirements

With the focus on conservation and management of the carbon stock, other types of markets are being reconsidered as well. These are markets that promote sustainable forest management and also favour climate mitigation and adaptation. Forest certification, for example, requires a number of the same forest management and conservation requirements as does REDD+, *e.g.* no deforestation, limited degradation by reduced impact logging practices and fire and pest management.

Several forest certification schemes exist, but globally the two best recognized schemes are the Programme for Endorsement of Forest Certification (PEFC) and the Forest Stewardship Council (FSC). The former endorses national forest management standards, includes the verification of origin of the timber products through a chain of custody certification and already covers more than 200 million hectares of forests, but does not have as good a standing in the market place as FSC. FSC only endorses national indicators that are linked to an international standard and that have been agreed upon through a national process during which there has been equitable participation of social, economic and environmental stakeholder groups. These two certification schemes differ essentially in strictness of social and environmental requirements, appeal procedures and stakeholder participation. FSC is stricter and has more elaborate participatory processes than PEFC while PEFC has greater independence between standard setting and certification bodies. Both schemes are adjusting and are beginning to resemble each other.

Forest certification in general, however, only applies to specific forest management units and therefore has a limited effect on overall deforestation or reforestation rates. These positive effects will depend very much on the scale and intensity of the operations. A greater positive effect may be perceived on forest degradation.

Since certification requires the application of reduced impact logging techniques, it has the potential to reduce damage due to felling and extraction to about half of that of conventional operations. Depending on the scale and intensity of the operations this may imply a considerable reduction in emissions. Increasing processing efficiency of the timber, once it has been logged, has a further potential to lower emissions. FSC certification has the potential to contribute to the reduction of emissions from forest degradation, since it has a performance based system.

Although forest certification was originally set up to increase market benefits - access and price - especially for tropical forest producers, currently only market access has been realized. Price increases have been limited to certain cases or in size. Easier access to credit and technical assistance has been seen as an additional benefit. All of these are factors that help increase the adaptive capacity of the forest manager; better organization, greater or more stable income and better access to supporting services.

Forest certification also has the potential to also increase the adaptive capacity of forest dependent people; additional training allows them to diversify their 26 economic activities, new employment opportunities help increase and diversify their income and local organizations involved in forest management are strengthened which enables them react to sudden environmental changes. An example of the latter is the village of Toncontin, in Honduras. This was the first village that was able to distribute emergency supplies after Hurricane Mitch hit in October 1998 because they could quickly identify potential beneficiaries and set up a distribution system based on the existing forest management organization.

Other certification schemes, such as schemes that certify biological agriculture or good agricultural practices, also have had a positive effect on the forest, both in area and in quality, and thus have the potential to contribute to both forest mitigation and forest adaptation activities. In Costa Rica, banana companies have purchased forest areas for protection and restoration to offset part of their emissions in the production process and contribute to biodiversity conservation.

Throughout the tropics, selected coffee plantations are increasing tree cover to be able to sell their products as 'shade grown' and more recently efforts are on the way to estimate GHG emissions from coffee production to be able to determine the level of carbon neutrality achieved. Carbon sequestration in trees is often seen as a good option to offset some or most of the unavoidable emissions. Such low emission schemes are very promising considering that they may contribute to carbon sequestration and storage - agroforestry systems with coffee or cacao have been reported to store as much carbon as 20 year old secondary vegetation - as well as to strengthening the adaptation capacity of the local agro-ecosystems and their inhabitants, contribute to biodiversity, water regulation and disease and pest control if the shade is well managed.

These schemes may also contribute to reducing the level of risk producers face when diversifying their production and securing more stable markets for their cash crops. They may be particularly useful in the context of landscape management, where they offer the opportunity to strengthen management of the ecosystem services throughout the landscape, including in agricultural fields. Another social responsibility scheme oriented at sharing costs and benefits of ecosystem service management, is the concept of PES. Such schemes may not necessarily be oriented towards carbon sequestration and storage but nearly all existing PES schemes promote the maintenance or enhancement of forest and tree cover. They may or may not require the measurement of the services provided. Some assume that if forest cover is maintained or expanded, or its use limited to carefully management operations (timber, NWFP, conservation, tourism), the desired services are provided. Such is the case of the Costa Rican PES scheme, which pays a flat rate per hectare per year for a mix of carbon sequestration and storage, water regulation, biodiversity maintenance and scenic beauty for each hectare of forest.

In Mexico, the first three services are being paid for through separate PES schemes, although all three schemes may have similar results in terms of carbon sequestration and storage, water regulation and biodiversity maintenance. In particular where water resources and biodiversity are at risk due to climate change, the contribution of PES to adaptation may become important. In general, such schemes also offer additional income to producers and forest owners, but in each case the benefits should be evaluated against the costs of meeting entry and monitoring requirements.

Managing Uncertainty and Risk

The consideration of risk has always been an important part of forest management activities. With climate change, uncertainty is increasing as are the risks of long term investments in forestry. Below are two examples of how the incorporation of uncertainty and risk into management decisions and improved monitoring for early warnings of changing conditions.

The Birris Micro Watershed

The Birris micro-watershed is located in Costa Rica. Its main landuses are cattle farming (milk and meat) and horticultural activities, while the micro-watershed provides a small hydro-electric power plant with water, later flowing into the Reventazón river with a larger hydro-electric power plant. The micro watershed is likely to suffer from climate change through changes in the onset of the growing season, as well as more severe droughts and high intensity rains. Erosion and sedimentation are likely to be the main direct impact of such changes and are considered by the different stakeholders as being a major issue: for the farmers because they lose fertile soil; by the electric power plants, because it fills up the reservoirs and may damage the machinery. These potential problems were analyzed by different stakeholders and indicators were developed to measure the potential effects of different land use scenarios on components potentially important for climate change adaptation and mitigation capacity of the micro-watershed.

Four scenarios were identified by their potential to reduce sedimentation:

- Business as usual,
- All critical areas reforested,
- All critical areas under improved soil management and,
- A combination of good soil management throughout the micro-watershed and reforestation in some of the critical areas.

Scientists estimated the values of the indicators for each of the four scenarios and once presented with the result of these studies, participants were requested to agree on one of the four land use options. They chose for an intermediate land use option that requires low initial investments while still reducing the risk that climate change may cause much erosion, and degradation of the agricultural lands and sedimentation of the hydro-electric power dam. Development objectives were thus combined with an assessment of risk of negative impacts of climate change, in this case erosion due to increased rainfall intensity.

Indicators of Socio-economic Impact of Land Use

Part of the research undertaken as part of a Mesoamerican Agro-environmental Programme (MAP) funded project is focused on identifying indicators that could predict the consequences of land use change, irrespective of the origin of the change. Studies have been carried out on the socio-economic and environmental impacts of different land uses in some Latin-American countries (*e.g.* Brazil, Costa Rica, Nicaragua) and this information was compared with information on past land use changes in those areas. This analysis should give rise to indicators on the timing and drivers of land use change as well as the potential consequences of these changes. The concept is very similar to the Pressure-State-Response set of indicators used by many countries at the national level within the framework of the UN sustainable development monitoring. The difference between the two lies in the scale and detail, with the MAP project allowing for the downscale of monitoring to landscape level, giving local authorities and stakeholder platforms the tools to predict change and estimate the risk of the negative impacts of those changes. This helps the operationalization of national sustainable development and climate change monitoring systems.

9

Global Discourse on Forestry

"Liberty and forest laws are incompatible," remarked an English country vicar, speaking on behalf of villagers shut out of woodland reserved for the exclusive use of the king, in 1720. The history of state forestry is indeed a history of social conflict. In monarchies and in democracies, in metropolitan Europe as well as in colonial South Asia, the state management of forests has met bitter and continuous opposition. On the one side are the professional foresters who believe that timber production can be ensured only through the exclusion of humans and their animals from wooded areas; on the other, the peasants, pastoralists, charcoal ironmakers, basketweavers, and other such groups for whom access to forests and forest resources is crucial to economic survival. Environmentalists have added to the criticisms of these latter groups, charging foresters with simplifying complex ecosytems in the direction of commercially valuable but biologically impoverished monocultures.

These contending parties have battled for more than two hundred years. In continental Europe, the eighteenth and nineteenth centuries were peppered with social protest movements against the state management of forests. These protests inspired, among other things, Karl Marx's first political writings and a memorable novel by Honore de Balzac capturing peasant hostility to forest officials. When the European model of strict state control over forests was exported to the colonies, the disaffected peasants and tribals responded with arson and violence. Movements over forest rights were a recurring phenomena in colonies ruled by the British, the Dutch, and the French. The conflicts persisted when the post-colonial governments of countries such as Malaysia and Indonesia followed the authoritarian model of forest management inherited from the colonizer.

In recent decades, however, the global discourse on forestry has moved towards a more accommodationist perspective. Foresters and peasant protesters now seem to talk to, rather than talk past, each other. A willingness to listen to and at least partially incorporate the other point of view has replaced the rigid and uncompromising attitude of the past. Within the forestry profession itself, skeptics doubt the contemporary relevance of the custodial and policing approaches previously followed. A system of natural resource management crafted in absolutist and colonialist times clearly needed to be seriously modified or even overthrown.4 Social activists and community leaders have, meanwhile, moved from demanding a total state withdrawal from forest areas to asking governments to more seriously and sympathetically consider the rights of forest-dependent communities.

With this move from conflict to collaboration have come shifts in the language of forestry itself. Terms such as "scientific forestry" and "rational land management," euphemisms for state control and commercial timber production, are being rapidly replaced by sweet-sounding phrases such as "community management," "participatory development," and "joint forest management." While these terms have come into vogue in the last two decades, they have, in fact, a very long geneaology. From the beginnings of state forestry, there have been serious attempts to democratize the regimes of resource management. Both dissidents within the bureaucracy as well as intellectual activists outside it tried hard to make the state respond more sensitively to the just claims of local communities. The ongoing programmes of joint forest management in India can draw legitimacy and sustenance from a struggle that is at least a century old.

THE LAW AND THE PROTESTS

The crucial watershed in the history of Indian forestry is undoubtedly the building of the railway network. In a famous minute of 1853, the governor general of India, Lord Dalhousie, wrote of how railway construction was both the means for creating a market for British goods and the outlet for British capital seeking profitable avenues for investment. Thus between 1853 and 1910 more than eighty thousand kilometers of track were laid in the subcontinent.6 The early years of railway expansion witnessed a savage assault on the forests of India. Great chunks of forest were destroyed to meet the demand for railway sleepers (over a million of which were required annually). The sal forests of Garhwal and Kumaun, for example, were "felled in even to desolation." "Thousands of trees were felled which were never removed, nor was their removal possible."

This depradation brought home most forcefully the fact that India's forests were not inexhaustible. At this time the British were unquestionably the world leaders in deforestation, having burnt or felled hundreds of thousands of acres of woodland in Australia, southern Africa, northeastern United States, Burma, and India. Knowing little of methods of sustained-yield forestry, they called in the Germans, who did. Thus in 1864 they established the Indian Forest Department, which for the first twenty-five years of its existence was serenely guided by three German inspectors general of forest-Dietrich Brandis, Wilhelm Schlich, and Bertold von Ribbentrop. For its effective functioning, the new department required a progressive curtailment of the previously untrammeled rights of use exercised by rural communities all over South Asia. An act was hurriedly drafted to establish the claims of the state to the forestland it immediately required, subject to the provision that existing rights not be abridged. This act was "infinitely milder and less stringent than that which is in force in most European countries." The search commenced for a more stringent and inclusive piece of legislation. In 1869, the Government of India circulated to the provinces a new draft act, which sought to strengthen the state's control over forest areas through the regulation and in some cases extinction of customary rights.

The new legislation was based on the assumption that all land not actually under cultivation belonged to the state. Of course, it was not easy to wish away the access to forests exercised in centuries past by peasants and other rural groups. The colonial state, however, argued that such use, however widespread and enduring, had been exercised only at the mercy of the monarch. Unless it had been expressly recorded in writing, customary use was deemed to be a "privilege," not a "right." And since the British government was the successor to Indian rulers, the ownership of forests and waste was now vested in it. "The right of conquest is the strongest of all rights," emphatically remarked one forest official. "It is a right against which there is no appeal."

There were, however, some notable dissenting voices within the colonial government. Sent the draft forest bill by the Government of India, the Madras Government in turn invited responses from various officers. The views of Narain Row, Deputy Collector of Nellore, are representative. The proposed legislation, he said, had no historical precedent, for "there were originally no Government forests in this country. Forests have always been of natural growth here; and so they have been enjoyed by the people."

Another Deputy Collector, Venkatachellum Puntulu, of Bellary, argued that the burden of the new legislation would fall most heavily on the poor. While large landlords would find it relatively easy to deny the state any claim over their forest property, unlettered peasants would not be able to prove rights of ownership, even though they traditionally used forests as common property.

Criticizing the detailed rules prohibiting the collection of different kinds of forest produce, Puntulu penetratingly remarked that "the provisions of this bill infringe the rights of poor people who live by daily labour (cutting wood, catching fish and eggs of birds) and whose feelings cannot be known to those whose opinions will be required on this bill and who cannot assert their claims, like [the] influential class, who can assert their claims in all ways open to them and spread agitation in the newspapers."

After several such responses came in, the Madras Board of Revenue told the Government of India that the claim of the state to uncultivated forests and wastes was virtually nonexistent:

There is scarcely a forest in the whole of the Presidency of Madras which is not within the limits of some village and there is not one in which so far as the Board can ascertain, the state asserted any rights of property unless royalties in teak, sandalwood, cardamoms and the like can be considered as such, until very recently. All of them, without exception are subject to tribal or communal rights which have existed from time immemorial and which are as difficult to define as they are necessary to the rural population.... [In Madras] the forests are, and always have been common property, no restriction except that of taxes, like the Moturpha [tax on tools] and Pulari [grazing tax] was ever imposed on the people till the Forest Department was created, and such taxes no more indicate that the forest belongs to the state than the collection of assessment shows that the private holdings in Malabar, Canara and the Ryotwari districts belong to it.

The Madras Government advanced three basic reasons for rejecting the bill drafted by the Government of India: First, because its principles, scope and purpose are inconsistent with the existing facts of forest property and its history. Second, because, even if the Bill were consistent with facts, its provisions are too arbitrary, setting the laws of property at open defiance, and leaving the determination of forest rights to a Department which, in this Presidency at all events, has always shown itself eager to destroy all forest rights but those of Government. Third, because a Forest Bill, which aims at the regulation of local usages ought to be framed.

The objections were disregarded, and in 1878, the new bill passed. The act divided the forests of the subcontinent into three broad classes. State or reserved forests were to be carefully chosen, in large and compact areas that could lend themselves to commercial exploitation.

The constitution of these reserves was to be preceded by a legal settlement that either extinguished customary rights of user, transferred them as "privileges" to be exercised elsewhere, or, in exceptional cases, allowed their limited exercise. In the second class, of "protected" forests, rights and privileges were recorded but not settled. However, all valuable tree species were to be declared as "reserved" by the state, while the Forest Department had the power to prohibit grazing and other ostensibly damaging practices.

The Forest Act also provided for a third class of forests-village forests. But as these lands had first to be constituted as reserved forests, the procedure aroused suspicion among the villagers, and this chapter remained a "dead letter."15 Meanwhile, the area of forests under strict state control steadily expanded. In 1878, there were 14,000 square miles of state forest. By 1890, this had increased to 76,000 square miles, three-fourths of which were reserved forests. Ten years later, there were 81,400 square miles of reserved forests and 8,300 of protected forests. Given increasing demand for wood products, the state sought to establish firmer control over forests, both by expanding the area taken over under the Forest Act and by converting protected forests to reserved forest. The Indian Forest Act of 1878 was a comprehensive piece of legislation that came to serve as a model for other British colonies.16 Within India, it allowed the state to expand the commercial exploitation of the forest while putting curbs on local use for subsistence. This denial of village forest rights provoked countrywide protest.

REBELLIONS AGAINST COLONIAL FORESTRY

The history of colonial rule is punctuated by major rebellions against colonial forestry-in Chotanagpur in 1893, in Bastar in 1910, in Gudem-Rampa in 1879-80 and again in 1922-23, in Midnapur in 1920, and in Adilabad in 1940. These rebellions sometimes extended over several hundred square miles of territory, involved thousands of villagers, and had to be put down by armed force.

Even where discontent did not manifest itself in open rebellion, it was expressed through arson, noncompliance, and breaches of the forest law.

The participants in these protests were unlettered peasants and tribals, and we know far more of their deeds than their words.

Nonetheless, their voices do figure here and there in the archives of the state, sometimes mediated by the language of the officials reporting them. Thus in the 1880s, when the government of the Bombay Presidency was aggressively demarcating the rich teak forests of the Dang district, preparatory to their constitution as state reserves, a Bhil tribal chief sent in a petition stating that "we do not wish to let the Dang jungle [be] demarcated, for thereby we shall lose our rights and we and our poor rayat [cultivators] shall always be under the control of the Forest Department and the Department will always oppress us."

Around the same time, the colonial state was attempting to take over the deodar (cedar) forests of the upper Jamuna valley. These trees had suddenly become market-worthy, to service the then expanding railway network. But as a peasant bitterly observed, "the forests have belonged to us from time immemorial, our ancestors planted them and have protected them; now that they have become of value, government steps in and robs us of them."18 Or consider, finally, these remarks of an administrator in the Bastar district of central India, on the determination of his tribal subjects to continue practicing swidden cultivation in what was now "government" forests: "On the road from Tetam to Katekalyan I found general dissatisfaction at the restriction of penda [swidden] cultivation. I was unable to convince them of its evils [sic]. Podiyami Bandi Peda of Tumakpal has to get his son married and for this purpose he wants to cultivate penda in the prohibited area. I told him he should not do it. He replied plainly that he would cultivate it and go to jail as he had to get his son married."

In 1871, the Madras Government predicted that the new act, if passed into law, would "place in antagonism to Government every class whose support is desired and essential to the object in view, from the Zamindar [landlord] to the Hill Toda or Korombar." This was an astonishingly accurate prediction, for the Forest Department was unquestionably the most unpopular arm of the British Raj.

The story of the numerous popular movements against state forestry, so long neglected by historians, is now attracting an array of chroniclers. The critics were principally of two kinds. On the one side were scholars and politicians with a deep knowledge of rural conditions, and who sometimes formed part of popular movements themselves.

Their criticisms of state forestry thus drew richly upon the feelings and grievances of the people most affected by it. On the other side were the rare (but, for that reason, significant) dissidents within the colonial bureaucracy, who opposed the centralizing thrust of government forest policy. The first set were outsiders so far as the apparatus of rule was concerned, but insiders with respect to popular opinion and popular consciousness. The second set were by virtue of race and status outsiders to Indian society, but insiders with regard to the policy of the state and the functioning of government.

PRECOCIOUS PROPHETS

In 1878, the Poona Sarvajanik Sabha, a vastly respected nationalist organization in western India, bitterly opposed the new Forest Act. Despite its middle-class origins, the Sabha had consistenly fought for the rights of the cultivator, urging that the colonial government lessen its burden of taxation on the peasantry.21 Now, in the context of the Forest Act debate, it pointed out that state usurpation was grossly violative of customary rights over forests, for both "private grantees and village and tribal communities" had "cherished and maintained these rights with the same tenacity with which private property in land is maintained elsewhere." The Sarvajanik Sabha did not, however, merely oppose the proposed Forest Act for its excessive emphasis on state control; it offered a more constructive and creative alternative.

Thus the Sabha argued that the better maintenance of forest cover could more easily be brought about by taking the Indian villager into confidence of the Indian Government. If the villagers were rewarded and commended for conserving their patches of forestlands, or for making plantations on the same, instead of ejecting them from the forestland that they possess, or in which they are interested, emulation might be evoked between neighboring villages. Thus more effective conservation and development of forests in India might be secured, and when the villagers have their own patches of forest to attend to, government forests might not be molested. Thus the interests of the villagers as well as the government can be secured without causing any unnecessary irritation in the minds of the masses of the Indian population. The Sabha was advocating a far more democratic structure of forest management than that envisaged by the colonial government. Indeed, it was proposing the institution of a Vrikshamitra (Friends of the Trees) Award, one hundred and ten years before the Indian Government's Ministry of Environment and Forests conceived and named such a scheme, for rewarding individuals and communities who had successfully protected or replenished forest areas. Three years after the 1878 act was passed, the impact of state forestry on rural communities was foregrounded by the social reformer Jotirau Phule. Phule himself was a gardener by caste, and in general exceptionally alert to the problems of the agricultural classes. The following is his description of the impact of the Forest Department on the livelihood of farmers and pastoralists in the Deccan countryside: In the olden days small landholders who could not subsist on cultivation alone used to eat wild fruits like figs and jamun and sell the leaves and flowers of the flame of the forest and the mahua tree [both common trees of the Indian forest].

They could also depend on the village ground to maintain one or two cows and two or four goats, thereby living happily in their own ancestral villages. However, the cunning European employees of our motherly government have used their foreign brains to erect a great superstructure called the forest department. With all the hills and undulating areas as also the fallow lands and grazing grounds brought under the control of the forest department, the livestock of the poor farmers do not even have place to breathe anywhere on the surface of the earth.

DEPENDENCE OF THE AGRICULTURIST ON THE PRODUCE OF FORESTS

These remarks drew attention to the dependence of the agriculturist on the produce of forests and other common lands. This dependence was even more acute in the tribal regions of middle India, where communities of hunter-gatherers, swidden agriculturists, and charcoal iron makers were likewise at the receiving end of the new forest laws. These peoples found an eloquent spokesman in Verrier Elwin (1902-1964), a brilliant Oxford scholar and renegade priest who became the foremost interpreter of adivasi (tribal) culture in India. Elwin was a pioneer of ecological anthropology, whose many works vividly showcased the intimate relationship between the forest world and the life of the adivasi.

All tribals, he argued, had a deep knowledge of wild plants and animals; some could even read the great volume of Nature like an "open book." Swidden agriculturists, for whom forest and farm shaded imperceptibly into each other, had an especial bond with the natural world. They liked to think of themselves as children of Dharti Mata, Mother Earth, fed and loved by her.

Elwin's ethnographies are peppered with references to the adivasi's love for the forest. Tragically, the forest and game laws introduced by the British had made them interlopers in their own land. He quotes a member of the tribal group Gond, whose idea of heaven was "miles and miles of forest without any forest guards." As the anthropologist himself wrote in 1941:

The reservation of forests was a very serious blow to the tribesman. He was forbidden to practice his traditional methods of cultivation. He was ordered to remain in one village and not to wander from place to place. When he had cattle he was kept in a state of continual anxiety for fear they should stray over the boundary and render him liable to heavy fines. If he was a Forest Villager he became liable at any moment to be called to work for the Forest Department. If he lived elsewhere he was forced to obtain a license for almost every kind of forest produce. At every turn the Forest Laws cut across his life, limiting, frustrating, destroying his self confidence.

During the year 1933-4 there were 27,000 forest offences registered in the Central Provinces and Berar and probably ten times as many unwhipped of justice. It is obvious that so great a number of offences would not occur unless the forest regulations ran counter to the fundamental needs of the tribesmen. A Forest Officer once said to me: "Our laws are of such a kind that every villager breaks one forest law every day of his life."

Elwin's writings were addressed equally to the colonial state and to the Congress nationalists, who in the 1940s were very much a government-in-waiting. The Congress, however, had not been especially sensitive to the rights of the tribals. But as Elwin reminded them, "the aboriginals are the real swadeshi [indigenous] products of India, in whose presence everything is foreign. They are the ancient people with moral claims and rights thousands of years old. They were here first: they should come first in our regard." He was deeply distressed when a Congress report on tribals followed the British authorities in asking for a ban on shifting cultivation.

Now Elwin's work had shown that, contrary to modernist prejudice, swidden as practiced by the Baiga, the Juang, and other tribes was an ecologically viable system of cultivation. When the nationalists recommended the ban, he wrote angrily that "the forests belong to the aboriginal. I should have thought that anyone who was a Nationalist would at least advocate swaraj [freedom] for the aboriginal!"

The significance of the forest in tribal life is a running theme in Elwin's work. Noting that a majority of tribal rebellions had centered around land and forests, he pleaded for the greater involvement of tribals in forest management in free India. Even if adivasis had no longer any legal rights of ownership, they had considerable moral rights. And as tribals were as much part of the national treasure as forests themselves, there should be an amicable adjustment between forest management and tribal needs. Even where commercial forest operations became necessary, he said, these should be undertaken by tribal cooperatives and not by powerful private contractors. After independence Verrier Elwin became the first foreigner to be granted citizenship of free India. In 1954, he was appointed Adviser on Tribal Affairs to the Government of India (with special reference to the North-east Frontier Agency). He was also to serve on more than one high-level, all-India committee on tribal policy. From his first official appointment until his premature death in 1964, Elwin repeatedly urged a reconsideration of forest policy, such that it might, at last, come to more properly serve tribal needs. In this he had little success for forest management became, if anything, more commercially oriented in independent India.32 Towards the end of his life, the anthropologist wrote with some bitterness of how the victims of government policy were being unfairly blamed for the destruction of forests:

There is constant propaganda that the tribal people are destroying the forest. When this was put to some of the villagers, they countered the complaint by asking how they could destroy the forest. They owned no trucks; they hardly had even a bullock-cart; the utmost that they could carry away was a headload of produce for sale to maintain their families and that too against a license. The utmost that they wanted was wood to keep them warm in the winter months, to reconstruct or repair their huts and carry on their little cottage industries. Their fuel-needs for cooking, they said, were not much, for they had not much to cook. Having explained their own position they invariably turned to the amount of [forest] destruction that was taking place all around them. They asked how the exzamindars [landlords], in violation of their agreements and the forest rules and laws, devastated vast tracts of forest land right in front of officials. They also related how the contractors stray outside the contracted coupes, carry loads in trucks in excess of their authorised capacity and otherwise exploit both the forests and the tribal people.

DISTRIBUTION OF THE WORLD'S MAIN VEGETATION TYPES OR BIOMES

Climate is the dominant control factor in the distribution of the world's main vegetation types or biomes. Biomes are defined as a distinctive ecological system, characterized primarily by the nature of their vegetation. On a global scale and in a historical and geological time frame, response to climatic stress is of overriding importance. The relevance of understanding tree and forest ecosystem response to climatic stress has increased because we are currently experiencing an unprecedented change of global climate which is, at least in part, the result of anthropogenic factors.

Most contemporary texts on the influence of climate and vegetation date our understanding of the relationship between climate and the distribution of vegetation from the work of Von Humboldt at the beginning of the nineteenth century. Holdridge (1947 and subsequent work) demonstrated a strong correlation between the main groups of life form or biomes (*e.g.* deserts, grasslands, deciduous or coniferous forests) and two major climatic characteristics, temperature and water availability. These climatic factors are the main influence at the biome scale, while soil type (nutrient availability) topography and anthropogenic factors are major influences on vegetation patterns within biomes on a smaller local scale.

It is of considerable interest and relevance that where temperature and moisture availability or moisture budget (defined as precipitation-evapo-transpiration) are similar, the same tree species or similar species of one tree genera are present or prove to be satisfactory forestry species if introduced. This reflects the relationship between climate and suitable physiology and anatomy, and also the pattern of species' evolution and migration. The timing of the separation of the earth's present-day continents relative to the evolutionary history of tree species and taxa determines presence or absence of particular species within suitable climatic zones. Eventually the land bridges between the continents became impassable to tree species during the period of their rapid evolution in the Cretaceous Era. In the absence of human influence, the geographical extent (natural distribution) of the various forest biomes is thus determined mainly by climatic conditions and the natural species composition will be further influenced by evolutionary and geological factors.

There are several critically important temperature thresholds that affect physiological processes and thus define the environmental limits of the major forest biomes. The first threshold is a critical minimum temperature in the range +12 to 1°C, which results in chilling injury to plant membranes. The next critical threshold is at about -15°C and roughly corresponds to the temperature at which frost damage occurs to leaves and buds (depending on the degree of frost acclimation).

The leaves of broadleaved species with a damage threshold at about -15°C are less resistant to frost than coniferous needles. The buds of broadleaved and coniferous species have similar minimum temperature thresholds but the xylem of broadleaved trees (angiosperms) is more susceptible to ice formation than that of conifers. This is because coniferous xylem is made up of tracheids, which have a smaller lumen diameter than the vessels that make up the xylem in broadleaved trees. Similarly broadleaved species with diffuse-porous xylem, which is of smaller diameter than ring-porous xylem, are more resistant to ice-induced xylem damage. Broadleaved trees with ring-porous xylem are notably absent from boreal forests.

The next critical temperature threshold is at -39 to -40°C, below which only a few boreal tree species can survive (*e.g. Picea glauca, Larix laricina* and *Larix sibirica)* because this temperature will freeze the xylem and buds. At their extreme northern limits, these cold-tolerant species often have a parenchyma pith cavity beneath the crown of the primordial bud that prevents ice formation from spreading from the xylem to the bud.

It has been argued that in harsh climates, particularly low temperatures, the evergreen habit gives a more favourable carbon balance and thus we see the dominance of coniferous evergreens in cold montane and boreal forests. Climates with ample rainfall, well distributed throughout the year and with rare frosts, as experienced in temperate regions (30-55° of latitude), also favour evergreen rather than deciduous forests. This is considered to have led to the dominance of broadleaved evergreen forests in the temperate regions of the Southern Hemisphere, with the notable exception of southern Chile where deciduous broadleaved forests occur. Broadleaved deciduous tree species predominate in the northern temperate regions.

The distribution of the various forest biomes is thus determined by climatic conditions. However within the major biomes individual species gradually decrease in numbers near their altitudinal or latitudinal limits. Woodward (1987, 1995) attributed this more to increasingly non-competitive carbon balance rather than to direct damage from low temperatures. Although the tree species present within the various forest biomes should not normally be experiencing climatic stress, climate remains of major importance to forestry and to the conservation of forest ecosystems for three main reasons. First, within a climatic region foresters are able to select species that grow better (faster) or provide other desirable benefits for particular sites, as influenced by local conditions of topography and soils. Second, the effect of climate on tree species limits the use of introduced or exotic species, which otherwise has proved a very successful strategy for improving yields in commercial forestry worldwide. Third, and perhaps of greatest interest, is that climate changes, not only naturally on a geological time-scale but also rapidly as a result of human activity, *i.e.* global climate change.

Landsberg and Gower (1997) followed Melillo *et al.* (1993) in adopting a classification of forest biomes based on major climatic region (tropical, temperate and boreal) and tree physiognomy (broadleaved, evergreen, broadleaved deciduous and needle-leaved evergreen conifer). Seven forest biomes were identified as follows: boreal, temperate deciduous, temperate coniferous, temperate mixed, temperate broadleaved evergreen forest, tropical evergreen and tropical deciduous. Of these, the boreal and tropical evergreens cover the greatest area. Forest biomes.

The increase of global surface land and ocean temperatures that has been observed during the last 100 years is faster than that observed during the geological past. Predictions of future climate indicate that some tree species, and some parts of the forest biomes, will experience climates outside those of their natural range. Over significant areas climatic stress will occur and dieback is likely. A number of authors have used existing relationships (correlations) between climatic factors and biome distribution to predict the future distribution of terrestrial biomes from the climate predictions provided by general circulation models. Changes in biome distribution might be expected to occur by migration, although migration at rates of 5 km annually will be required and palaeoecological records indicate postglacial migration rates of tree species of only 40-150 m annually. Thus migration rates are likely to be insufficient, resulting in significant areas of stress and dieback, or rather, that stress and dieback will be part of the process of migration. A recent example of such predictions is that of Friend *et al.* (1997) who mapped the global distribution of eight biomes and of desert for existing (today's) climate and for climate predicted for the year 2080.

This model, called 'HYBRID', predicts vegetation type at any particular location on the basis of the outcome of competition for light, nitrogen and water and of the plants' ability to survive extreme conditions. Unlike earlier, less sophisticated work of this type, HYBRID predicts that tropical forests will decline in area, with dieback beginning in the 2050s as a result of decreased rainfall and increased temperatures. Temperate and mixed forests are likely to move northwards and increase their total area. Boreal forest area is predicted to change very little provided that these forests can establish in more northern areas with shallow poorly developed soils. The palaeoecological records show that the species composition of forest ecosystems varied during their postglacial advance so we could also predict some changes of species composition as a result of the stress caused by climate change.

These predictions suggest that forest managers will need to plan for, and respond to, climate change if extensive areas of forest dieback are to be avoided; some such problems are likely to occur in any event. Indeed, there is firm evidence that climatic conditions have been a major, or perhaps *the* major, factor responsible for forest dieback in Europe and the north-eastern USA. Changes of species choice will be an obvious course of action in plantation forestry.

The successful use of 'exotics' in commercial forestry, for example Sitka spruce *(Picea sitchensis)* in western Europe, *Pinus radiata* in New Zealand and Chile, and *Eucalyptus* in Portugal and South America, indicates that forest managers can, in any event, achieve increased yields by planting species outside their current natural distribution.

RECENT ESTIMATES OF GLOBAL FOREST AREA

The following section is based on 1990 baseline figures, updated to 1995, prepared by the Food and Agriculture Organisation (FAO) Forest Resource Assessment Programme, reported in and largely drawn from *State of the World's Forests 1997.*

In 1995 forests were estimated to cover 3454 million ha, or 26.6 per cent of the total land area of the world (Greenland and Antarctic excepted). Almost two-thirds of the world's forests were located in seven countries: Russia, Brazil, Canada, USA, China, Indonesia and Zaire; 29 countries had more than half of their land covered by forest, of which 21 were in the tropical belt. However 49 countries, in addition to the many non-forested small island states and territories, had less than 10 per cent of their land covered by forests. Five entire subregions were in this category: North Africa (1.2 per cent of the land area), Near East (1.9 per cent), Temperate Oceania (6.2 per cent), Non-tropical Southern Africa (6.8 per cent) and West Sahelian Africa (7.5 per cent). The latest information on the distribution of forest and of forest cover change by ecological zones was provided in 1990; the results of the Forest Resources Assessment 2000 were released by FAO in 2000. In 1990, temperate and boreal forests occupied 1.64 billion ha and tropical forests 1.76 billion ha. A breakdown by ecological zone was available only for tropical forests.The figures on tropical forests show that most (88 per cent) are in lowlands; of these, tropical rain forests accounted for 47 per cent of all lowland tropical forests, followed by moist deciduous forest (38 per cent) and dry and very dry formations (15 per cent).

NATURAL FORESTS

The forest area estimates described above include undisturbed forests, forests modified by humans through use and management (or 'seminatural' forests) and forests created artificially by humankind (*i.e.* forest plantations) by afforestation or reforestation. (Afforestation is defined as the establishment of a tree crop on an area from which it has always, or for a very long time, been absent. Reforestation is defined as the establishment of a tree crop on forest land.) In most industrialised countries, particularly in continental Europe, forests are being managed in such a way that at management-unit level a continuum exists from low-intensity management, involving natural regeneration, through more intensive methods involving some artificial planting to highly intensive methods with complete planting and cultivation; this makes it difficult to isolate figures for natural forest and plantations. The distinction between natural or seminatural forests and forest plantations can more easily be made for developing countries and some industrialised countries such as New Zealand in which forest plantations have been established using introduced species.

Interest in natural forests, particularly their role in the conservation of biological diversity, has led to efforts to compare forests today with what is thought to be their original character and to give complete protection to areas of forests which have had no, or minimal, human interference. Although there are difficulties in identifying the extent of natural forest, compounded by problems of definition, some information exists that can be used as an indication of broad patterns of natural forests in various regions.

An attempt has been made by the World Wide Fund for Nature (WWF) to quantify the area of forests in western Europe that has been relatively undisturbed by humans or which has retained much of its natural character. Their report distinguishes between 'virgin forest', defined as 'forest ecosystems whose characteristics are determined exclusively by natural location and environmental factors... without human influences present or visible any more', and 'natural and ancient seminatural forests', which 'have not been planted or sown by man for the past two centuries' and 'which continue to have a large number of the natural elements'.

The study found that only a small proportion (probably < 1 per cent) of the total forest land in northern and western Europe could be considered as virgin forest, which has arisen since the last glaciation. Almost all was located in Sweden, Finland and Norway, with small areas in Greece, Austria and Switzerland and (according to another author) in France. In eastern Europe, Slovakia and Belarus have considerable areas of virgin forest while Poland and Croatia have small areas. In addition, in northern and western Europe, the WWF report identifies natural and ancient seminatural forests representing 2.1 per cent of the total forest cover (1990) of the 16 countries concerned. There are a further 3 million ha of land in the region in national parks and other protected areas and another 50 000 ha in small forest reserves (mostly for nature conservation and scientific research), whose use is tightly restricted.

The situation in temperate and boreal North America is quite different from that of densely populated Europe and Japan, where use and management of forests for many centuries have left very little of the original forest area untouched. 'Old growth forests', as they are called in North America, still cover extensive areas.

On the lands managed by the US National Park Service alone, old-growth forests covered 1.97 million ha in 1988. Although not a direct measure of the extent of old growth forest, it may be noted that the area of forest included in national parks and other protected areas in North America (USA and Canada) was reported to be nearly 49 million ha in 1990.

The FAO Forest Resource Assessment 1990 did not distinguish between undisturbed and disturbed 'natural' forests in developing countries. However, the Forest Resource Assessment 1980 made estimates of the areas of undisturbed closed forests (primary forests and old secondary forests where there had been no logging for the last 60-80 years) and of closed forests that were included in national parks and other protected areas (thus relatively undisturbed, at least in theory). At that time, these two categories together represented 60 per cent of the total closed forest area in the tropics, a proportion varying from 39 per cent in tropical Asia to 59 per cent in tropical Africa and 69 per cent in tropical America.

These different proportions by region reflected a slower development of large-scale harvesting in tropical America compared with tropical Africa and Asia, and also the fact that, in tropical America, spontaneous colonisation did not follow in the wake of logging as systematically as in the two other regions due to lower population pressure. Although the two categories do not match the concept of 'virgin forests' of Europe and of 'old growth forests' of North America, the sum of the two categories nevertheless gives an indication of the amount of forest disturbance (or management, depending on the point of view of the observer) that existed around 1980 in the humid tropics. Although corresponding estimates for 1990 and 1995 are not available, it is likely that the share of undisturbed forests remains higher in the three tropical regions than in Europe and probably in North America too.

FOREST CONDITIONS AND AREA

The area covered by forests is very likely to change under climate change, with shifts occurring between forest types due to changing temperature and precipitation regimes, while in some regions, forest area is expected to expand (*e.g.* temperate regions) and in others to contract (*e.g.* boreal, tropical and mountain forests). Such changes have been occurring in the past following the natural changes in temperature and precipitation that accompanied the different ice ages. Currently, however, it is very difficult to separate forest area change due to climate change from area changes due to other factors.

Globally, planted forests and natural regeneration have increased the forest areas in the United States, Europe, China, and some countries in Latin America and the Caribbean *e.g.* Chile, Uruguay, Cuba and Costa Rica. On the other hand, some countries in Africa, Asia and the Pacific and the tropical countries of Latin America continue to be subject to deforestation, mainly due to conversion to small- and large-scale agriculture and livestock while deforestation in the boreal forests of Siberia is mainly due to forest fires. Although the boreal forests are expected to move northward, temperate forests are expected to increase their area northward to a greater extent than the boreal forests, thus reducing the total area of boreal forests. In the future, it is expected that the combination of climate change, land use conversion and un-sustainable land use practices will interact. Changes in water availability are considered to be a key factor for the survival and growth of many forest species, although the response to prolonged droughts will vary among species and also among different varieties of the same species. Climate change will increase the risk of frequent and more intense fires, especially where changing climate is accompanied by lower precipitation or longer dry periods as in the boreal, Mediterranean and sub-tropical forests and traditional land clearing practices as in the Amazon. In the northern Atlantic region of Nicaragua, for example, Rodriquez *et al.*, found that the combination of the amount of rainfall during the previous three months and the average monthly temperature of the current month showed a strong relation with 64 per cent of the fires between 1996 and 1999.

Although data are not conclusive, it is expected that frequency of strong hurricanes will increase in hurricane prone areas such as Central America and the Asia Pacific region. Hurricanes may destroy forest areas completely or cause heavy degradation. If left untouched, however, such areas will ecologically recover over time, albeit slow in terms of biomass. The main effect is likely to be economic (infrastructure, crops and timber lost) and social (lost lives and livelihoods). Together with land use changes, however, the effects may be much longer lasting and devastating - degraded and young forests are easily converted into agricultural land and pastures.

HEALTH AND VITALITY OF CLIMATE CHANGE

Climate change may have profound impacts on the health and vitality of the world's forests. In some cases, vitality may increase due to a combination of a more favourable climate for growth and CO2 fertilization. In most cases however, increasing temperatures favour the growth of insect populations that is detrimental to the health of forests.

This is more likely to occur in forests dominated by few tree species or where specific temperatures or moisture levels control insect populations. For example, the spread of the mountain pine beetle, Dendroctonus ponderosae, in boreal forests, has been largely attributed to the absence of consistently low temperatures over a long period of time, which allowed an existing outbreak to spread across montane areas and into the colder boreal forests. Similarly, Finland is expecting an increase in infestation of root and bud rots in their coniferous forests, due to the spread of a virulent fungus, Heterobasidion parviporum, favoured by longer harvesting periods, increased storm damage and longer spore production season. In the tropics, on the other hand, increased warming reduces the life cycle of many insect pests, while at the same time increased fire damage makes trees more susceptible to insect attacks and vice versa.

Biological diversity of Climate

Species growth and survival depends for a large part on climate variables. Most species have a particular climatic range within which they grow best, are competitive and are able to adapt to slight environmental changes and respond to insect attacks, diseases and other adverse environmental and human influences. Many of the ecological processes that are needed for tree and other plant and animal species to live together are influenced by climatic conditions.

The importance of climate for forest ecosystems and their composition and diversity is exemplified by the various global and regional vegetation classifications. The Holdridge ecological life zones, are limited by temperature, precipitation and humidity. Several researchers have attempted to estimate the impact of climate change on the forests of Central America, based on estimated shifts of the life zone boundaries. Such studies, however, fall short of projecting real changes that may occur, since geographical shifts due to climate change are likely to occur on an individual species level, rather than on forest type level.

This is mainly because some species will be able to adapt better to changing conditions than others, resulting in changes of composition of forest types, rather than geographic shifts of forest types.

In general, many species have a tendency to move to higher latitudes or higher altitudes. Lucier *et al.*, in their revision of climate change impacts on forests, found reports of phenological changes in a number of species, with more and greater changes observed in higher latitudes. Common changes observed were changing flowering times and changing time of bud break, affecting productivity and carbon sequestration potential. Phenological changes observed in oak, apple and pears and a range of 29 Mediterranean species, did not affect ecosystem processes other than bringing them a few days forward, although such behaviour was easier to predict in insect-pollinated species than in wind-pollinated species. Ecological processes such as pollination, flowering and fruit setting may be more affected in tropical systems, by changes in the phenological cycles because species interactions may be more complex and involve more than one species, while at the same time seasonality is not as clearly marked.

FOREST ECOSYSTEM SERVICES AND UNDERLYING PROCESSES

Following the Millennium Ecosystem Assessment report, and forest ecosystem services are defined as the benefits that people obtain from ecosystems. While many ecosystem services can be identified and are often grouped into four broad types of services, only those services with well documented evidence of their management and their relation with climate change and human well-being.

PRODUCTIVITY OF CLIMATE CHANGE

The impact of climate change on productivity varies according to geographic area, species, stand composition, tree age, soils (in particular water holding capacity), effects of CO_2 and nitrogen fertilization and interactions between any of these factors. Some of the changes may be temporal, reverting once saturation levels have been reached. This is projected to be the case for water availability, where reduction of water generally reduces plant growth but in areas of water surplus may initially increase growth when waterlogging is being reduced. Similar reactions have been noted for CO_2 and nitrogen fertilization as well as temperature increases. In general, productivity was found to increase with rising temperatures in most forest areas, including the Amazon, probably due to CO_2 fertilization. However, in contrast to temperate areas, production increases in tropical forests will be temporal and will decrease once CO_2 saturation levels have been reached. Some studies have already registered decreasing growth rates in tropical forests. Water deficits over extended periods have also been shown to decrease productivity and may be the cause for the declined productivity recorded by the studies above. Some authors argue that based on paleontological evidence this may not result in the forest dieback often mentioned in connection to expected changes in the Amazon region. Natural disturbances often decrease forest area, but through the damage they cause to standing trees, they may also decrease productivity.

CARBON STORAGE AND SEQUESTRATION IN FOREST

There is an important interaction between carbon storage and sequestration by forests and changing temperatures and precipitation. On the one hand, the more carbon is stored in forests; less will be in the atmosphere. Increasing this stock will thus contribute to reducing the rate at which the global temperature is increasing. This relation has become extremely important in the climate change discussions and many tropical countries are preparing themselves to reduce emissions and increase forest carbon stock in order to capture part of the funding pledged for GHG emissions reductions. In Costa Rica, recognition of this service led to the implementation of innovative financing mechanisms for forest management, planted forests and conservation during the mid-nineties. This has led to increased efforts to ascertain the extent and content of the existing natural and planted forests.

On the other hand, increasing temperatures, longer dry seasons and increasing CO2 concentrations in the atmosphere in the long term, are expected to reduce the capacity of forests to store and sequester carbon, possibly converting forests from carbon sinks to carbon sources. Since carbon sequestration depends on productivity, all factors that affect productivity will also affect carbon sequestration. In addition, in the short term, increasing temperatures may reduce carbon storage capacity, although the effect may vary depending on the season in temperate regions. Early spring warming, for example, has been found to increase carbon sequestration of terrestrial ecosystems, while early autumn warming increased respiration more than sequestration.

Soil and Water Protection

Forests have long been recognised as contributing to water and soil protection and in several countries this has been translated into systems that pay for these services. Their positive influence on water regulation, however, is still discussed by foresters and hydrologists. The role of water regulation and soil protection may become increasingly important under climate change conditions. However, the capacity of forests to fulfil this role may be affected by the changing conditions.

Reductions in rainy season flows and increases in dry season flows are of little value when total annual rainfall is low and significantly evaporated and absorbed by forests. In areas with frequent fog, the absorption of water by trees from the clouds (horizontal rain) may contribute significantly to the total amount of rainfall. The palaeoecological study of Amazon vegetation changes, indicated that in cloud forest areas, where trees often are submerged in fog, warming may cause the clouds to rise above the trees. This will reduce the potential for horizontal precipitation.

Multiple Socioeconomic Benefits

In some areas, climate change may increase growth, while in others decreases are expected. While the expected global increase in wood production may lower prices, benefitting consumers, the combination of lower prices and regionally differentiated effects on productivity will cause differentiated effects on timber harvest related income and employment. The same authors project rises in timber production of up to 50 per cent in all continents, except for Australia and New Zealand. However, most of this increase is expected to come from plantations, with increasingly shorter rotations and is therefore likely to be distributed unevenly amongst the continents. In South America, where greatest increase is expected, current plantation production is concentrated in southern Brazil, Argentina, Uruguay and Chile. Natural forests are found in the tropical regions of the continent, where forest dieback may decrease timber production.

Harvests of non wood forest products (NWFP) have three major functions: provision of part of the daily necessities of forest dependent people, off-farm income and a safety net in times of adverse conditions for agricultural production. Osman-Elasha *et al.*, suggest that climate change will have impacts on the productivity of NWFPs and that NWFP users will largely be impacted through increased pressure on forest products from people that look for emergency supplies or alternative ways of income. The latter is likely to occur in areas of high poverty, high dependence on NWFPS and increased frequency and intensity of extreme climate events and other natural disturbances, such as pests, diseases and fires. The impacts of climate change on the provision of these products and the subsequent socioeconomic effects, however, require more studies.

Climate change impacts on cultural and recreational services of forests have also been little studied and are difficult to measure, in particular for those services that by themselves are difficult to measure. Osman-Elasha *et al.*, report some studies on well defined recreational services, such as skiing in mountainous areas, where skiing at lower altitudes is likely to be affected by temperature increases. Recreational values placed on forests are usually local and unfortunately in most countries no reliable climate change projections have been made at such a scale. The same authors indicate that the effect of climate change on forest biodiversity and structure in Africa and the subsequent effect on attractiveness for tourists of many of the national parks need to be further studied.

WORLD ENERGY RESOURCES AND CONSUMPTION

The world has a number of energy resources which provide us with the ability to perform work (a narrowly-defined measure of the ability to effect physical change). Energy resources range from fossil fuels and nuclear fuels to renewable energy such as wind, hydro-and solar energy. When this energy is drawn upon to do work, and is converted to a less useful form, energy consumption is said to have occured.

WORLD ENERGY CONSUMPTION

In 2004 the worldwide energy consumption of the human race was estimated as 15 TW (TW=1012 Watts) by the United States Energy Information Administration. This is equivalent to 0.5 ZJ (ZJ =1021J) per year. There is at least 10 per cent uncertainty in this number because the underlying data is continuously changing and not all of the world's economies track their energy consumption with the same rigour. Consumption by fuel type Eighty-seven per cent of the world's energy is supplied by fossil fuel. The 15 TW total energy consumption of 2004 was divided as follows:

	TW=10^{12} Watt	**ZJ=10^{21}J per year**
Oil	5.6	0.18
Gas	3.5	0.11
Coal	3.8	0.12
Hydroelectric	0.9	0.03
Nuclear	0.9	0.03
Geothermal, Wind, Solar, Wood	0.2	0.006

Ever since the advent of the industrial revolution, the worldwide energy consumption has been growing steadily. In 1890 the consumption of fossil fuels roughly equaled the amount of bio mass fuel burned by households and industry. In 1900 global energy consumption equaled 0.7 TW. The twentieth century saw a rapid twenty fold increase in fossil fuels. Between 1980 and 2004 the worldwide annual growth rate has been 2 per cent. The most significant growth of energy consumption is currently taking place in China which has been growing at 5.5 per cent over the last 25 years. Its 1.3 billion people are currently consuming energy at a rate of 2 KW per person. The growth in energy consumption over the last quarter century. Over the last twenty years Fossil fuels have continued to grow and increased their share of the energy supply, coal has been growing the fastest. Nuclear and hydro electric energy have stagnated due to environmental concerns. With the exception of France no major western country has ordered a new nuclear power plant since 1980.

In 2004 renewable energy supplied around 7 per cent of the world's energy consumption. Most (87 per cent) of the renewable energy was hydroelectric power. Solar and wind power provided 4 and 65 GW (GW=109 Watt) respectively. Consumption by country energy consumption broadly tracks with gross national product, although there is a significant difference between the consumption levels of the US with 11.4 KW per person, and Japan and Germany's with 6 KW per person. In developing countries such as India the per person energy use is closer to 0.5 KW. The per capita energy consumption against the GDP per person for all countries with more than 20 million inhabitants, this covers 95 per cent of the world population. Canada has the highest energy consumption per capita whereas the lowest energy consumption takes place in the third world.

Energy Consumption by Sector

Transportation, industry, residential and commercial (offices and shops) each consume approximately equal shares of the total 15 TW.A third of the world's energy is used to produce electricity. In 2005, global electricity consumption equaled 2 TW. The energy used to generate 2 TW of electricity is approximately 5 TW, as the efficiency of a typical existing power plant is around 38 per cent. The new generation of gas fired plants reaches a substantially higher efficiency of 55 per cent. Coal is the most popular fuel for the world's electricity plants. World energy resources Fossil fuel resources. Despite several voices predicting the imminent decline of fossil fuels, there are still significant reserves of all the traditional energy components. Remaining reserves of conventional fossil fuels are estimated as:

Coal	290 ZJ
Oil	57 ZJ
Gas	30 ZJ

Again significant uncertainty exists for these numbers. This uncertainty is not surprising, since the estimation for the remaining fossil fuels on the planets depends on a detailed understanding of the earth crust. This understanding is still less than perfect. While modern drilling technology makes it possible to drill wells in up to 3000 meters of water to verify the exact composition of the geology, half of the ocean has depth exceeding 3000 meters, leaving about a third of the planet beyond the reach of detailed analysis. The make up of the estimated 57 ZJ of oil on earth. The estimations for the world's oil reserves vary from low of 8 ZJ, consisting of currently proven and recoverable reserves, to a maximum of 110 ZJ consisting of available, but not necessary recoverable reserves, and including optimistic estimates for unconventional sources such as tar sands and oil shale. Both estimates provide oil for the foreseeable future at current oil consumption rate of 0.18 ZJ per year. There is a broad consensus among scientists that we are not close to running out of fossil fuels.

Coal is especially abundant and by itself can sustain the current energy consumption of the entire planet for the next 600 years. Renewable energy resources political and/or environmental considerations might move the world's energy consumption away from fossil fuels. For example, the European Commission has proposed in its Renewable Energy Roadmap, a binding target of increasing the level of renewable energy in the EU's overall mix from less than 7 per cent today to 20 per cent by 2020. In 2005 the Swedish government announced their intention to become the first country to break their dependence on oil and other 'fossil raw materials' by 2020. Renewable energy sources are even larger than the traditional fossil fuels and in theory can easily supply our energy needs. The sunlight interacts with the planet. There is 89,000 TW of solar energy that falls on the planet's surface. In other words, we need to capture less than 0.02 per cent of the available solar energy to meet our current energy needs. The available wind energy estimates range from 300 to 370 TW.

Using the lower estimate, just 5 per cent of the available wind energy would supply the current worldwide energy needs. Most of this wind energy is available over open ocean. Not only does the ocean cover 71 per cent of the planet, wind also tends to blow stronger over open water because there are less obstructions. The above percentages for solar and wind energy ignore the formidable challenges of energy distribution and storage that need to be solved to overcome the intermittent and seasonal variations of these energy sources. The numbers do however illustrate that it is technically possible to move away from fossil fuels should society decide to make the necessary investment. The required investment to change energy sources is enormous. It is estimated that the cost to replace the global infrastructure for liquid transportation fuels alone is $3-5 trillion.

Alternative Energy Paths

Whether a significant investment in renewable energy is wise or not, is currently the subject of much debate. Trials are taking place in several countries; Japan and Germany have started to make some investments in solar energy, making them the largest consumers of photovoltaic cells in the world despite their unfavourable geographic location.

Denmark and Germany have installed 3 GW and 17 GW of wind power respectively. In 2005 wind generated 18.5 per cent of all the electricity in Denmark. Brazil has made a significant investment in ethanol fuel which supplies a significant part of the transportation fuel in that country. Starting in 1965,

France made large investments in nuclear power and to this date three quarters of their electricity comes from their nuclear pressure water reactor plants. In the 21st century some of these different energy paths might become more mainstream and start replacing the ubiquitous fossil fuels.

EARTH'S ENERGY BUDGET

A schematic representation of the energy exchanges between the Earth's surface, the Earth's atmosphere, and outer space. The recycling of energy between the Earth's surface and the atmosphere is characteristic of the greenhouse effect. Note that the total energy entering each level is equal to the energy leaving that level as should be expected for a system in balance.

The Earth can be considered as a physical system with an energy budget that includes all gains of incoming energy and all losses of outgoing energy. The planet is approximately in equilibrium, so the sum of the gains should be approximately equal to the sum of the losses.

Note: Although the term "energy budget" is widely used, the flow of energy in and out of the Earth is actually measured in units of power (watts), not units of energy (joules). Therefore, "power budget" would be a more accurate term.

The Power Budget

The total flux of power entering the Earth's atmosphere is estimated at 174 peta watts. This consists of:

- Solar radiation (99.978 per cent, or nearly 174 petawatts; or about 340 W m^{-2})
  - This is equal to the product of the solar constant, about 1366 watts per square metre, and the area of the Earth's disc as seen from the Sun, about 1.28 × 1014 square metres, averaged over the Earth's surface, which is four times larger. The solar flux averaged over just the sunlit half of the earth's surface is about 680 W m-2
- Geothermal energy (0.013 per cent, or about 23 terawatts; or about 0.045 W m^{-2})
  - This is produced by stored heat and heat produced by radioactive decay leaking out of the Earth's interior.
- Tidal energy (0.002 per cent, or about 3 terawatts; or about 0.0059 W m-2)
  - This is produced by the interaction of the Earth's mass with the gravitational fields of other bodies such as the Moon and Sun.
- Waste heat from fossil fuel consumption (about 0.007 per cent, or about 13 terawatts; or about 0.025 W m-2).

Note that the solar constant varies (by approximately 0.1 per cent over a solar cycle); and is not known absolutely to within better than about one watt per square metre. Hence the geothermal and tidal contributions are less than the uncertainty in the solar power.

Outgoing Power

An average albedo (reflectivity) of the Earth is about 0.3, which means that 30 per cent of the incident solar energy is reflected back into space, while 70 per cent is absorbed by the Earth and reradiated as infrared.

The planet's albedo varies from month to month, but 0.3 is the average figure. It also varies very strongly spatially: ice sheets have a high albedo, oceans low.

The contributions from geothermal and tidal power sources are so small that they are omitted from the following calculations.

The 30 per cent reflected energy consists of:

- 6 per cent reflected from the atmosphere
- 20 per cent reflected from clouds
- 4 per cent reflected from the ground (including land, water and ice)

All of the 70 per cent absorbed energy is eventually reradiated:

- 64 per cent by the clouds and atmosphere
- 6 per cent by the ground

The same 70 per cent of absorbed energy can be split this way:

- 51 per cent absorbed by land and water, then emerging in the following ways:
  - 23 per cent transferred back into the atmosphere as latent heat by the evaporation of water
  - 7 per cent transferred back into the atmosphere by heated rising air
  - 6 per cent radiated directly into space
  - 15 per cent transferred into the atmosphere by radiation, then reradiated into space, and
- 19 per cent absorbed by the atmosphere, including:
  - 16 per cent reradiated back into space
  - 3 per cent transferred to clouds, from where it is radiated back into space

Anthropogenic Modification

Emission of greenhouse gases, and other factors (such as land-use changes), modify the energy budget slightly but significantly. The IPCC provides an estimate of these forcing, insofar as they are known. The largest and best known are from the well-mixed greenhouse gases (CO_2, CH_4, halocarbons, etc.), totalling an increase in forcing of 2.4 W m-2 relative to 1750. These are less than 1 per cent of the solar input, but contributes to the observed increase in atmospheric and oceanic temperature.

Electricity Generation

Electricity generation is the first process in the delivery of electricity to consumers. The other processes are electric power transmission and electricity distribution.

The importance of dependable electricity generation, transmission and distribution was revealed when it became apparent that electricity was useful for providing heat, light and power for human needs. Centralised power generation became possible when it was recognised that alternating current electric power lines can transport electricity at low costs across great distances by taking advantage of the ability to transform the voltage using power transformers. Electricity has been generated for the purpose of powering human technologies for at least 120 years from various sources of energy. The first power plants were run on wood, while today we rely mainly on petroleum, natural gas, coal, hydroelectric and nuclear power and a small amount from hydrogen, solar energy, tidal harnesses, wind generators, and geothermal sources.

Electricity Demand

The demand for electricity can be met in two different ways. The primary method thus far has been for public or private utilities to construct large scale centralised projects to generate and transmit the electricity required to fuel economies. Many of these projects have caused unpleasant environmental effects such as air or radiation pollution and the flooding of large areas of land.

Distributed generation creates power on a smaller scale at locations throughout the electricity network. Often these sites generate electricity as a by-product of other industrial processes such as using gas from landfills to drive turbines.

Bibliography

A. Gilmour and R.J. Fisher: *Villagers, Forests and Foresters*, Sahayogi Press, 2004.

Amrish Kumar Ahuja: *Educational Management Planning and Finance*, Authorspress, 2007.

Anand Kumar Sharma: *Project Planning Analysis and Management*, Anmol, Publication, Delhi, 2006.

Anindita Majumdar: *British Forest Policy and Tribal Community in Bengal, 1880-1947*, Readers Service, 2006.

Bina Agarwal: *Gender and Green Governance : The Political Economy of Women's Presence Within and Beyond Community Forestry*, Oxford University Press, Delhi, 2010.

C.A. Rahman: *Compilation of Forest Policy and Law: Including Important Sections of Wildlife (Protection) Act.*, International Book, Delhi, 2009.

G P D Vyas: *Community Forestry*, Agrobios, Delhi, 2013.

Hinal D Pandya: *Deforestation Forest Policy and Government Inaction*, International Book, Delhi, 2008.

John W Bruce: *Community Forestry: Rapid Appraisal of Tree and Land Tenure*, Daya, Publication, Delhi, 2005.

K. D. Raju: *Genetically Modified Organisms: Emerging Law and Policy in India*, TERI, 2007.

K. Krishna Murty: *Labour Management Relations Under Globalisation: Law and Policy Perspectives*, Akansha Publication, Delhi, 2009.

Kailash Thakur: *Environmental Protection Law and Policy in India*, Deep & Deep, Publication, Delhi, 2004.

Klaus Seeland and Franz Schmithusen: *Indigenous Knowledge, Forest Management and Forest Policy in South Asia*, D K Printworld, 2003.

Md. Zafar Mahfooz Nomani: *Natural Resources Law and Policy*, Uppal,Publication, Delhi, 2004.

Neelam: *Revival of Sick Units: Law and Policy*, Regal Publications, Delhi, 2014.

P Subramanian and S Senthilnathan: *Forest Project Analysis and Management*, International Book, Delhi, 2004.

Prem Nath Dhar: *Global Cargo Management: Concept, Typology, Law and Policy*, Kanishka, Publication, Delhi, 2008.

R. Bawa and P.K. Khosla: *Biodiversity of Forest Types A Community Forestry Approach* , BSMPS, 2004.

Rajib Handique: *British Forest Policy in Assam*, Concept, Publication, Delhi, 2004.

Ravinder Dhanai: *Forest Project Analysis and Management*, Cyber Tech Publication, Delhi, 2009.

S. Abdul Thaha: *Forest Policy and Ecological Change: Hyderabad State in Colonial India*, Cambridge Univ Press, 2004.

S. Bhatt, V.S. Mani and V. Balakista Reddy: *Air Law and Policy in India*, Lancers, Publishers, 2004.

Shyam Divan and Armin Rosencranz: *Environmental Law and Policy in India: Cases, Materials and Statutes*, Oxford University, 2002.

Stuart Bell and Donald McGillivray: *Ball and Bell on Environmental Law: The Law and Policy Relating to the Protection of the Environment*, Oxford University Press, 2004.

The Indian Forest Act, 1927 Alongwith the Forest Conservation Act, 1980, Natraj Publication, Delhi, 2010.

Index

A

Adapting Forest Policy and Legislation 4
Adapting Forestry Institutions 6
Agricultural Policy 195
Approaches, Methods and Tools 41

B

Bank Financing 2
Biodiversity Conservation 227, 242
Biological Diversity 201
Biomass Resources 236, 237,238

C

Carbon Sequestration 224, 242, 261, 262
Carbon Storage 262
Classical Methods for Determination 158
Commercial Harvesting 2
Community Forestry Project in Potosi 67
Community Forestry Projects 20
Community Problem Analysis 121
Conceptual Framework 17

D

Designing Projects to Meet Local Needs 8

E

Ecological Requirements 218
Environmental Assets 230
Environmental Change 227

F

Farm Forestry 199, 200, 203, 204
Forest Carbon 239, 240, 262
Forest Cover 196, 198, 203, 242, 257, 258
Forest Ecosystem Services 261
Forest Products 224, 237, 238
Forest Soils 223

G

Global Forest Area 256
Global Warming 199
Guidelines for Forest Management Planning 164

H

Historical Cost Valuation 148

I

Implementation of Forest Management Plans 170
Implementation of Programmes 58
Indigenous Peoples 194, 206, 207
Industrial Wood 195

J

Joint Forest Management 198, 205, 206, 259

L

Land Tenure 237, 238, 239
Legislation should be Modified to Support 5
Log Measurement 182

M

Malakand Social Forestry Project 23
Management 193, 194, 205, 206, 207, 208, 209, 213, 214, 216, 217, 218, 219, 229, 245, 246, 251, 252, 253, 257, 258, 259, 266

N

National Agricultural Policy 195
National Commission 195
National Environment Policy 198
National Park 258

P

Participatory Forest Management 208
Participatory Planning 15
Planning and Organization 89
Planning Commission Reports 199
Policy and Legislation Issues 10
Potosi Community Forestry Project 20
Production forestry 195, 196, 203, 204, 205
Project Design 9

R

Restrictions on Forest Access 5
Results and Lessons Learned 89, 98
Rights of Ownership or Stewardship of Forest Land 5

S

Scientific Research 258
Sustainable Development 229
Sustainable Forest Management 219, 224, 225

T

Techniques for Estimating Measures 126
Temperate Forests 259
Tenure Rights 237, 238
Transport Operations 167, 185
Tropical Forests 259, 262

V

Valuing Forest Goods and Services in Practice 130
Valuing Marketed Goods and Services 130

W

Water Supply 217
Watershed Management 225
Wood Import 204
World Energy Resources 264, 265